AUTOMATED MUSIC COMPOSITION

AUTOMATED MUSIC COMPOSITION

Phil Winsor

UNIVERSITY OF NORTH TEXAS PRESS

For Michele-Louise and Bethany

Written 2/1/89–7/30/89 under a Research Grant from
the National Science Council of the Republic of China

Library of Congress Cataloging-in-Publication Data

Winsor, Phil, 1938–
    Automated music composition / by Phil Winsor.
       p.   cm.
    ISBN 0-929398-38-6.
    1. Computer composition. 2. computer music—Instruction and study. 3. BASIC
(Computer program language) I. Title.
MT56.W53   1992
781.3'4—dc20   92-7263
                                    CIP
                                     MN

ACKNOWLEDGEMENTS

The author would like to thank: Dr. Daniel Yuan, President of National Chiao Tung University, for inviting him to be Visiting Computer Music Research Professor during the writing of this book (January through August, 1989);

Dr. Ting-Lien Wu, Director of the Computer Music Studio at National Chiao Tung University, who encouraged this project as a learning resource for composers on Taiwan;

Garland Andrews, of ProGenitor Software, for typesetting the musical examples, editing the English version of the book, and guiding the manuscript to completion; and

Frances Vick and Kate Lynass, of the University of North Texas Press, for their support and diligence in making this book a reality.

Phil Winsor
2/10/92

Contents

PART I

Fundamentals

1

Overview of Computer Music Applications

MUSIC INTELLIGENCE

What is Music Intelligence, and how can it benefit the musician? This question is the first to arise from musicians and nonmusicians alike when they are told that the computer has assumed as important a role in the art of music as it has in other intellectual disciplines. The answer is that the computer is suited to the performance of a wide range of tasks, and that it will perform those tasks just as readily for musicians as it will for scientists. In the process, it can exhibit characteristics of (human) intelligence to the extent it is programmed to do so.

To precisely denote Music Intelligence is as difficult as to exactly say what Artificial Intelligence is, because the complex mixture of skills and talents which comprise human intelligence is little understood. Through introspection and careful observation, we can identify superficial logical and cognitive functions such as the ability to store, recall, compare, model, extrapolate, and parse various data structures; but the workings of the most powerful wellspring of creative activity, the subconscious intelligence, remains elusive and largely uncharted. Until a deeper comprehension of the breadth of human intellectual activity and the dynamics of its component processes is achieved, we must settle for a temporary definition:

> Music Intelligence is research into methods of making the computer more cognizant of and powerful over the manipulation and organization of musical materials, structures, and systems.

Uses of Music Intelligence

Although the immediate goals and rewards of computer applications in the arts may seem more tangential to society than those of science, the methods and procedures of data processing impose no utilitarian prerequisites—they will serve the creative artist at play as unquestioningly as they serve the biochemist in search of a cure for cancer or the material scientist at work on the purification of microprocessor chips.

What can the computer, a rigidly mechanistic device contribute to the musical arts, born of the human psyche and intuitive ephemera? Is it really possible to treat music as something that can be quantified, tested, and systematically codified in the same way that one would develop and study a computer-simulated model of a new space craft?

While it may be argued that the act of creating a spiritually moving piece of music remains a mystery (Esthetics, the philosophy of artistic value systems, is still not able to adequately explain how and why an art object comes to be considered beautiful), care must be taken not to transpose this view to other, more accessible dimensions of musical structure.

Leaving aside the act of creation, almost every domain of the musical event is susceptible to computational methods. The question to ask is not, "Is it possible to apply the computer to musical problem-solving," but rather, "How can it be applied in a meaningful way, and what is the best frame of reference for its application?"

Conceptual Overview

Computer music in general can be divided into two primary categories: sound production methods (commercial synthesizers) and music composition methods. As explained in a later chapter, when computer music began, both the sound production and compositional processes were carried out in a single environment—the mainframe computer. However, over several decades these areas became distinct through the advent of viable real-time, microprocessor-based music performance devices. Today, the personal computer often fills the role of composer/performer while the synthesizer acts as the instrument of performance, in the same way that people have traditionally played acoustic instruments. It is likely that, as technology advances, we will see a reunification of these separate functions within a single piece of hardware. On a small scale, it already exists in the form of built-in sequencing capability found in some synthesizers. These devices allow the performer to play a musical passage which will be retained in the instrument's memory, and which can be recalled for execution at a later time. This internal sequencer acts as a performance command center, issuing instructions about when to play specific notes, how loudly to play them, and how long to continue them.

Music Research Applications

Investigators in each musical subdiscipline are devising ways to enlist the computer's help in solving musical problems.

Some of the major research areas are:

(1) Algorithmic and Automated Composition
(2) Music Theory Expert Systems
(3) Computer-Aided Instruction
(4) Musicology
(5) Performance
(6) Psychoacoustic Phenomena (Cognition)
(7) Physics of Sound
(8) Architectural Acoustics
(9) Performance Environment Simulation
(10) Ecological (sonic environment) Acoustics
(11) Esthetic Perception Theory
(12) General System Theory, Information Theory
(13) Intermedia Explorations (multidisciplinary events comprised of multiple information media, such as choreography, video, film, laser imagery, light sculpture, and music)

We will now consider several of these fields in greater detail.

Composition

Composition heads the list of Music Research Areas, because the "putting-together" (modeling, simulation, designing) of musical structures provides solutions to problems encountered in the remaining music research areas, which are heavily model-oriented. Research situations normally require the formulation of a strategy or paradigm (conceptual frame of reference) before there is work for the computer to perform, and in music the composer has traditionally filled this role.

Some of the important research categories are:

(1) Algorithmic Composition: application of data transformation procedures to sound structures
(2) Automated Music: study of self-determining, self-controlling music composition systems based on algorithms which favor a particular musical style
(3) Experimental Music Systems and Structures: General System Theory, Stochastic Music and Information Theory
(4) Studies in the Internal Structure of Musical Sound: Music Tone Color Research Aided by Direct Synthesis Techniques

Algorithmic Composition. Music composition can be defined as the process of selecting from a finite set of elements (pitches, rhythms, tone-colors, etc.) certain possibilities over others for presentation as a work of art.

In music composition as in computer science, algorithms are detailed instructions for the successful execution of a particular series of tasks. One simple example is to create a melodic line by programming the computer to apply certain criteria in the selection of tones from a pitch scale. Instructions for this algorithm can be written in pseudocode as:

(1) Select at random a note from the seven tones of the C-Major pitch scale;
(2) Search the program rule-base (list) for criteria to test the viability of selected tone;
(3) Apply the rule to the candidate melody note;
(4) If the note passes the test, add it to the list of accepted melody notes; advance notelist counter; Goto 1:
(5) If the note fails the rule test, Goto 1:

Whether aware of it or not, composers have always used algorithms to create (select) music, but in the past they had to rely entirely on the power of their internal personal computer (brain) for the execution of various procedures. As a consequence, many potentially fruitful structural and organizational models lay dormant in the minds of composers because of the inordinate amount of human time and effort required for their realization.

Symbiosis. Beginning about 1950, composers began to bring the computer into their employ as a tireless assistant in the fleshing out of musical structures. Of these, two composer/experimenters—Lejaren A. Hiller in the United States of America, and Iannis Xenakis in France—independently contributed many important precedents to the methodology of computer music composition. They are generally considered by the professional music community to be the fathers of algorithmic composition by computer. As a consequence of their work, it quickly became apparent that, not only could the computer precisely and unerringly generate complex musical textures, but it was also an unforeseen source of inspiration. Through speculative experiment and the simulation of novel contexts, composers discovered a virtually unlimited means of expanding their aural imagination. A symbiotic relationship quickly developed between man and machine.

At present, the all-important compositional function cannot be provided by microprocessor-based synthesizers. Perhaps in the future, manufacturers will market devices containing algorithmic composition software, but for now the personal computer, serving as host to one programming language or another (BASIC, FORTRAN, C, or PASCAL), is the environment increasingly used by contemporary composers for the creation of music scores.

Music Theory

The primary research focus of Music Theory is the description of musical systems as exhibited by the works of composers from various periods in music history. Tools employed are the analysis and subsequent resynthesis of stylistic models as a test of the efficacy of theoretical systems.

Music Theory's practical side relates to its position at the core of the academic musical curriculum. Its central goal is to impart a deeper understanding of music interpretation by teaching students to compose examples modeled after ancient musical forms. Due to the widespread reliance on core theory courses, interest in the related area of Computer-Assisted Instruction has grown rapidly since 1975.

Some Music Theory research areas are:

(1) Formulation of Descriptive Theoretical Systems;
(2) Development of Analytical Tools for the validation of theoretical hypotheses;
(3) Design of Expert Systems for the simulation of significant musical styles of ancient historical periods: Palestrina, Bach, etc.; and,
(4) Analytic/Synthetic Expert Systems.

Computer-Aided Instruction

Researchers in each of the primary musical areas are interested in application of the computer to teaching situations. As instructional systems continue to develop, more time will become available for classroom teachers to deal with problems worthier of their time than the routine preparation of testing and training exercises. The most intense efforts to prepare effective computerized teaching materials are to be found in the area of Music Theory, but teachers of the performance of traditional musical instruments may soon be able to benefit from software which analyzes and diagnoses particular problems that a performer may have with regard to tone production and quality.

Musicology

Musicology can be thought of as the archaeology of music. It is the broadest of all musical subdisciplines, encompassing aspects of each of the others. It deals with the discovery and study of musical information having a bearing on contemporary understanding of ancient musical styles, performance practices and their relationship to the culture of a particular epoch.

Some current research areas are:

(1) Comparative Study Usage (related to area (3) of Music Theory Research—Expert Systems);
(2) Research in Cross-Referencing and Indexing of salient stylistic features (database); and,
(3) Comparative Study of Linguistic/Musical Structural Models.

Psychoacoustic Phenomenology

The composer as well as the theorist is concerned with matters arising from the characteristics of human perception. Not only are people perceptually constrained by the physical limitations of their perception systems, but the relationship between external stimuli and the interpretation placed on them by the brain requires much more research before scientific knowledge about cognitive processes can be considered adequate. For instance, the roles played by long- and short-term memory in the human's perception of esthetic events is of great interest to composers and music theorists alike. At present, all artists rely upon an intuitive comprehension of the dynamics of perception, a risky situation at best; undoubtedly, future discoveries in this area will enhance the composer's ability to predict the effects of musical structures on the listener, thereby eliminating a great deal of guesswork in the projection of musical patterns and forms.

Performance Environment Simulation

Until recently, the acoustics of enclosed music performance spaces were solely the province of architectural acousticians—professionals who study the characteristics of various shapes and sizes of rooms, as well as the attributes of diverse building materials, to arrive at concert hall designs which will satisfy the musical ear with respect to acoustic presence, clarity, and a host of other qualities. Formerly, musicians served primarily as consultants to these acousticians, lending their ears to help evaluate room characteristics such as sound dispersion, attenuation, resonance, image placement, reverberation decay time, and so on.

Over the past few years, the role of the musician in determining acoustical properties of performance spaces has expanded dramatically, due to the development of sophisticated digital devices for the simulation of a broad range of room types. The application of sound reinforcement, imaging, and aural location theory to sonic environment configuration has produced a state-of-the-art in which the virtual size, shape, and acoustical characteristics of diverse performance environments can be simulated regardless of the raw physical characteristics of the host enclosure.

In the past, concert halls were designed with the objective of accommodating soloists, chamber ensembles, and full orchestras. To achieve this goal, compromises were made which rendered an ideal acoustical setting nearly impossible for any specific medium. At most, one could hope that the acoustics would not be disastrous for all types of musical events. The day is now at hand when the musician can "tune" the performance space to suit the qualities of the music to be performed, from a warm, intimate atmosphere amenable to a solo piano recital to the dryer acoustical environment required for some types of orchestral music. In fact, it is conceivable to digitally reconfigure a performance space between concert pieces in order to support the musical intentions of the composers.

Ecological (sonic environment) Acoustics

At first glance this research area might seem to be remote from the interests of musicians, since it deals with levels, types, and severity of sound pollution in the human habitats of home, workplace, and city. However, musicians are likely to be more sensitive to hazardous noise environments than nonmusicians, giving them the motivation to use their discriminatory talents for abatement research.

There is a second side to the ecology of sound: if some sound environments produce negative effects on the human being, what are the characteristic of environments which generate a sense of well-being, reduced stress, and increased productivity? This area is probably most attractive to the composer/musician, because he has spent a good deal of time increasing his sensitivity to the characteristics of sound in general, and to positive sonic environments in particular.

Information Theory and Esthetic Perception

Derived from the *Mathematical Theory of Communication* (Shannon and Weaver), this area was born around 1955 through the work of Abraham Moles. Dr. Moles' classic, "Information Theory and Esthetic Perception," laid the groundwork for a fresh approach to theoretical work in the field of esthetics by bringing to bear on artistic objects the analytic methods normally associated with mathematics—probability theory and integral calculus. At the risk of oversimplification, it can be said that Information Theory (relative to musical esthetics) deals with the quantification and categorization of time-related transformation processes, and the autocorrelation of constituent layers of musical experiences. A theoretical distinction is drawn between information flow across a perceptual channel as a materially quantifiable phenomenon and the signification or meaning of the messages carried by information medium. To understand this concept, consider the traditional dot-dash signals which make up the International Morse Code alphabet. To an observer unskilled in deciphering coded messages, the patterns transmitted are nothing more than raw information containing a high degree of repetition (redundancy); but, to the trained telegrapher, the quantitative information flow is loaded with meaning, carried by a set of symbolic conventions agreed upon in advance by sender and receiver for the transmission of intelligible ideas.

Practical Applications of Research Outcomes

Pure research eventually spawns many useful products and devices for the carrying out of routine tasks in everyday life. The music industry has been beneficiary of an uncommonly large number of these gifts over the past decade.

The most notable catalyst to musical productivity was developed during the 1970s by a Stanford University Computer Music Researcher, Dr. John Chowning. His theoretical work in the area of FM (frequency modulation) sound synthesis techniques gave rise to a generation of powerful digital sound generating devices produced by a number of MIDI synthesizer manufacturers, such as the Yamaha Company's TX81-Z and New England Digital Corporation's Synclavier II.

Polyphonic (many-voiced), multitimbral (multiple tone-color) synthesizers have revolutionized every dimension of commercial music production as a consequence of their ability to convincingly emulate the sound qualities of traditional acoustic instruments such as the violin, clarinet, or trumpet. Indeed, when listening to music broadcast by radio and television, it is frequently difficult even for the trained musician to discover whether the music springs from a natural or synthetic source.

The crafts of orchestration and arranging have been especially well served by technology in recent years. In pre-MIDI days, arrangers and orchestrators usually experienced a substantial time gap between the conception and realization of music designed for a television or movie production. This condition could be hazardous, especially if the arranger's future employment depended on the production director's immediate approval of a particular musical sequence. Understandably, arrangers were not inclined to take risks; they relied heavily on hackneyed techniques which were certain to work reliably, if not interestingly, in a particular dramatic context, leading to a shopworn handbook of musical cliches called "stock arrangements."

The invention of the MIDI-interfaced synthesizer configuration has eliminated the delay between conception and manifestation to the extent that today it is possible for the arranger/orchestrator to explore more challenging musical ideas without chancing loss of face (and livelihood). All experiments can be performed and evaluated quickly in the privacy of the arranger's studio, away from the critical ear of the producer.

Classroom Environment. One important fringe benefit of the rapid evolution of digital music-handling software and hardware since 1982 (the birth of MIDI) is the ease with which musical examples and training materials can be presented. Formerly, courses such as harmony, counterpoint, and orchestration relied upon the teacher's ability to perform materials at the piano keyboard, while giving instructions to the students to imagine one example or another as performed by various instrumental or vocal ensembles. Today, the same illustrations are experienced and manipulated effortlessly by digital equipment and software designed for pedagogical use. Every subject in the music curriculum has been effected by this technology.

Future Research and Development

Although it is impossible to foresee with certainty the direction research will take in the coming years, products will undoubtedly be developed in the following areas:

(1) Music notation optical scanning devices, along with software to interpret various notation systems and automatically perform music scores on MIDI synthesizers;
(2) Devices and software to digitally sample music improvised by various acoustic instrument ensembles and convert it to music notation;
(3) Complex sound synthesis devices built into personal computers; and,
(4) Automatic Composition Software geared to the needs of the entertainment industry (programs that will instantly compose music in a variety of styles).

ROLE OF MIDI

MIDI, Musical Instrument Digital Interface, was originally devised to allow synthesizers to transmit data to each other. During the late

1970s, popular musicians approached instrument manufacturers to find a way to eliminate the need for the elaborate configuration of keyboards (usually of different makes) that had to be transported from concert to concert to assure maximum variety in the orchestration of various songs. Each synthesizer typically produced a characteristic sound quality, and the insatiable ear of the rock musician demanded an array of equipment that filled the stage with stacks and rows of keyboards. To play them all, the performer constantly moved from position to position as each new sound quality was needed.

In 1982, the needs of commercial musicians were answered in the form of MIDI protocol—a communications standard that designers agreed to follow when developing future synthesizers. By accepting the MIDI standard, a manufacturer could be assured that his device would be able to compatibly send and receive musical data from synthesizers made by other manufacturers.

The performing musician was finally able to produce a musical passage on one keyboard and hear it simultaneously played on several other MIDI synthesizers; they were responding to the transmitted musical data, played at the master keyboard, recorded as digital command information (what key was pressed, how long it was held down, etc.), and passed on to the slave devices.

Shortly after MIDI emerged, it was extended to include the personal computer as the controlling link in the chain connecting one synthesizer to another. Software was quickly written to record, store, edit, and playback lengthy musical passages (called sequences, or notelists) on command, opening a dimension of musical texture previously out of reach to the individual performer: the ability to behave as an entire ensemble from a single keyboard. Countermelodies and harmonizations could be prepared in advance and stored in disk files until needed during the performance of a particular piece, thereby releasing the musician from the task of remembering which keyboard to reach for to get the appropriate sound quality.

Around 1985, software designers began to provide programs which would convert (text) music score-files, generated as the output of compositional algorithms coded in a programming language such as BASIC or Pascal, to sequence-files performable by synthesizers. Although initially of more interest to researchers and composers affiliated with universities, this resource is rapidly growing in popularity among commercial musicians, and will certainly become the stimulus for a wave of Automatic Composition software for the popular music market.

2

The MIDI Communications Interface: Music Representation Within the Computer

MUSIC NOTATION

Our present music notation is a synthesis of logical, symbolic, and graphic (also called iconic) elements—a hybrid system which has evolved over hundreds of years and which requires considerable practice to master. Although it allows people to communicate their musical thoughts to one another reasonably well, it is of no use in communicating with computers unless it is converted to machine language.

Because the computer is actually only a complex network of many on/off switches, whose positions are symbolically represented as either low or high, 0 or 1, a method must be devised to meaningfully translate musical information into patterns of binary state switches. There are many considerations with regard to this process, but it is convenient to think of it on two different planes: the conceptual and the practical.

CONCEPTUAL PERSPECTIVE

The computer is indifferent to our mental processes. It is not concerned at all with our logical patterns and methods of conceptualizing musical data. We look upon musical styles and systems from many viewpoints; we classify, organize, and group musical events in ways that reflect our physical, psychological and intellectual biases. Therefore, the issue of musical structure and its comprehension by human beings is "precomputational"; and, while critically important to effective application of the machine to algorithmic composition, it

13

is an isolated step in the interaction between man and the switching network. Moreover, the method of music conceptualization is usually bound to the orientation of the computer user.

A great deal of research has been done relative to effective systematization of the conceptual framework for the symbolic representation of music. Many different perspectives have emerged in an attempt to model accurately within the computer the salient features of identifiable musical styles and systems. Two important modeling categories are: (1) Symbolic and (2) Procedural approaches.

Symbolic (Grammatical) Representation

This perspective considers musical systems to be representative of specific musical "languages," or systems in which the music score contains symbols (signs) that conform to a particular style or grammar. The grammar is defined by the rhetoric it employs, that is by the hierarchically determined, interrelated sets of principles that govern the choices of specific values on the horizontal (melodic) and vertical (harmonic) planes from moment to moment in a sample composition. Often, large data bases must be employed to hold the constraints and other style delineating facts which will be consulted for instantiation of specific events in a projected new, albeit similar, style example. This (linguistic) approach to musical system is currently of great interest to Artificial Intelligence researchers in the areas of Music Theory and Musicology and, to a lesser extent, to composers who wish to design Expert Systems to analyze and project further extensions of their personal composing styles.

Theory Versus Composition. The theorist and musicologist see musical structures differently from the composer. While the composer's primary concern is to invent and apply procedures for the formation of musical structures (the "How-to-do-it," a *priori* approach), the analyst's primary concern is with the documentation of what has happened (the "Let's-see-if-we-can-find-rules-to-describe-it," a *posteriori* approach) during a piece of music. One example of this divergence of viewpoint can be found in the "outside-time" notion of musical system as implemented during the so-called common practice period (roughly 1650-1900). Functional tonality dominated musical structure to an extent that it was virtually impossible to consider, or even conceive of alternatives. The analytical, declarative method which evolved to characterize the important relationships of forms and event-structures during this period illustrates the role of symbolic notation in the identification and communication of patterns within familiar musical systems. When we refer to the musical syntax, grammar, or rhetoric of musical examples from functional tonality, we rely almost totally on the symbolic notation of tertian chordal structures and their connective relationships, both on the immediate, local level as well as on a deeper, global (Schenkerian) structural level. The well-worn symbol sequence:

$$I - IV - ii - V - iii - vi - IV - V - I$$

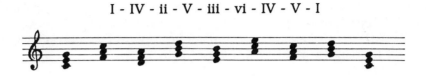

Example 2-1.

is immediately converted by the trained musician into a mentally audible harmonic progression. This system of classification is essential to theorists or musicologists who wish to devise Expert Systems for the analysis and re-creation of musical styles from the common practice period, because it provides the macroscopic "handles" to facilitate database encoding of salient stylistic features on a much higher level than sheer statistical data-recording techniques. (Since the music was not constructed from a probabilistic frame of reference, it is pointless to expect a meaningful description of the interrelations among musical processes to issue from a statistical measurement of it.) In short, the analytical method must provide insight to the hierarchically organized, context-dependent, natural language oriented textures of traditional music.

Procedural (Formative) Representation

By contrast to the symbolic (grammatical) approach to musical event-structuring, the procedural (formative) approach treats the computer as an extension of the composer's mental workshop. It does the composer's bidding in the application of complex processes to musical event-streams, assists in the controlled traversing of organically related sound-mass moments, and generally allows the composer to accomplish goals speedily which might consume a lifetime if performed by hand. This approach toward the computer relies only to a small degree on the computer's "knowledge" of what the composer is doing; it simply obeys the master's prescriptions, which may incidentally involve some analytical operations, but which are generally not aimed either at increasing the computer's awareness of what it is doing, or at teaching it to be an expert in producing one particular musical style or another.

While the symbolic representation of sound organization must unquestionably play a great role in the design of computer programs for use by theorists and musicologists, the composer often employs the computer in a more flexible manner, by separating the symbolic, conceptual stage from the iconic, generative phase of musical construction. Rather than become committed to a single-focus, style-dependent program for generating musical textures, the composer often wishes to conceive the specific musical system embodied by the encoded processes as existing outside the purview of the computer. Similarly, the composer may wish to subdivide the compositional process into separate, cumulative procedures. As Curtis Roads has written (1979):

> For compositional uses, the situation is slightly less restrictive, in that composers can coordinate symbolic and sonic representations by working in each domain separately and mapping the symbolic to the sonic. In this case it makes sense to treat the sonic domain as being composed of discrete "sonic objects." Naturally, objects can be linked and blended for a continuous musical flow.

It follows, then, that the intuitive, formative, process-oriented outlook of the composer requires an inherently different application of the computer from that of other musical sub-disciplines.

One consequence of the procedural approach to music representation is that control over, and responsibility for, the final result remain in the composer's province. The computer digests and processes data which is low level and primarily iconic in nature, then slavishly generates and outputs data which stands for instantaneous states of the extra-computational musical system. In this circumstance, the machine simply acts as a "black-box" which performs the composer's list of procedures, processes and organizational dicta according to parameters controlled (often interactively) by data introduced during the initialization stages of program execution. Figure 2-1 provides a symbolic view of this process.

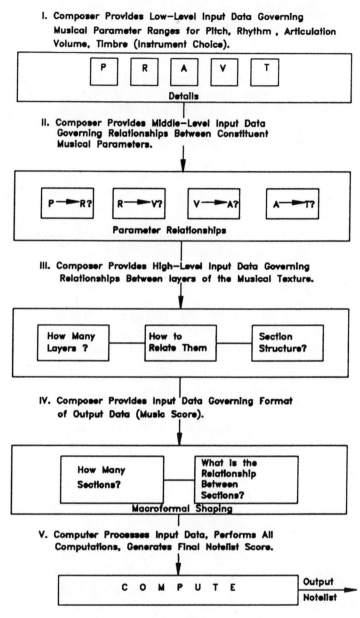

I. Composer Provides Low-Level Input Data Governing Musical Parameter Ranges for Pitch, Rhythm, Articulation Volume, Timbre (Instrument Choice).

P   R   A   V   T

Details

II. Composer Provides Middle-Level Input Data Governing Relationships Between Constituent Musical Parameters.

P ▶ R?   R ▶ V?   V ▶ A?   A ▶ T?

Parameter Relationships

III. Composer Provides High-Level Input Data Governing Relationships Between layers of the Musical Texture.

How Many Layers?   How to Relate Them   Section Structure?

IV. Composer Provides Input Data Governing Format of Output Data (Music Score).

How Many Sections?   What is the Relationship Between Sections?

Macroformal Shaping

V. Computer Processes Input Data, Performs All Computations, Generates Final Notelist Score.

C O M P U T E   Output Notelist

Figure 2-1.

Classes of Compositions

Composer Sever Tipei has pointed out in his paper, "The Computer: A Composer's Collaborator," that the processes and decisions performed by the computer can be applied to widely varied input data on separate occasions, resulting in what is termed "a class of compositions":

...by allowing for the existence of multiple, equally acceptable variants of a work, one no longer concentrates on writing a particular piece but rather on generating an entire "class of compositions." The term was introduced during the 1960s by composers of aleatory music (music that contains some indeterminacy at the performance level): the performer is asked to make decisions related either to the form of a piece (its sections can be arranged in more than one sequence) or to elements of detail (duration, pitch, dynamics, etc. are only approximately notated)...

Originally a class of compositions designated all possible works resulting from the interpretation of instructions and symbols offered in lieu of a traditionally notated score.

The assumption is that the infrastructure of a particular music composition program imprints an indelible "stamp," or overall character on the output data, irrespective of input data variants. That is, the algorithm configuration represents a characteristic schema that will always communicate to the musical result.

While this computer-as-super-performer notion is true for comprehensive composition-generating programs, many lower levels of computer participation are employed in algorithmic composition.

PRACTICAL PERSPECTIVE

Quite apart from the particular high-level representational stance taken while conceptualizing musical systems, the instantiation of particular system states must be accomplished in a utilitarian manner. This can be facilitated by isolating and classifying the most significant musical elements, which are referred to as parameters.

Encoding of Musical Data

Musical Parameters. Composers use the term "parameter" to refer to any quantifiable dimension of a musical structure which can be isolated and scaled according to a range of discrete values (such as the integer set, 1 to n). The lower level parameters are similar to what have been called "the elements of music" for centuries: pitch, rhythm, articulation, dynamics, and tone color. Often, these low-level parameters are unified in some way, so that they can be stored as a group, called a vector. It is said that a vector contains the key to an aggregate of "attribute/variables" which totally defines the important characteristics of one note-event. For example, a hypothetical event vector containing data for five parameters can be thought of as follows:

NOTE EVENT #1

PITCH	DURATION	VOLUME	ARTICULATION	TIMBRE
C#3	EIGHTH	FFF	STACCATO	FLUTE

Figure 2-2.

In computer terms, a vector can be visualized as a multidimensional array used to store the specific values (states) of every musical variable associated with each note-event. The total collection of array addresses along an imaginary line 1 to n which contain the succession of note-events is termed the "Notelist." Here is a 2-dimensional array which holds values for the Pitch and Rhythm parameters of a notelist (sequence of pitches) of order (length) ten:

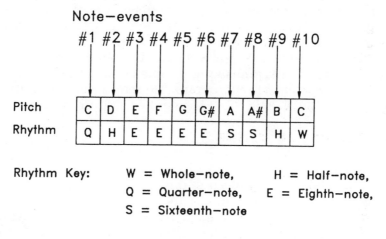

Figure 2-3.

In musical form, the notelist of Figure 2-3 is:

Example 2-2.

In the same manner, parameters at levels higher than the note-event level can also be captured and subjected to interpretation as a scalar range of values. For instance, one identifiable, higher-level parameter of music from the Western contemporary period is Texture

Density. It is sometimes used by composers to regulate the number and type of instruments that will participate at any given moment in the performance of a music score.

In the case of MIDI-system applications, when musical data is output from software designed for compositional use, it will most likely be iconic rather than symbolic in form, and will consist of a list of musical data scaled according to the value range of the parameter which it is destined to control.

The final "score"—the output list—will assume a format suitable to the targeted performance device, human or electronic. One commonly used format, sometimes referred to as a list of event vectors, is the Notelist Format: a first-to-last, time-sequenced succession of note-event attributes. Within this method, each note-event is viewed as a point in the time-space continuum which contains all the necessary information to determine the values of a confluence of musical parameters. As mentioned above, in practical terms the event vector can be visualized as a location (address) in computer memory which contains a list of specific scalar values for each of the significant attributes of a given note-event.

In reality, computer output destined for a device such as a MIDI sound synthesizer, would probably only contain numbers corresponding to the above alphanumeric characters. Therefore, the representation of the preceding NOTE-EVENT #1 inside the computer would take the form:

$$61 \quad 8 \quad 127 \quad .50 \quad 18$$

While musicians may think it odd to call a list of event vectors a "music score," the notelist is as specific in every way as traditionally notated music; moreover, its format is better suited to performance by digital devices. Admittedly, from a human perspective, the format is difficult to read and discourages one's taking an analytical viewpoint of the musical system represented by the data, primarily because of the one-dimensionality of the score configuration. To demonstrate this problem, consider the following traditionally notated musical example, which is the transcribed output of a C language program:

Example 2-3.

Now, compare the notation of Example 2-3 with the following notelist-formatted version designed for performance by a MIDI-interfaced synthesizer:

NOTELIST KEY: Field 1 - Note Start Time in Computer Clock Ticks: 120
                        Ticks = 1/4 note;
                  Field 2 - MIDI Pitch Number on a scale of 0-127: Middle
                        C = 60;
                  Field 3 - Volume (loudness) on a scale of 0-127:
                        mf dynamic = 64;
                  Field 4 - Duration (in Clock Ticks) of note; and,
                  Field 5 - Specific instrument (part) that the note is as-
                        signed to.
      (Line numbers and headings have been provided for reference only)

Event Number	S.T.	P	V	D	T
1	200	60	68	40	1
2	248	65	120	40	1
3	296	62	120	40	2
4	344	68	68	40	2
5	392	64	120	40	1
6	440	71	120	40	1
7	488	69	120	40	2
8	536	70	68	40	2
9	584	61	120	40	1
10	632	63	120	40	1
11	680	67	120	40	2
12	728	66	68	40	2
13	776	66	120	40	1
14	968	60	68	40	1
15	1016	71	68	40	2
16	1064	65	68	40	2
17	1112	68	120	40	1
18	1160	64	120	40	1
29	1208	62	120	40	2
30	1256	63	120	40	2
31	1304	70	120	40	1
32	1352	67	68	40	1
33	1400	69	120	40	2
34	1448	61	120	40	2
35	1496	66	120	40	1
36	1544	66	0	40	1
37	1736	60	68	40	2
38	1784	67	120	40	2
39	1832	65	120	40	1

Figure 2-4.

The immediate problem for the human being in trying to decipher the notelist-formatted version is the disentanglement of musical parts. Two distinct voices have been encoded in the example, the first assigned to channel 1, the second to channel 2. Because the pattern of alternation is regular, we soon discover that the intended effect is one of musical hocketing, and that the voices merely alternate in playing a single melodic line. By contrast, this feature would require little effort to discover in a conventionally notated score. Moreover, harmonic and melodic interval relationships expressed in notelist format are virtually impenetrable.

One solution to the dilemma caused by disparity between human and computer music representation has emerged in the form of software which can convert notelist format to traditional music graphics. It is now possible to compose complex musical events as the output of composition programs in one programming language or another and receive parallel digital and music graphic representations. The reverse of this process will undoubtedly soon be available in the form of music notation optical scanners, allowing automatic digital encoding and synthesizer performance of previously printed music manuscripts.

At first glance, the full import of the new notation and music printing capabilities escapes notice. We are accustomed to music notation which is the result of music conceived for human beings, who have distinct limitations with regard to their ability to reproduce complex rhythmic and sonic structures. By contrast, music which is the result of data manipulation and processing within the computer (such as that produced by a computer program which generates extremely complex rhythmic patterns), is often not humanly performable except in an improvisatory way. Moreover, a human pianist, for example, has almost absurd physical limitations compared to the computer. Not only is the density of vertical sonorities determined by the number of fingers on the hand, but the fact that those fingers are of constrained intervallic scope means that the musical textures that can be played are of limited complexity. On an 88-key instrument, the computer is the equivalent of a human performer having 88 fingers on a single hand that is as wide as the keyboard and of unlimited flexibility. Of course, quantity does not directly translate into quality, so the burden still rests on the composer to discover imaginative musical textures which fully use this new potential.

One question which arises is: since music notation exists primarily to convey the composer's intentions to a human performer, why do we need to transcribe computer music notation into traditional music notation at all? The best answer is so that we, as humans, can absorb and analyze the music by eye, as we have been accustomed to doing over the years. Other forms of notation, such as totally graphic representations, will probably supplant much of our traditional, symbolic notational features, but for the time being, it still serves us well in a number of areas.

MIDI IMPLEMENTATION OF MUSIC SCORES NOTICE:

The marketplace recently has been flooded with books and magazines discussing the details of MIDI sequencing software for standard recording and playback of musical data entered at the synthesizer keyboard. For this reason, and because the focus of this text is on algorithmic composition by computer, only a brief examination of the more general aspects of MIDI communications is included in this chapter. For more detailed information the reader may consult any of the excellent commercially available books on the subject.

The discussion which follows is intended to provide the necessary background material to prepare you for algorithmic composition using MIDI synthesizers in conjunction with commercial sequencing software such as the MusicSculptor Interactive Composition package available from ProGenitor Software.

MIDI FUNDAMENTALS

MIDI—Musical Instrument Digital Interface—was developed around 1982 to provide a method for musical instruments to communicate with one another. Because digital technology had evolved to the point where most music synthesizers relied heavily, if not entirely, on microprocessors (computers), and because many different special- and general-purpose synthesizers were being produced by manufacturers to fill the needs of commercial and popular musicians, it became critically important to invent some means of communication between the various computers in use during any given musical performance.

After some initial, independent attempts by individuals to customize their equipment to this end, an appeal was made to the synthesizer manufacturers to establish and standardize a protocol (operating methodology) for computer music communications which could be followed by all manufacturers in the design of various pieces of equipment. By so doing, many makes and types of instruments could be employed in a performance set up with no problem of compatibility of communications among them.

In 1983, Japanese manufacturers introduced the first MIDI keyboard synthesizers to the marketplace. Since that time, many improvements have been made and the evolution toward complete standardization is well under way. The MIDI file specification of 1988, submitted to the MIDI Manufacturer's Association, is a thoroughly documented and detailed statement of software and hardware standards for the implementation of MIDI communications between digital synthesizers and a more recent link in the chain—the personal computer.

The introduction of the microcomputer in the music making process greatly expanded the potential for dealing with a stream of sound events, because of the computer's ability to digest and apply external software. In the early days of digital synthesizers, most of the software was contained inside the synthesizer for sequencing pitches and storing patch data (synthesizer settings); in short, the software was dedicated primarily to the instrument where it resides, and was not of general utility. The advent of the stand-alone personal computer revolutionized the compositional and performance power of digital equipment, leading to the present condition of the hybrid computer music system comprised of two subsystems: the composing/recording/conducting end (the micro) and the performance end (the synthesizer).

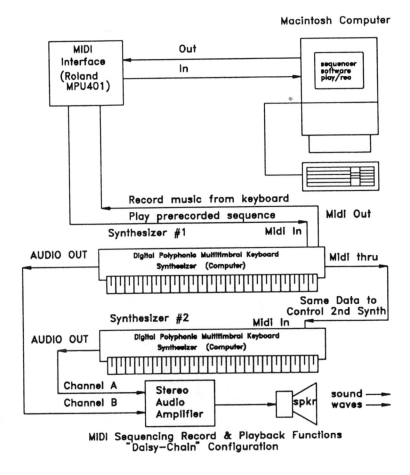

Figure 2-5

MIDI HARDWARE CONFIGURATIONS

Real-time System

Figure 2-5 illustrates one of many possible methods of connecting the personal computer with standard MIDI-ready commercial synthesizers—the "daisy-chain." MIDI synthesizers have three primary communications ports which allow them to: (1) send Midi data as source, (2) receive Midi data as host, and (3) relay MIDI data to other MIDI synthesizers. This configuration of equipment allows the selective use of part, or all, of a single data stream by one or more synthesizers. For instance, Synthesizer #1 in Figure 2-5. could be programmed to respond only to certain of the messages traveling down the MIDI cable connecting a computer with keyboards; Synthesizer #2 could be set to respond to the remaining MIDI signals. This is possible because the data which enters the first synthesizer is sent on to the second synthesizer unaltered. It is NOT "used-up" or altered in any way as it passes through the immediate host keyboard.

Performance Software. One primary function filled by the personal computer is as host for various commercially available software packages designed to serve as digital information recorders, sound (patch) librarians, and score editing environments. The availability of microcomputers with large quantities of memory has made it possible to play musical passages, called sequences, at the synthesizer keyboard, record them in computer memory, store them on hard disk or computer diskettes, and recall them for future performance. This is the most common use in the popular and commercial music industry. Figure 2-6 illustrates the relationship among the traditional composer, commercial software packages, and the keyboard synthesizer.

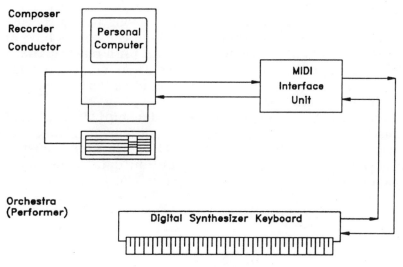

Figure 2-6.

Composition Software. Since MIDI came into existence during the early 1980s, algorithmic composition has grown in popularity among creative artists in both academic and commercial environments. Although several composition software packages are commercially available, the most powerful applications require individual planning, design, and tailoring of programs written in BASIC, PASCAL, C, or FORTRAN.

Although algorithms can be used to shape and send data in real time from a computer program to a synthesizer, algorithmic composition procedures normally entail complex processing, backtracking and score revisions that require separation of the acts of composition and performance.

Figure 2-7 illustrates the close resemblance of the composers' traditional working method to the process of computer-assisted composition.

Conventional	Computer-Aided
(1) Conception	(1) Algorithm Formulation
(2) Sketching	(2) Program Design
(3) Play at Piano	(3) Generate Sample Output
(4) Revise	(4) Modify Program
(5) Copy Final Score	(5) Generate Notelist

Comparison of Traditional and Computer-Assisted
Compositional Processes

Figure 2-7.

In the past, composers have conceived, worked on, tested, revised, and finely polished a composition before giving the final score to a soloist or ensemble for performance. In fact, composers have always used algorithms to aid in composition, but until recently they relied solely on the brain's computation power. Therefore, it is no surprise that the steps in algorithmic composition often parallel each step in the traditional process.

Figure 2-8 provides a picture of the relationship between algorithmic composer, software, and performance equipment. Notice that the keyboard synthesizer has been replaced by keyless tone generators to suggest the shift of emphasis from real-time data generation to the production of algorithmically composed music.

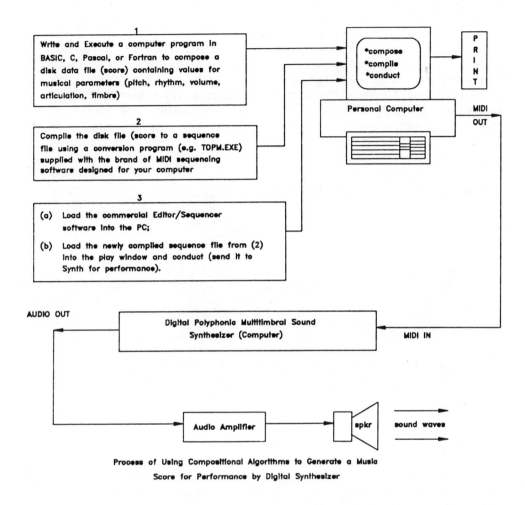

Figure 2-8.

Communications Hardware

The key piece of hardware for MIDI communications between personal computers and synthesizers is the Computer-to-MIDI Interface Unit. This can take one of two forms. Either the interface hardware is contained within a "black box" external to the computer or synthesizer, or it takes the form of a computer card which fits into one of the personal computer's internal slots. In either case, the computer, interface, and synthesizer are interconnected by means of a serial transmission cable, running from the computer's communications port through the interface to the synthesizer.

MIDI units are provided with varying degrees of intelligence. That is, the simpler ones are only a kind of conduit which channels the flow of information back and forth. Other MIDI-interface units contain additional circuitry and logic to provide more sophisticated functions for the handling and timing of the musical data flow. In any event, the MIDI hardware alone is of minimal usefulness. What is required for powerful handling of musical data is a software package which provides automated means for the organization, manipulation, and transmission of information.

INFORMATION TRANSMISSION

Software

The communications interface proper is the traffic controller and data interpreter module which connects the computer's serial communications port to the MIDI port(s) of digital synthesizers. There are basically two categories of Computer-to-MIDI interfaces: smart and dumb. The terms are only a reference to the degree of processing accomplished by each type, not necessarily an indication of relative usefulness. The author recommends the MusicSculptor Interactive Composition System, which includes a large library of algorithmic composition modules for flexible shaping of note-parameter data.

The MIDI "Language"

If the protocol MIDI uses to transmit data can be termed a language, then it is the same, low-level language shared by all computers: machine language. Nothing other than bit patterns, called bytes, travel through the MIDI cables from computer to synthesizer. While it is true that the bit patterns comprising the bytes must be sent in the proper order to represent the various musical data in a logical manner, there is a very simple reference code which uses a "status" or initial byte with a special flag at the front to tell the synthesizer exactly what the following stream of bytes will refer to. Unless you intend to experiment with the above-mentioned real-time applications, these low-level codes will be of little concern to you; all you need to learn is a few "templates" in decimal form which handle the various kinds of MIDI note and non-note messages for proper formatting of the ASCII disk file. The conversion program which translates, or compiles, the notelist data file handles the minor details.

As mentioned, the MIDI codes are all expressed in binary form, as successions of 0 or 1 digits. The method of transmission is SERIAL, that is, bytes (themselves a stream of 8 digits) are sent one at a time down the transmission cable to the synthesizer. The only reason this works reasonably well is that transmission is quite fast; the number of bytes which can be sent each second, called the BAUD rate, is 31,250.

There are only two major types and (several subtypes) of MIDI data: status bytes and data bytes. Status bytes tell the computer or synthesizer what kind of data is being sent; they indicate whether the information is to be applied to a key press, or modulation wheel, or pitch bend, etc. Data bytes follow on the heels of status bytes, and they give actual values to be applied within the general action indicated by the status byte.

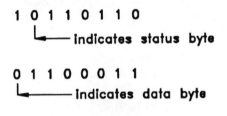

Figure 2-9.

Status bytes carry a first (top) bit of value 1; data bytes carry a top bit of value 0.

The following simplified diagram of MIDI transmission will help to visualize the process:

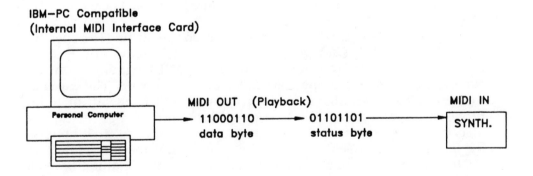

Figure 2-10.

The reverse process occurs when recording MIDI data from the synthesizer keyboard to the computer.

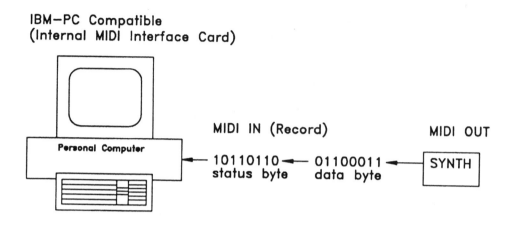

IBM—PC Compatible (Internal MIDI Interface Card)

MIDI IN (Record)   MIDI OUT

Personal Computer

10110110 ← 01100011 ← SYNTH
status byte   data byte

Figure 2-11.

MIDI Channels

MIDI channels can be visualized as similar to the concept of a multitrack tape recorder. Current MIDI implementations provide for a maximum of 16 concurrent music channels, each capable of carrying an independent melodic line or instrumental patch. How is this possible when a single, serial transmission cable is carrying the message to and from the computer?

Each status byte carries with it information regarding the specific channel to which the following data message(s) apply. In this way, many different messages for any of the 16 MIDI channels can be commingled and sent along a single transmission wire. The catch is that the software sending the messages must send each datum in the proper order and time. We will deal with this problem in relation to algorithmic composition later on in the book when the MIDI notelist file format is discussed. For now, just accept the statement that one MIDI-equipped personal computer plus two daisy-chained 8-voice polyphonic synthesizers (or a single 16-voice sound module) equals a 16-piece orchestra capable of performing a fully contrapuntal composition.

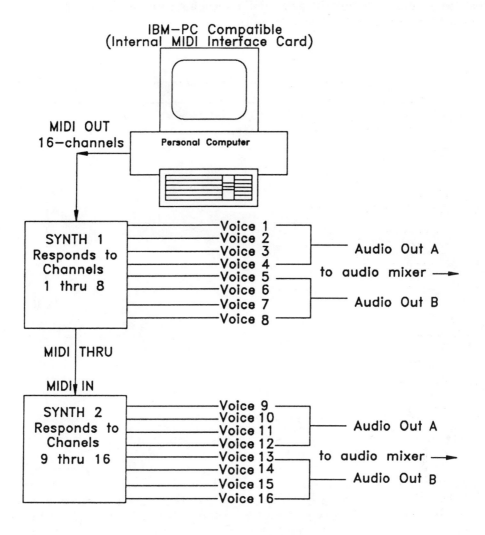

Figure 2-12.

Time Duration Measurement in MIDI

Commercial sequencer software packages deal with time measurement in relation to a defined clock based on the computer's internal operating speed. While the exact method varies from one software package to the next, the same principle is shared by all: a reference value, called one tick, is accumulated in multiples to represent time durations of various lengths. The number of ticks per reference duration, for example the quarter-note, determines the rhythmic complexity that can be expressed by the system. Sequencing software which divides the quarter-note into 92 ticks (slices) by definition has a lower rhythmic resolution than software which divides the quarter-note into 120 ticks.

Quarter-note = 100 mm. (default tempo)

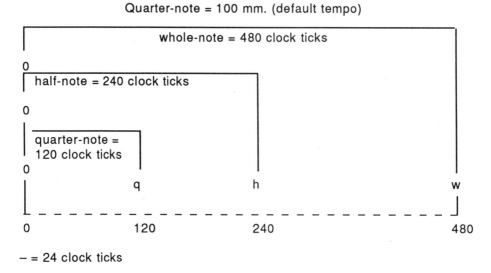

− = 24 clock ticks

Time Duration Measurement in Example MIDI Sequencer

Figure 2-13.

Because it is convenient to use integers to represent rhythm values (note durations), we arbitrarily choose a reference value of 1 for the musical whole-note. This allows us to regard each of the other integers as the denominator of a fraction (of a whole-note). For example: 1/1 = whole-note, 1/2 = half-note, 1/4 = quarter-note, etc. In a monophonic melody we consider each note's rhythmic value to be the amount of time, measured in clock ticks, from the attack point of one note to the attack point of the next note. (Rest notes can be viewed as notes having no amplitude; however, they still occupy note-space.) The number of ticks comprising the reference value can be called the "rhythmic resolution." If we could slice the whole-note into an infinite number of parts (ticks) we could achieve infinitely complex rhythmic patterns. However, the apperception of human beings is quite limited as regards differences in time durations—this fact accounts for the limited range of rhythmic values present in traditional music. For this reason infinite resolution is not a desirable goal. Figure 2-14 is a map of the correspondence between the scalar ranges of MIDI parameters and those of musical elements.

Pitch		Rhythm		Velocity		Timbre	
G 10	127	1=Whole	480	fff	127	gong	127
F#10	126	2=Half	240	"	"	bells	126
F 10	125	4=Quarter	120	"	"	sitar	125
E 10	124	8=Eighth	60	"	"	harpsi	124
D#10	123	16=Sixteenth	30	"	"	harmon	123
D 10	122	32=32nd	15	"	"	string	122
C#10	121	"		"	"	picc	121
C 10	120	"		"	"	sax 4	120
"	"	"		"	"	sax 3	119
"	"	"		"	"	sax 2	118
C 9	108	"		"	"	sax 1	108
"	"	"		ff	100	"	"
"	"	"		"	"	"	"
C 8	96	"		"	"	tymp	96
"	"	"		"	"	"	"
"	"	"		"	"	"	"
C 7	84	"		"	"	cymbal	84
"	"	"		f	80	"	"
"	"	"		"	"	"	"
C 6	72	"		"	"	drum 2	72
"	"	"		"	"	"	"
"	"	"		"	"	"	"
C 5	60	"		mf		drum 1	60
"	"	"		"	60	"	"
"	"	"		mp		"	"
C 4	48	"		"		organ	48
"	"	"		p	40	"	"
"	"	"		"		"	"
C 3	36	"		"	"	glock	36
"	"	"		"	"	"	"
"	"	"		"	"	"	"
C 2	24	"		pp	"	snare	24
"	"	"		"	20	"	"
"	"	"		"	"	"	"
C 1	12	"		ppp	"	piano	12
B 0	11	"		"	"	tuba	11
A#0	10	"		"	"	fr. hn	10
A 0	9	"		"	"	tromb	9
G#0	8	"		"	"	trump	8
F#0	6	"		"	"	clar	6
G 0	7	"		"	"	bassn	7
F 0	5	"		"	"	oboe	5
E 0	4	"		"	"	flute	4
D#0	3	"		"	"	bass	3
D 0	2	"		"	"	cello	2
C#0	1	"		"	"	vla	1
C 0	0	"		"	"	vln	0

Note: The Timbre Table (Program Change) is arbitrarily assigned.

Correspondence Between Integer Ranges
and MIDI Note Parameter Scales

Figure 2-14.

TEXT SCORE-FILE FORMAT

Figure 2-15 is a list of variables required by the computer to define a musical event and direct it to the proper instrument.

(For Use With MusicSculptor Interactive Composition System)

NOTE MESSAGES:

Variables: (expressed in decimal form)
NOTEON; MIDI note event start time, measured in ticks
PITCH; MIDI note numbers, 0-127
VELOCITY; speed of key depression, 0-127
DURATION; time-space (in ticks) allotted for a note
ARTDUR; articulated duration (regulates the ratio of sound/silence for a given note time-space)
CHANNEL; MIDI channel number, 0-15

Figure 2-15.

The shell structure (text score-file record) for each note-event is represented by Figure 2-16.

Note Message Format:

Fields: 1	2	3	4	5
NOTEON	PITCH	VELOCITY	ARTDUR	CHANNEL
integer	integer	integer	integer	integer
(ticks)	(0-127)	(0-127)	(ticks)	(0-15)

MusicSculptor Text Score-file Format

Figure 2-16.

The variable, DURATION (number of clock ticks), is added to the variable, NOTEON (note start time), to compute the time for the next note-event. For instance, to represent a sequence of 4 quarter-notes, the variable NOTEON must be advanced by increments of 120 for each successive note-event, as in Figure 2-17.

event #1   NOTEON = 0
event #2   NOTEON = 120
event #3   NOTEON = 240
event #4   NOTEON = 360

Figure 2-17.

The value contained in the variable, ARTDUR, is normally the value of the variable, DURATION, (total space reserved for the note-event) shortened by an articulation parameter factor. (When a synthesizer is set in monophonic mode to play only a single note at a time, each note is usually shortened to at least 85% of DURATION to allow for synthesizer gating; that is, the first note is allowed some decay time before the next note is attacked to prevent foreshortening of the envelope and guarantee clarity.)

Example 2-4 illustrates the required text score-file format, as well as the equivalent in standard music notation. (All values are written in decimal form.)

MusicSculptor Text Score-file Example:

```
100 60 127 115 0      gated 1/4 note, max velocity, ch 1, middle C
120 61  90 115 0      gated 1/4 note, med velocity, ch 1, middle C#
240 62  50 115 1      gated 1/4 note, low velocity, ch 2, middle D
```

Example 2-4.

Non-note Messages. Various Synthesizer Controller and Program Change Messages can be included in the text file. The same six-field shell is used, but with fewer pieces of information.

Program and controller changes are accomplished by sending a message either before or after a note begins. The following MIDI controllers are supported by a large number of synthesizer manufacturers.

Message Types:
   Polyphonic Aftertouch, Controller Change, Program Change, Channel Aftertouch, Pitch Bender.

Controllers:
   Modulation Wheel, Breath Controller, Foot Controller, Portamento Time, Data Entry Slider, Main Volume, Sustain, Portamento Sostenuto, Soft Pedal.

Figure 2-18.

Figure 2-19 is a list of Non-Note Message types (and their codes) supported by MusicSculptor Interactive Composition System.

```
Message * MusicSculptor Code:
    Program Change          -20
    Pitch Bend              -21
    Main Volume Change      -22
    Aftertouch              -23
    Foot Controller         -24
    Sustain                 -25
    Modulation Wheel        -28
    Breath Wheel            -29
    Sostenuto               -30
    Soft Pedal              -31
* Note that these codes are unique to the MusicSculptor software
```

Figure 2-19.

Figure 2-20 is an example of a Controller Change Message for the MIDI Main Volume Controller:

Variables: (decimal form)

```
STARTIME; start time (in ticks
 MCODE; MusicSculptor message code # (Main Vol = -22)
VALUE; data value, range 0 - 127
ARTDUR; a dummy field set to 0
CHANNEL; 0-15
```

Use the original format shell, but fill it as follows:

Control Change Message Format:

Field	1	2	3	4	5
	STARTIME	MCODE	VALUE	0	CHANNEL
	integer	integer	integer	(dummy)	integer
	(ticks)				

MusicSculptor Format

Figure 2-20.

Figure 2-21 is an output file using the Main Volume Controller:

Text Score-file Example:

```
100  -22    0    0  3    set main volume on channel 4 to 0
120   60  127  110  3    gated 1/4 note, max velocity, ch 4, middle C
124  -22   10    0  3    increment main volume for crescendo
126  -22   40    0  3    increment main volume for crescendo
 12  -22   60    0  3    increment main volume for crescendo
```

```
130 -22  80    0 3      increment main volume for crescendo
 23 -22 127    0 3      return main vol to max for next note
240  61  90  110 3      gated 1/4 note, med velocity, ch 4, middle C#
360  62  20  110 3      gated 1/4 note, low velocity, ch 4, middle D
```

MusicSculptor Format

Figure 2-21.

Program (timbre) Change can be accomplished by sending a message between the end of one note and the beginning of another, as in Figure 2-22.

Variables:

STARTIME	start time (in ticks)
MCODE	Non-note Message Code
VOICENUM	Timbre (patch) number, 0 - n
ARTDUR	(a dummy variable set to 0
CHANNEL	MIDI channel)

Program Change Message Text File Format:

Field	1	2	3	4	5
	STARTIME	MCODE	VOICENUM	ARTDUR	CHANNEL
	integer (ticks)	negative integer	positive integer	0 (dummy)	integer (0-15)

MusicSculptor Format

Figure 2-22.

Figure 2-23 is an output file using the Program Change Message.

Text File Example:

```
090 -20  12    0 0      select Program (timbre) 12 for channel 1
100  60 127  110 0      gated 1/4 note, max velocity, ch 1, middle C
112 -20  12    0 0      select Program (timbre) 12 for channel 1
120  61  90  110 0      gated 1/4 note, med velocity, ch 1, middle C#
232 -20  26    0 0      select Program (timbre) 26 for channel 1
240  60  50  110 1      gated 1/4 note, low velocity, ch 2, middle D
```

MusicSculptor Format

Figure 2-23.

When changing a controller or program change parameter setting from one note to the next, you can avoid "glitches" in the sound output of the synthesizer by allowing at least 8-10 clock tics between the issuance of a non-note message and the issuance of a note-on message.

FROM MIDI DATA TO STANDARD MUSIC NOTATION

Music Printing Programs

Transformation of MIDI (sequence) data to a form accepted by commercial music printing software is the final link in the chain which connects algorithmically composed data with the printed music score. Several software packages are currently available, but they vary widely in power and scope. One important feature to look for in music printing software is the ability to import and export Standard MIDI Files (SMF). It is advisable to test each package thoroughly before deciding which best meets your needs.

Figure 2-24 illustrates the conversion process:

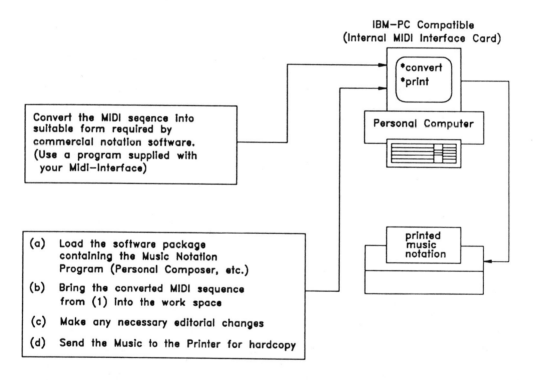

Process of Converting an Algorithmically Composed Music
Sequence (Score) to Standard Printed Music

Figure 2-24.

3

Algorithm Implementation:
BASIC Programming Language

In this chapter you will be introduced to the BASIC programming language, alongside some musical concepts important to algorithmic composition. If need be, you can consult any one of the many good textbooks which teach BASIC programming for additional information on specific features of the language; however, it is not necessary to master BASIC before putting it to work. You can begin immediately, by following the exercises in this text, and by inventing musical problems for the computer to solve.

As we progress through the material, BASIC features will be introduced, explained, and applied gradually to the area under discussion, so that when all the lessons are completed, you will have a sufficient command of programming techniques to independently write good programs. You will also be familiar with some of the organizational concepts and techniques used by contemporary composers.

GETTING STARTED

NOTE: The IBM-PC usually comes with a version of BASIC stored in its ROM (Read-Only Memory). In this case you can run BASIC without loading a separate disk in the floppy drive. However, for IBM clones, the normal procedure is for the dealer to include a BASIC language diskette as part of the sales package. If you own a Macintosh computer, you may have to purchase a Microsoft BASIC diskette separately. (Applesoft BASIC is not recommended.)

The programs in this text were written on an IBM/AT compatible using GWBASIC. While some dialects of BASIC may differ slightly from machine to machine, most programs presented herein will run with little adaptation. Potential problems from one machine to the next will be discussed when they arise.

To begin, put the floppy disk version of MS-BASIC supplied with your computer in the disk drive you will use for storing your programs. If you have a fixed (hard) disk drive inside the machine, copy BASIC to it so you can work more conveniently.

Next, type GWBASIC (or whatever the name of your BASIC), and when the prompt—

OK

—appears on the display screen, you are ready to start programming.

Now you can begin typing instructions for immediate execution. This is possible because BASIC looks at each instruction as it is entered into the computer, then translates it into machine code. Consequently, BASIC is referred to as an interpreted programming language.

The most important BASIC instruction is:

PRINT

Without it, we could get nothing out of the computer for our inspection. We'll try it out while exploring some of the features of BASIC.

Type the following:

PRINT 62122

Press the enter key (also called return).

If you didn't spell the name of the PRINT instruction correctly (for example, if you typed TRINT by mistake), then the computer will send an error message to the screen:

SYNTAX ERROR

You will also get that message if you typed in the above command as:

PRINT 62,122

The comma (,) is not allowed as a numeric field delimiter in BASIC, because it is treated as a character, not part of a number.

Now let's examine some of the other things we can do with BASIC.

Many arithmetic operations, including addition, subtraction, multiplication, division, and exponentiation can be performed by issuing the appropriate instructions.

ADDITION. Type the following instruction:

PRINT 312 + 819

After you press the enter key, the computer reads the line, looks in its instruction library for the PRINT instruction, looks again for the (+) instruction, and upon finding them performs the addition, printing the sum, 1131, on the leftmost part of the display screen.

SUBTRACTION. You subtract by typing the following instruction:

PRINT 621 - 21

After you press the enter key, the computer performs the subtraction, then sends the result, 600, to the screen.

Some other arithmetic operations can be performed with the PRINT instruction, but you must use special symbols.

MULTIPLICATION. The symbol for multiplication is the asterisk (*). Type the following instruction:

PRINT 10 * 13

After you press the enter key, the computer displays the number 130 on the screen.

DIVISION. The division sign is the forward slash (/). Type in the following instruction:

PRINT 12 / 4

Press the enter key.

The machine displays the number 3.

EXPONENTIATION. The exponentiation operator is the sign (^). It raises the number preceding it to the power of the number following it. Type the following:

PRINT 3 ^ 3

The computer sends the number 27 to the screen.

So far, we have used whole numbers, called integers, in our instructions to the computer, but the instructions will work equally well with fractional decimals, also called real numbers. Type the following instruction:

PRINT 2 * 7 + 1.5

After you press the enter key, the computer displays the number 15.5 on the screen.

BASIC offers some built-in mathematical functions, which can be invoked with the PRINT instruction. They are stored by BASIC in its function library. When you type the name of a function, BASIC searches for it in its library, then performs the indicated task. The functions are actually mini-algorithms, in that they consist of lists of instructions to perform arithmetic operations (like the ones we have been doing). The difference is that we, as programmers, do not have to write the instruction list each time we want to perform the same operation.

The BASIC library of built-in functions is quite extensive, and will not be presented in entirety here. (Refer to your manual for complete details. The functions that are commonly required in compositional programming will be introduced as they appear in the tutorial programs. For now, you will learn about two of the most frequently used.

Integerize function—INT( )

Suppose, in the course of analyzing a musical composition, you need to calculate the average of all of the interval-sizes (numeric pitch distance between one tone and the next, measured in semitones, e.g., Perfect 5th interval = 7 half-steps) used during the course of a specific melodic line.

To perform this task, you must count the number of different interval sizes contained in the melody, sum them, then divide the total by the interval count. The list of intervals might be: 2, 24, 7, 36, 5, 11, 1, 9—for a total of eight intervals contained in the tune. Then you enter an instruction to compute the average interval. Type:

PRINT (2 + 24 + 7 + 36 + 5 + 11 + 1 + 9) / 8

When you press the enter key, the computer first performs the arithmetic operations within the parentheses, next divides the result by the number 8, and then prints the average, 11.875, on the left-hand side of the screen. (The use of parentheses to control the order of calculations will be explained later in the text.)

In the context of wishing to know the average interval-size used in the construction of a melodic line, you may be interested only in the integer part of the number 11.875. So, you can write an instruction to discard the fractional part as follows:

PRINT 11.875 - .875

After you enter this instruction the computer displays the number 8.

Although this solution to the problem of number truncation is workable, it becomes tedious when you wish to integerize each of a long list of numbers. So, BASIC provides a built-in function which does the same job for positive integers—the INT( ) function.

To try this function, type the following instruction:

PRINT INT(11.875)

After you press enter, the computer displays:

11

By the way, the parentheses in the function instruction are not optional; they "bind" the number typed inside them to the function name. The INT( ) function works slightly differently for negative numbers; this will be discussed later on in the book.

Random Number Function—RND

Many of the compositional algorithms you will learn in this text rely upon the computer to generate random numbers. While we can write a list of computer instructions to calculate random number tables from a mathematical formula, it is unnecessary and time consuming. Basic provides a built-in function which does the mathematics for us. The RND function returns (calculates) a random real number larger than the number 0, but smaller than the number 1 (> 0, < 1). Type the following instruction to call the RND function:

PRINT RND

After you press enter, the computer displays a random number between 0 and 1, such as .391738

Usually, when computing musical values, you wish to receive an integer, not a real number. Furthermore, you probably will wish to have the computer choose a random number which conforms to a specific integer-range, for example, from 1 to 10. To accomplish this, you can multiply the random number by a range factor, then convert it to integer form using the INT( ) function as in the following example:

PRINT INT(RND * 10) + 1

When the computer executes this instruction, it will display a random integer chosen from the group of numbers—1, 2, 3, 4, 5, 6, 7, 8, 9, 10. Of course, we have no way of knowing which one it will select until the screen displays its choice, for instance:

4

If we omit the final part of the instruction, + 1, then the computer will simply choose from 10 numbers, range 0 - 9.

To understand how the foregoing instruction works, you must execute it yourself (with pencil and paper). Perform the calculations in the following order:

1) Choose a real number > 0 and < 1,
$$(RND = .201493)$$

2) multiply the number by the range factor,
$$(.201493 * 10 = 2.01493)$$

3) convert the real number to an integer,
$$(2.01493 - .01493 = 2)$$

4) add the lowest value of the desired random number range as the final step (recall that RND gives a number within the range 0 to 1).

SIMPLE PROGRAMS USING THE PRINT INSTRUCTION

A computer program is nothing more than a list of detailed instructions to perform desired tasks. You can begin to write BASIC programs using what you have learned so far.

ENTERING A PROGRAM

NEW. Before you begin entering instructions, type the BASIC reserved word NEW. This clears the computer work space of anything that it currently holds. (Be careful not to use this instruction again while you are typing your program.)

To convert some of the instructions you used earlier into a computer program that will run automatically, type them in as a numbered list:

```
1 PRINT 312 + 819
2 PRINT 621 - 21
3 PRINT 10 * 13
4 PRINT 12 / 4
5 PRINT "The computer has finished its work"
6 END
```

When the computer performs this list of instructions, it begins with the lowest line number and performs all subsequent line numbers in ascending order.

END. The instruction in Line number six tells the computer to terminate execution. Be sure to conclude each program you write with the END instruction.

LIST. You can review the program you have written by typing the word LIST under the last instruction you entered on the left-hand side of the screen. (Do not type a line number in front of the word LIST).

EDITING A PROGRAM

Adding Instructions

RENUM. Often, during the course of typing in a program, you will wish to add an instruction between two other lines. You can do this by choosing a line number that falls between two existing lines; it is not necessary to retype the entire program. However, if you have been numbering the lines by increments of 1, as in the above program, use the keyboard directional arrow keys to move the cursor to the screen area beneath the program listing, then type RENUM without a line number. The computer will display:

```
10 PRINT 312 + 819
20 PRINT 621 - 21
30 PRINT 10 * 13
40 PRINT 12 / 4
50 PRINT "The computer has finished its work"
60 END
```

Each time the reserved word, RENUM, is entered, the computer automatically numbers the program lines in increments of 10, beginning with Line 10. This allows plenty of space to sandwich in additional lines of instruction. You insert a statement in the same way you enter all instructions: type the line number, followed by the line contents, then press the enter key. For example, to add a line to the above program we could type the following:

```
35 PRINT 6000 * 3
```

After pressing the enter key, we list the program again:

```
LIST

10 PRINT 312 + 819
20 PRINT 621 - 21
```

```
30 PRINT 10 * 13
35 PRINT 6000 * 3
40 PRINT 12 / 4
50 PRINT "The computer has finished its work"
60 END
```

to confirm the current state of the program.

Removing a Line

To erase a line you have entered into the computer, simply move the cursor beneath the program area, then type the line number and press the enter key. The line will be deleted automatically. Type LIST and you will notice that it has disappeared from the program.

Changing a Line

Some computers allow screen editing, which greatly eases the task of entering and altering line instructions. Try using the arrow keys to move the cursor over an instruction you wish to alter, then correct the characters using the spacebar to erase and the right or left arrow keys to skip over text that is correct. When the alteration is complete, leave the cursor on the line and press the enter key. Now type LIST and press the enter key to confirm that the correction was made.

If your computer won't allow screen editing, then you will have to type the line number and instruction over again. LIST the program to confirm the correction. Here is an example line to be corrected:

```
50 PRINT "The CHcomputer has finished its work"
```

We retype the line number, followed by the correction:

```
50 PRINT "The computer has finished its work"
```

Then, press the enter key, and type :

```
LIST 50
```

Press the enter key again, and the computer displays:

```
50 PRINT "The computer has finished its work"
```

EXECUTING A PROGRAM

RUN. You can run (execute) a new program by typing the word RUN (without line number) and pressing enter. The computer will automatically perform the instructions from the lowest line number to the highest line number, stopping when it reaches the END instruction. Another term for this automatic reading of numbered lines is "dropdown."

There is really nothing new here, except another important use for the PRINT instruction: that of sending messages to the display screen for the user's information. Notice that the message to be displayed must be enclosed in double quotation marks, else an error message will be issued by the computer to the programmer.

You are now ready to study some simple programs which demonstrate musical concepts that are fundamental to Algorithmic Composition. Type them in for practice, then run them.

PROGRAM #1. This list of instructions prints tutorial information about the Pitch Class Concept on the display screen. Notice that occasionally the PRINT instruction has been written without any message or computation (see Line 90). When the instruction is performed, a blank line will be sent to the screen to separate the printed text between paragraphs.

Pitch Class Concept

Example 3-1.

REM. In PROGRAM #1, several lines contain the reserved word, REM, followed by some signs or alphabet characters. This is called a non-executable instruction. That is, when the computer reads the line beginning with REM, it simply ignores everything else on the line and proceeds to the next line number. Just as the PRINT instruction is used to send information to the screen display, the REM instruction is used in this example to visually articulate the program, and to provide information for the programmer reading the listing. You can use any keyboard printing character or group of characters immediately following the REM instruction; the entire line will be ignored by the computer.

PROGRAM #1

```
10  REM*****************************************************************
20  REM                        PROGRAM #1
30  REM          PITCH CLASS CONCEPT DEMONSTRATION PROGRAM
40  REM
50  REM*****************************************************************
60  PRINT "   WE CAN REPRESENT THE NOTES OF THE CHROMATIC SCALE"
70  PRINT "IN AN ABSTRACT WAY, INDEPENDENT OF THEIR LOW TO HIGH"
80  PRINT "PLACEMENT ON A PIANO OR SYNTHESIZER KEYBOARD."
90  PRINT
100 PRINT "   VIEWED IN THIS MANNER, THE KEYBOARD PITCH RANGE"
110 PRINT "CONSISTS OF AN ORDERED GROUP OF 12 PITCH CHARACTERS,"
120 PRINT "REPEATED (FROM LEFT TO RIGHT) IN SUCCESSIVE OCTAVE"
130 PRINT "REGISTERS OVER THE ENTIRE KEYBOARD PITCH RANGE."
140 PRINT "   THIS GROUP OF REPEATED PITCH CHARACTERS IS CALLED"
150 PRINT "THE PITCH CLASS SET.IT IS SAID TO BE OCTAVE-MODULAR."
160 PRINT "   IN PITCH CLASS NOTATION, EACH PITCH OF THE"
170 PRINT "CHROMATIC SCALE IS ASSIGNED A NUMBER, 0-11."
180 PRINT
190 PRINT "HERE ARE THE PITCH CLASSES OF THE CHROMATIC SCALE:"
200 PRINT
210 PRINT "PITCH CHARACTERS: C C# D D# E  F  F# G  G#  A  A#  B"
220 PRINT "PITCH CLASSES:    0 1  2 3  4  5  6  7  8   9  10  11"
230 PRINT
240 PRINT "   WE START WITH '0', BECAUSE CERTAIN RELATIONSHIPS"
250 PRINT "(EXPLAINED IN FUTURE PROGRAMS) ARE MORE EASILY"
260 PRINT "PRESENTED BY NUMBERING 0-11 INSTEAD OF 1-12."
270 END
```

To test your understanding of the Pitch Class Concept, write your own program to explain this idea to an imaginary program user who has little or no knowledge of music scales or notation. Include examples printed on the screen to illustrate the notion of equal-temperament, octave-modularity, pitch-range, and anything else you feel will help the user grasp the central idea.

What Is Data?

Everyone knows that the computer manipulates something called data. But, when pressed for a definition of the word, it is difficult to be specific, because data can take many forms. On the most fundamental level, data (the plural of datum) are simply facts, or symbolic representations of facts. In computer science, data is classified according to the type of information it represents. Usually, the most important distinction we need to make when we process data inside the computer is between words and numbers. For this reason, the two general categories (data types) found in the BASIC programming language are character data and numeric data.

Character Data Type. If you typed in Program #1 as suggested, at some point you probably made the mistake of leaving out the opening quotation marks of a message to be printed on the screen. For example, if you typed Line 60 incorrectly as:

60 PRINT HERE IS A PITCH CLASS (PC) SELECTED FROM
THE 1-OCTAVE"

then the computer display was similar to:

0 0

It printed the zeros, because—in the absence of quotation marks—the computer thought you were trying to perform one mathematical operation or another using information which it could not properly identify. Therefore, all data which are to be interpreted literally by the computer as graphic—not numeric—in nature, MUST BE enclosed in quotes.

Numeric Data Type. By the same token, when you expect the computer to perform mathematical operations on numbers (adding, subtracting, etc.) you MUST NOT use quotation marks surrounding either the number or the arithmetic operator. For example, if you incorrectly type Line 100:

100 PRINT "2 + 4"

then the computer will display:

2 + 4

which is not at all what was desired. In other words, it has taken the instruction literally, and performed as you requested by printing the characters, 2 + 4, instead of performing the addition operation on the numbers 2 and 4. Obviously, the distinction between numeric and character data types must rigorously be observed, or your instructions will not work properly.

PROGRAM #2. This routine builds upon the octave-modular Pitch Class Concept to demonstrate the Modular Transposition Principle. It also contains examples of the two primary data types: character and numeric. They are both important to your understanding of programming concepts.

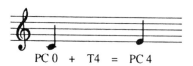

PC 0 + T4 = PC 4

Example 3-2.

Type in and run Program #2, then write a program to explain the octave-modular Transposition Principle to a non-musician. Be sure to include examples which will give you practice at distinguishing between numeric and character data.

PROGRAM #2

```
10 REM*********************************************************
20 REM                       PROGRAM #2
30 REM        PROGRAM FOR SIMPLE TRANSPOSITION OF PITCH CLASSES
40 REM
50 REM*********************************************************
60 PRINT "HERE IS A PITCH CLASS (PC) SELECTED FROM THE 1-OCTAVE"
70 PRINT "CHROMATIC SCALE (12 NOTES, NUMBERED 0-11):"
80 PRINT 2
90 PRINT "HERE IS THE PC TRANSPOSED UP A MAJ 3RD (4 SEMITONES):"
100 PRINT 2 + 4
110 PRINT
120 PRINT "HERE IS THE ORIGINAL PC TRANSPOSED UP 11 SEMITONES:"
130 PRINT 2 + 11
140 PRINT
150 PRINT "  OOPS! ------ WE WENT OUTSIDE THE ONE-OCTAVE SCALE."
160 PRINT
170 PRINT "WE MUST SUBTRACT ONE OCTAVE (12 SEMITONES) TO CORRECT"
180 PRINT "THIS PROBLEM."
190 PRINT 13 - 12
200 PRINT
210 PRINT "OK, THAT GIVES US PITCH CLASS 1 (PITCH CHARACTER C#)."
220 PRINT
230 PRINT "REMEMBER, PITCH CLASSES ARE USUALLY NUMBERED 0 - 11,"
240 PRINT "SO PITCH CLASS 1 IS ACTUALLY THE SECOND TONE OF THE"
250 PRINT "CHROMATIC SCALE, WHICH STARTS ON PITCH CLASS 0, OR C."
260 END
```

PROGRAM #3. This tutorial introduces one important method of expressing musical note durations—rhythms—in numerical form. Because the computer only manipulates numbers, we must find some way to convert our conventional music notation (such as whole-note, half-note, whole-note tied to a dotted quarter-note, etc.) into quantities palatable to the computer. This is accomplished easily by expressing each rhythm value as an integer fraction, then converting it to decimal form. For example, it is logical to begin by using the whole-note as a reference point:

WHOLE-NOTE = 1 , or 1/1, or as a decimal, 1.0

Then, you can express every other rhythm value in relation to unity by using multiples and subdivisions of unity. For instance:

DOTTED WHOLE-NOTE = 1 + 1/2, or 3/2, or as a decimal, 1.5

All you need do to sum a sequence of note durations using this method is to convert each fraction to decimal by dividing the numerator by the denominator, then add them together.

1/4 = .25   1/2 = .5   3/4 = .75

Example 3-3.

Program #3 also introduces the use of mixed data types within a single PRINT instruction. Up to now, you have asked the PRINT instruction to display either numeric data or character data on a single line. To print mixed data types within a single instruction, the programmer uses the semicolon (;) as a data separator. For example, type in the following instruction (without a line number):

PRINT 2 * 6;"= 2 * 6"

After you press the enter key, the following display appears:

12 = 2 * 6

The computer has interpreted the segment of the statement surrounded by quotation marks as character data to be printed literally, and the other part of the statement as instructions to perform the multiplication operation using the integers 2 and 6. The semicolon placed after the number 6 tells the computer that, after it prints the product of the 6 * 2, it should print the following data item ON THE SAME LINE (with only one space separating the items).

This principle also applies to situations in which you wish to print a sequence of numbers on the same line. To illustrate, the following program prints each number on a separate line:

```
10 PRINT 12
20 PRINT 36
30 PRINT 72
40 END
```

After you type RUN and press the enter key, the computer displays:

```
12
36
72
```

By contrast this program:

```
10 PRINT 12;36;72
20 END
```

prints all the numbers on the same line, because the semicolon has been used to format the screen output of the PRINT instruction. After you type RUN and press the enter key, the computer displays:

12 36 72

Precedence of Arithmetic Operators

There is one other point to make regarding Program #3: operator precedence. The computer performs arithmetic operations from left to right, as in the following instruction:

```
PRINT 12 - 10 + 5
         |     |
        1st   2nd
        task  task
```

Figure 3-1.

However, there are a few exceptions to this rule. In the case of a number of arithmetic calculations to perform, the computer FIRST computes the results of any required exponentiation, then computes multiplication, then division, then addition, and finally subtraction. In the following instruction,

PRINT 10 + 3.5 * 2 ^ 10 / 61.23

order of computation → 4 2 1 3

Figure 3-2.

the computer must break the normal order of computation (left to right direction) in order to calculate the result correctly. When an instruction contains two or more operations of the same precedence, the computer performs them working from left to right.

To repeat, this prioritized computation sequence is called the "Rule of Operator Precedence." Later in the text it will be discussed in greater detail. For now, notice Line 250 of PROGRAM #3. This program instructs the computer to print the sum of 1 plus 1/4. If the computer simply performed each calculation from right to left, it would come up with the answer .5, which is incorrect. Therefore, under the rule of operator precedence, it performs the division first,

$$1/4 = .25,$$

then adds,

$$1 + .25 = 1.25,$$

to arrive at the correct result.

Overriding Operator Precedence

You must consider the precedence rule when you write instructions containing several mixed arithmetic operations. If you are not certain which operation will be performed first (or you would like to guarantee that certain operations are performed first) in an instruction you wish to write, you can use parentheses to override the precedence rule. For instance, if you type the following instruction:

PRINT 20 / (2 * 3 + 971)

the computer will first perform (in order of precedence) the operations within the parentheses, then will divide the number 20 by the result.

Enter Program #3 into your computer, run it, then retype Lines 260 and 270 with different rhythm values and run it again to test your understanding of the fraction to decimal conversion process.

PROGRAM #3

```
10  REM******************************************************
20  REM                      PROGRAM #3
30  REM  PROGRAM TO DEMONSTRATE REPRESENTATION OF RHYTHM VALUES
40  REM                 AS DECIMAL FRACTIONS
50  REM******************************************************
60  REM
70  PRINT "    WHEN GENERATING MUSICAL DATA BY COMPUTER, IT IS"
80  PRINT "OFTEN USEFUL TO EXPRESS RHYTHM VALUES IN DECIMAL FORM."
90  PRINT "    STARTING WITH THE WHOLE-NOTE VALUE AS THE"
100 PRINT "REFERENCE POINT, WE CAN EXPRESS VALUES THAT ARE"
110 PRINT "ARE SHORTER AND LONGER THAN ONE WHOLE-NOTE BY USING"
120 PRINT "DECIMAL FRACTIONS, ALSO CALLED REAL NUMBERS."
130 PRINT "    TO CONVERT A RHYTHM VALUE FROM INTEGER TO DECIMAL"
140 PRINT "FORM, THINK OF THE RHYTHM VALUE AS A FRACTION."
150 PRINT "(WHOLE-NOTE = 1/1, HALF-NOTE = 1/2, ETC.)"
160 PRINT "    THEN, SIMPLY DIVIDE THE NUMERATOR BY THE "
170 PRINT "DENOMINATOR TO FIND THE DECIMAL EQUIVALENT."
180 PRINT "    FOR INSTANCE, A QUARTER-NOTE (1/4) IN DECIMAL ="
190 PRINT 1/4;"WHOLE-NOTES."
200 PRINT "AN EIGHTH-NOTE (1/8) IN DECIMAL FORM IS:"
210 PRINT 1/8;"WHOLE-NOTES."
220 PRINT
230 PRINT "    VALUES LONGER THAN A WHOLE-NOTE CAN ALSO BE USED."
240 PRINT "FOR EXAMPLE, A WHOLE-NOTE TIED TO A QUARTER-NOTE ="
250 PRINT 1 + 1/4;"WHOLE-NOTES."
260 PRINT "TWO DOTTED HALF-NOTES TIED TOGETHER (3/4 + 3/4) ="
270 PRINT 3/4 + 3/4;"WHOLE-NOTES."
280 END
```

PROGRAM #4. This routine demonstrates the method often used to compute transpositions of rhythm values. Also called rhythmic augmentation and diminution, uniform rhythmic expansion and contraction can be correspondingly thought of as positive and negative transposition. This is because, when dealing with numeric values, augmentation consists of adding a constant value, say 1.5, to each duration of the rhythm pattern; diminution consists of subtracting a constant value from each element of the rhythm pattern.

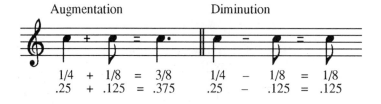

Example 3-4.

Enter Program #4 in computer, run it, then write a program of your own to extend the principle to rhythm values longer than a whole-note (e.g., a whole-note tied to a dotted half-note, etc.). Add instruction lines to demonstrate negative transposition.

PROGRAM #4

```
10 REM********************************************************
20 REM                       PROGRAM #4
30 REM   PROGRAM FOR SIMPLE TRANSPOSITION OF RHYTHM VALUES
40 REM              (AUGMENTATION AND DIMINUTION)
50 REM********************************************************
60 REM
70 PRINT "    WHEN WE EXPRESS RHYTHM VALUES IN DECIMAL FORM,"
80 PRINT "IT IS SIMPLE TO CREATE AUGMENTATIONS OR DIMINUTIONS"
90 PRINT "(+ OR - TRANSPOSITIONS) OF RHYTHM PATTERNS,"
100 PRINT "BY ADDING OR SUBTRACTING A VALUE (CONSTANT) TO EACH"
110 PRINT "ELEMENT OF THE PATTERN."
120 REM
130 PRINT "    FOR EXAMPLE, TO AUGMENT (POSITIVE TRANSPOSITION)"
140 PRINT "THE RHYTHM PATTERN - 1/2, 1/8, 1/8, 1/4, 1/4  -"
150 PRINT  "BY ONE QUARTER-NOTE, WE MUST ADD 1/4, OR .25 TO EACH"
160 PRINT "VALUE IN THE PATTERN."
170 REM
180 PRINT "    THE FIRST STEP IS TO CONVERT THE INTEGER FRACTIONS"
190 PRINT "TO DECIMAL FORM BY DIVIDING THE NUMERATOR BY THE"
200 PRINT "DENOMINATOR, RESULTING IN:"
210 PRINT 1/2,1/8,1/8,1/4,1/4
220 PRINT "    THEN, WE ADD THE DECIMAL EQUIVALENT OF A"
230 PRINT "QUARTER-NOTE:"
240 PRINT 1/4
250 PRINT "TO EACH DURATION OF THE PATTERN, YIELDING:"
260 PRINT 1/2 + 1/4,1/8 + 1/4,1/8 + 1/4,1/4 + 1/4,1/4 + 1/4
270 REM
280 PRINT "    DIMINUTION OF A RHYTHM PATTERN IS THE OPPOSITE"
290 PRINT "OF AUGMENTATION; IT IS DONE BY SUBTRACTING A CONSTANT"
300 PRINT "VALUE FROM EACH PATTERN ELEMENT."
310 END
```

LEARNING TO USE VARIABLES

The programs you have entered into the computer so far have not required an inordinate amount of time to type in. However, imagine the situation of wishing to print several hundred pitches (as numbers) on the computer screen. Without some mechanism for simplifying this task, there would be little reason to use the computer. Fortunately, BASIC provides many labor-saving shortcuts for the programmer. The use of variables is an important one.

NUMERIC VARIABLES

Recall that in your study of mathematics, variables were used to store quantities which often changed during the course of solving a problem. Like the letter variables you encountered in math, numeric variables in BASIC can be single letters that represent changeable values. For example, you can type:

$$X = Y + Z$$

Choosing Variable Names

Variables in BASIC differ slightly from their math counterparts. They can be named by more than one letter, so that the name itself reminds us (is mnemonic) of the variable's function. For example, if you wish to compute data for the pitches of a melodic line, then you can type a variable named PITCH to store the data. There is one important restriction in this regard. You may store only one item at a time in a given numeric variable. If you try to place a second number in the variable while it is full, you will succeed, but the original datum will be discarded.

While it is best to choose a variable name which clearly reflects the variable's program function, BASIC allows you to use up to 40 letters and numbers in almost any combination, provided that the name begins with a letter. Blank spaces and non-alphabet characters (!($^%&@) should not be part of the name.

Examples of legal variable names.	A1
	COUNTER
	RHYTHM
	V3S1G5
	X

Examples of illegal variable names	PITCH	(no spaces allowed)
	1B	(always begin with a letter)
	G*#@1F	(use only letters and numbers)

One more restriction should be mentioned: variable names MUST NOT contain the same letters as computer instructions, which are referred to as RESERVED WORDS. For instance, you may not use RUN, LIST, PRINT, NEW, or any other instruction as part of a name. For a complete list of reserved words, consult the BASIC User's Manual.

Think of variables as initially empty boxes, with a letter printed on them so we can find them and recall what they are being used for. A variable named PITCH, symbolized in the following manner:

PITCH $\boxed{0}$

Figure 3-3.

is simply a place in computer memory (the computer decides exactly where) that you have told the computer to reserve for the storage of numeric values. Until you put a number in the box, it will be empty—represented by the number 0.

The LET Instruction

BASIC provides an instruction for the assignment of values to variables. It is the reserved word LET, followed by the variable name, then the assignment operator (=), then the number to put in the variable. To demonstrate, type:

LET PITCH = 12

Press the enter key, then type:

PRINT PITCH

After you press the enter key, the computer will display:

12

This instruction literally asks the computer to place a copy of the number 12 in the memory address called PITCH.

The Assignment Operator (=)

In mathematics we think of the equal sign strictly as an equality indicator. However, in BASIC the equal sign actually means "make a copy of the number on the right side of the sign, then place it in the variable name (address) on the left side of the sign."

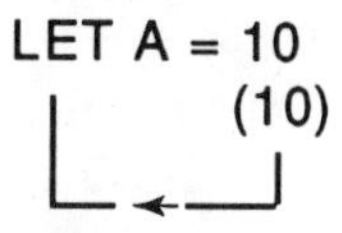

LET A = 10

Figure 3-4.

When the assignment instruction is executed, any value that was previously stored in the memory location (variable name A, in this case) is pushed out and lost forever. This happens each time a new assignment is made. Type the following list of instructions to observe the replacement of contents in the variable named PITCH:

```
LET PITCH = 0
PRINT PITCH
LET PITCH = 60
PRINT PITCH
LET PITCH = 61
PRINT PITCH
LET PITCH = 62
PRINT PITCH
```

You can see that the contents of variable PITCH were continually overwritten by the assignment operator from one LET instruction to the next. It may seem trivial to dwell on this point, but many programming errors can result from an incomplete grasp of the overwrite principle.

Here is a symbolic picture of what occurs in the preceding variable assignment example:

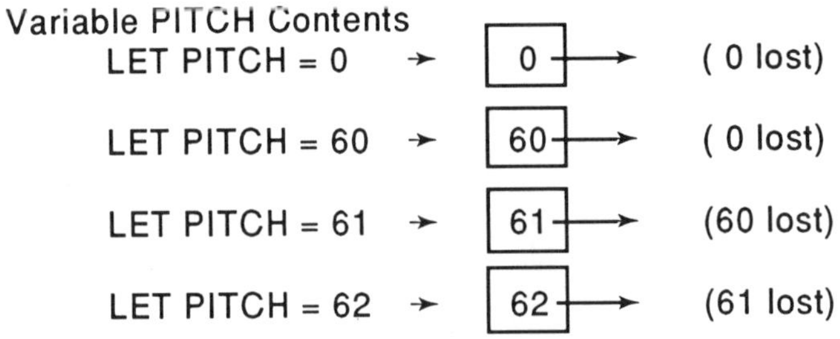

Variable PITCH Contents

LET PITCH = 0 →	0 →	(0 lost)
LET PITCH = 60 →	60 →	(0 lost)
LET PITCH = 61 →	61 →	(60 lost)
LET PITCH = 62 →	62 →	(61 lost)

Figure 3-5.

The reserved word, LET, is optional in BASIC. Here is a shorter way to assign a number to a variable:

10 PITCH = 23

This shortcut is less preferable from the beginner's point of view, because it blurs the important distinction between math variables and those used in BASIC. So, for the time being, include the reserved word, LET, in all assignment statements.

Variable Initialization

BASIC automatically initializes available memory locations to the number 0 when program execution begins. Nevertheless, it is good programming practice to identify all variables, and set them to 0 at the start of a new program. For example, if you wish to use program variables to hold values for the musical parameters of pitch, rhythm, and volume, then the first (initialization) segment of your program should be:

```
10 LET PITCH = 0
20 LET RHYTHM = 0
30 LET VOLUME = 0
```

These instructions simply set aside three storage places in computer memory, identified by the names you gave them, then set the contents of the three variables to 0.

Copying From One Variable to Another

The LET instruction and assignment operator (=) can also be used to copy the contents of one variable into another variable. In this situation, the two variables are referred to as the sender and the receiver.

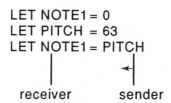

```
LET NOTE1 = 0
LET PITCH  = 63
LET NOTE1 = PITCH
```

receiver   sender

Figure 3-6.

The receiving variable must ALWAYS be to the left of the assignment operator (=), without exception. Therefore, statements like the following are illegal:

LET 12 = PITCH

It is also illegal to combine the PRINT instruction with the assignment instruction:

PRINT PITCH = 12

Just remember that the contents of the variable on the left of the equal sign will always be lost after the assignment is made; otherwise, you can manipulate variable contents with ease.

Positioning of Variables and Math Operators

Although you can use variables on both sides of the assignment operator (=), arithmetic operations can only be performed on the right side of the equal sign. For instance:

```
10 LET PITCH = 62
20 PRINT "Original pitch is";PITCH
30 LET TRANSPOSE = 4
40 PRINT "Transposition interval is";TRANSPOSE
50 LET PITCH = PITCH + TRANSPOSE
60 PRINT "Transposed pitch is";PITCH
70 END
```

When you type this instruction list, the computer will display:

```
Original pitch is 62
Transposition interval is 4
Transposed pitch is 66
```

Notice that Line 50 uses variables to the right and left of the equal sign, but that the math is restricted to the right side. You must always follow this rule.

CHARACTER VARIABLES

You have learned that numeric variables are used to store numbers and the results of mathematical computation during program execution. BASIC also provides a way to store character data during program execution. Sometimes referred to as string variables, they can hold a sequence of alphanumeric characters for displaying screen messages to the program user.

The rules for naming character (string) variables are the same as for naming numeric variables:

1) The name must begin with a letter,
2) Combinations of letters and numbers may be used,
3) The name may not contain a BASIC reserved word, and
4) You may not use special symbols (#@!&).

There is one exception. Character variable names normally must end with a dollar sign ($). Here are some legal character variables:

```
TEXT$
PITCH$
VOLUME$
TONE1$
X$
```

(There is a way to avoid ending character variables with a dollar sign if you find this requirement limiting. See your BASIC User's Manual for information on the declaration of variables.)

In most versions of BASIC for micros, a single string variable has space to store up to 255 characters. For instance, the sentence:

This line contains many characters.

will easily fit into the space reserved in computer memory for the variable TEXT$. All you do is enclose the characters in quotation marks, place them to the right of the equal sign, then place the variable name to the left of the equal sign. For instance:

LET TEXT$ = "This line contains many characters."

Any character can be assigned to a string variable, as in the following program fragment:

```
10 TEXT$ = "I CAN STore the image of numBERS, Letters & SIGNS."
20 PRINT TEXT$
30 TEXT$ = "But, math operations can't be done on the numbers."
40 PRINT TEXT$
50 END
```

After you type RUN and press the enter key, the computer displays:

I CAN STore the image of numBERS, Letters & SIGNS.
But, math operations can't be done on the numbers.

Notice four important points in the preceding program segment:

1) The contents of character variables are stored as letters; therefore, any numbers included within the quotes are not directly available to perform arithmetic operations,

2) Character variables can be overwritten in the same way as numeric variables,

3) The PRINT instruction causes the entire contents of the character variable to be printed on the screen, and

4) The quotation marks enclosing the character string are not printed.

Control over Screen Output

PROGRAM #5. This is a tutorial which introduces the user to the concept of data types and their application. You may need to write similar programs if you are a teacher who wishes to save time by providing an opportunity for students to learn at their own pace outside the class. This increasingly popular teaching strategy is called Computer-Aided Instruction, or CAI.

The CLS and INKEY$ Instructions

Notice that two new BASIC instructions have been used in this program.

The instruction on Line 30 of Program #5,

```
30 CLS
```

simply erases everything that happens to be on the display screen when the command RUN is executed.

The instruction on Line 90 of Program #5,

```
90 IF INKEY $  < >  " "  THEN  90
   |      |      | |         |__|
   if ____|    not space    repeat line
```

Figure 3-7.

is a preview of a statement type called a conditional transfer, which is combined with a special string variable name, INKEY$. This variable is reserved in BASIC for getting and storing a single character from the computer keyboard. The symbol < > is a BASIC relational operator which means "not equal to"; it is explained in greater detail along with other relational operators in the section on Relational Operators.

Line 90 works by checking to see whether the variable INKEY$ contains a blank character (yes, a space is considered a character), then, if it holds anything other than a space, branches back to the beginning of Line 90 in an endless loop. The loop is broken only when the user presses the space bar. Conditional test and branch instructions will be introduced and explained in the section on Interactive Programming. For now, you can simply mimic the use of INKEY$ in Line 90 and CLS in Line 30 in your own instructions to control the flow of information on the display screen.

DATA TYPES SUMMARY

The word "data" has been used several times in reference to information manipulated by the computer. You have been moving it around inside the computer since you began this chapter. On the most general level, data are simply facts. For these facts to have meaning for human beings they must symbolize some external phenomenon, such as a statistical population or a business letter. Because we usually perform math operations on numbers and text operations on alphabetic character strings, BASIC classifies data into the two primary data types: 1) numeric, and 2) character. The numeric data type contains an additional subcategory called real numbers, which are simply numbers which consist of both integer and fractional parts. A numeric array can store both integers and real numbers, without discrimination. However, as you have learned, a character array can store only character REPRESENTATIONS of number, not the actual values numbers represented.

Type Program #5 into your computer and run it to test your understanding of BASIC's data types. Then, write a tutorial program to demonstrate the principles of screen display you have learned up to this point.

PROGRAM #5

```
10  REM****************************************************
12  REM                      PROGRAM #5
14  REM          PROGRAM TO DEMONSTRATE PRIMARY DATA TYPES
20  REM****************************************************
30  CLS
40  PRINT "    THIS PROGRAM EXPLAINS THE 2 PRIMARY DATA TYPES"
50  PRINT "USED IN BASIC - NUMERIC AND CHARACTER."
60  REM:***************************************************
70  PRINT
80  PRINT "+++++  PRESS THE <SPACE> BAR TO CONTINUE  +++++"
90  IF INKEY$ <> " " THEN 90
100 CLS
110 PRINT
```

```
120 PRINT "                    I. NUMERIC DATA TYPE
130 PRINT
140 PRINT "     NUMERIC VALUES ARE NUMBERS EXPRESSED IN"
150 PRINT "ARE NUMBERS EXPRESSED IN INTEGER OR FLOATING-POINT"
160 PRINT "(REAL NUMBER) FORM."
170 PRINT
180 PRINT "     NUMERIC VARIABLES ARE USED TO STORE INTEGERS"
190 PRINT "OR REAL NUMBERS IN COMPUTER MEMORY DURING PROGRAM"
200 PRINT "EXECUTION."
210 PRINT
220 PRINT "     FOR EXAMPLE, BOTH THE NUMBER 12 AND THE NUMBER"
230 PRINT "12.3212 ARE NUMERIC VALUES WHICH CAN BE PLACED"
240 PRINT "IN NUMERIC VARIABLES FOR MANIPULATION."
250 PRINT
260 PRINT "     TO PLACE A NUMBER IN A MEMORY ADDRESS"
270 PRINT "SPECIFIED BY A LEGAL VARIABLE IDENTIFIER (NAME),"
280 PRINT "SIMPLY WRITE A LINE-NUMBERED STATEMENT USING THE"
290 PRINT "ASSIGNMENT OPERATOR (=) AND THE OPTIONAL KEYWORD"
300 PRINT "(LET)."
310 PRINT
320 PRINT "+++++  PRESS THE <SPACE> BAR TO CONTINUE  +++++"
330 IF INKEY$ <> " " THEN 330
340 CLS
350 PRINT "               FOR INSTANCE:"
360 PRINT "THE KEYS ON A PIANO KEYBOARD (LOW TO HIGH) CAN BE"
370 PRINT "REPRESENTED BY THE NUMBERS - 0 THROUGH 88. IF WE WANTED"
380 PRINT "TO STORE THE NUMBER OF THE HIGHEST NOTE ON THE"
390 PRINT "PIANO KEYBOARD IN A VARIABLE NAMED - "
400 PRINT
410 PRINT "          PITCHNUMBER"
420 PRINT
430 PRINT "WE COULD WRITE THE STATEMENT:"
440 PRINT
450 PRINT "     100 LET PITCHNUMBER = 88
460 PRINT
470 PRINT "     BY THE SAME TOKEN, IF WE ALSO WISHED TO STORE THE"
480 PRINT "RHYTHMIC VALUE 8.5 (TO REPRESENT A DURATION OF EIGHT"
490 PRINT "WHOLE NOTES TIED TO A  1/2 NOTE) IN A VARIABLE CALLED -"
500 PRINT
510 PRINT "          DURATION
520 PRINT
530 PRINT "WE COULD WRITE THE STATEMENT:"
540 PRINT
550 PRINT "     110 LET DURATION = 8.5
560 PRINT
570 LET PITCHNUMBER = 88
580 LET DURATION = 8.5
590 PRINT "+++++  PRESS THE <SPACE> BAR TO CONTINUE  +++++"
600 IF INKEY$ <> " " THEN 600
```

```
610 CLS
620 PRINT "   TO BE CERTAIN THAT THE ASSIGNMENT OPERATION WAS"
630 PRINT "ACTUALLY PERFORMED, WE CAN WRITE STATEMENTS TO"
640 PRINT "PRINT THE CONTENTS OF THE 2 VARIABLES ON THE"
650 PRINT "COMPUTER DISPLAY SCREEN:"
660 PRINT
670 PRINT "        130 PRINT PITCHNUMBER"
680 PRINT "        140 PRINT DURATION"
690 PRINT
700 PRINT "   WHEN THE COMPUTER EXECUTES LINES 100-140,"
710 PRINT "THE SCREEN DISPLAY WILL SHOW:"
720 PRINT
730 PRINT PITCHNUMBER     'this variable contains 127
740 PRINT DURATION      'this variable contains 8.5
750 PRINT
760 PRINT "+++++  PRESS THE <SPACE> BAR TO CONTINUE  +++++"
770 IF INKEY$ <> " " THEN 770
780 CLS
790 PRINT "               II. CHARACTER DATA TYPE
800 PRINT
810 PRINT "   CHARACTER DATA IS DEFINED AS INFORMATION WHICH"
820 PRINT "IS LITERAL IN NATURE, AND WHICH WILL NOT BE DIRECTLY"
830 PRINT "USED IN COMPUTATION, SUCH AS A WRITTEN MESSAGE TO"
840 PRINT "BE PRINTED ON THE SCREEN."
850 PRINT
860 PRINT "   A SEQUENCE OF CHARACTERS (INCLUDING SPACES) IS"
870 PRINT "CALLED A CHARACTER 'STRING'.
880 PRINT
890 PRINT "   TO TELL THE COMPUTER THAT A CHARACTER OR STRING OF"
900 PRINT "CHARACTERS IS NOT NUMERIC DATA, WE USE DOUBLE"
910 PRINT "QUOTATION MARKS BEFORE AND AFTER THE CHARACTER(S)."
920 PRINT
930 PRINT "   WHEN THE INSTRUCTION TO PRINT THE INFORMATION"
940 PRINT "WITHIN THE QUOTES IS EXECUTED, THE STRING OF CHARACTERS"
950 PRINT "WILL BE SENT TO THE SCREEN, BUT THE QUOTATION MARKS"
960 PRINT "MARKS THEMSELVES WILL NOT BE PRINTED."
970 PRINT
980 PRINT "+++++  PRESS THE <SPACE> BAR TO CONTINUE  +++++"
990 IF INKEY$ <> " " THEN 990
1000 CLS
1010 PRINT "          FOR EXAMPLE:"
1020 PRINT
1030 PRINT "200 PRINT 'THIS IS A CHARACTER STRING.'"
1040 PRINT
1050 PRINT "   (SINGLE QUOTES HAVE BEEN USED FOR THE SCREEN"
1060 PRINT "DISPLAY IN THIS CASE, BUT YOU MUST USE DOUBLE QUOTES"
1070 PRINT "AROUND THE STRING WHEN YOU WRITE THE ABOVE"
1080 PRINT "LINE-NUMBERED INSTRUCTION.)"
1090 PRINT
```

```
1100 PRINT "     CHARACTER DATA MAY BE STORED IN COMPUTER MEMORY BY"
1110 PRINT "THE USE OF CHARACTER VARIABLES.  THESE VARIABLE NAMES"
1120 PRINT "ARE RECOGNIZED BY THE INCLUSION OF THE SYMBOL "
1130 PRINT
1140 PRINT "                    $"
1150 PRINT
1160 PRINT "AS THE FINAL CHARACTER OF THE VARIABLE. FOR INSTANCE:"
1170 PRINT
1180 PRINT "              NOTE$"
1190 PRINT
1200 PRINT "IS A LEGAL CHARACTER VARIABLE NAME WHICH WE COULD USE"
1210 PRINT "TO STORE THE CHARACTERS OF MUSICAL NOTE NAMES."
1220 PRINT
1230 PRINT "+++++  PRESS THE <SPACE> BAR TO CONTINUE  +++++"
1240 IF INKEY$ <> " " THEN 1240
1250 CLS
1260 PRINT "     WE USE THE ASSIGNMENT OPERATOR (=) AND THE"
1270 PRINT "OPTIONAL (LET) KEYWORD TO PLACE THE CHARACTER STRING"
1280 PRINT "(ENCLOSED IN DOUBLE QUOTATION MARKS) IN THE VARIABLE"
1290 PRINT "NOTE$:"
1300 PRINT
1310 PRINT "     300 NOTE$ = 'C  C#  D  D#  E  F  F# G '."
1320 PRINT
1330 LET NOTE$ = "C C# D D# E F F# G "
1340 PRINT " — REMEMBER, YOU MUST USE DOUBLE QUOTES IN YOUR"
1350 PRINT "BASIC PROGRAM —"
1360 PRINT "     WE PRINT OUT THE CONTENTS OF THE VARIABLE"
1370 PRINT
1380 PRINT "              NOTE$
1390 PRINT
1400 PRINT "IN THE SAME MANNER AS NUMERIC VARIABLES:"
1410 PRINT
1420 PRINT "     310 PRINT NOTE$
1430 PRINT
1440 PRINT "WHICH, WHEN EXECUTED, WILL RESULT IN:"
1450 PRINT
1460 PRINT NOTE$
1470 END
```

4

Interactive Programs

Most music composition programs require some sort of interaction with the program user. Programmers communicate with one another through the inclusion of REM (remark) statements at key points of the instruction code to clarify program function and processing operations. These comments are available only by listing the program, however, so they usually are not seen by the casual program user. Therefore, interactive programs must provide additional information in the form of screen prompts to allow the user to understand what the program does and what kind of interaction the computer requires.

In the case of very long, complex programs which involve a great deal of explanation as to their execution, a User Help Routine can be appended for invocation on request. More often, a simple screen display introduction will be sufficient to guide the user toward effective application of the program. In either case, interactivity depends heavily on:

1) prompts to the user describing the computer's expectations regarding input data,

2) the inclusion of computer instructions to test the input data for validity, and

3) the issuance of error messages to the program user upon the detection of improperly entered or inappropriate input data.

Because of the need to guarantee user-friendliness and input data error-detection, a well-written program normally is increased in size by at least 50% of its original length, due to the inclusion of user prompts, programming remarks, input data tests, and error messages.

The INPUT Instruction

This instruction is used during program execution to store data entered from the keyboard in numeric or character variables. The INPUT instruction consists of the keyword INPUT, followed by the name of a legal variable to hold the user-entered data. For instance, to get an alphanumeric pitch name from the program user, we could write:

10 INPUT PITCHCLASS$

When the line is executed, the screen display will be:

?

The question mark is the computer's way of telling the program user that it is waiting for some data to be entered. Unfortunately, the user has no way of knowing either the type of data expected or the permissible range of values. For this reason, the INPUT statement normally requires a preliminary line of code to serve as the user prompt for data entry:

5 PRINT "Enter a Pitchclass in alphanumeric form:"
10 INPUT PITCHCLASS$

When the lines are executed, the user sees the following:

Enter a Pitchclass in alphanumeric form:
?

The computer suspends program execution after it prints the question mark to the screen; when the user enters the anticipated data immediately next to the question mark:

?C#

the computer stores it in the accompanying variable name, then proceeds to the next line number. For convenience, the INPUT statement allows the inclusion of a prompt as part of the instruction itself,

10 INPUT "Enter a Pitchclass in alphanumeric form:";PITCHCLASS$

thereby eliminating the need for a separate line to print a message to the display screen. Notice the semicolon placed between the closing quotation mark of the prompt string and the variable name. The semicolon causes the INPUT instruction to print a question mark immediately following the last character of the prompt string. The execution of Line 10 will produce:

Enter A Pitchclass in alphanumeric form:?F#

(The user has entered the data after the prompt.) You may substitute a comma for the semicolon if you wish to suppress screen printing of the question mark, but program execution will still be suspended until the data is entered by the user.

The INPUT instruction can accept data for more than one variable in a single instruction. Suppose we wish to have the program user enter data for each attribute/variable of an event vector. (Recall that an event vector is a single note-event, characterized and defined by a number of individual scalar parameter values.) For example, we could prompt the user to input data for each of the five common note-event parameters: Pitch, Rhythm, Articulation, Volume, and Timbre.

Example 4-1.

A single Input instruction will do the job:

10 INPUT "Enter 5 parameter values (P,R,A,V,T): ";P,R,A,V,T

When the instruction is executed, the computer will print a single question mark to the screen, but it will expect to receive five numbers (separated by commas) similar to the following execution example:

Enter 5 parameter values (P,R,A,V,T):?60,2,50,100,5

PROGRAM DESIGN

Programming Style

Now that you have learned a method of two-way communication between the computer and its human user, it is time to think about effective program organization. Some programmers simply write what is called "in-line" code, which is often very compressed, fast-running, and almost impossible to fathom for anyone other than the program author. Because compositional applications often require that our programs be comprehensible to others wishing to learn algorithmic methods, use of articulative white-space, sufficient remarks, and a partitioned program structure is advisable in all cases.

Pseudocode. Prior to the job of encoding computer instructions in BASIC, the programmer must have a clear understanding of the nature of the activities to be undertaken. The first step in designing a good program is to write down a description of the problem in ordinary language. Often, it will be most convenient to consider the desired result before proceeding toward a breakdown of the overall work schedule into separate stages, or subproblems. Try to describe as accurately as possible the exact nature of the results you wish to achieve. For instance, a generalized characterization of a plan to make a computer-composed pitch sequence based on the C-major scale might be:

> I would like the computer to compose a melody consisting of any or all of the seven tones of the C-major diatonic scale. The pitch sequence length will be specified by the program user, but it should begin on pitch class C and end on pitch class G, otherwise the computer can select any of the available notes in any order.

Procedural Problem Formulation. A pseudocode translation of the above goal, phrased in procedural terms (do this, do that, etc.), would be:

> 1) give the computer the seven pitch classes of the diatonic C-major scale as possible pitch choices,
> 2) tell the computer to select notes randomly from the scale a given number of times to construct the melody, but
> 3) instruct the computer to begin on the pitch class C and end on the pitch class G.

Block Diagram of Tasks. Block diagrams can help us visualize program construction in the initial stages of development. Unlike Flow Charts, which we will examine a bit later, they are quite general in nature. Nonetheless, they are valuable because they allow the beginning programmer to discover flaws in conception and areas of vagueness in output characterization, all of which must be corrected before program development can proceed. Here is a Block Diagram of the problem under consideration:

Random C—major Scale Pitch Sequence
Program Block Diagram

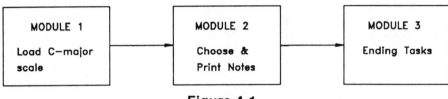

Figure 4-1.

A stepwise implementation of the pseudocode procedures follows:

1) Load the seven pitches of the diatonic C-major scale into an array,
2) prompt the program user to enter a number to determine the length of the sequence,
3) print the starting note (C) of the melody on the display screen,
4) set the range of selection for the random numbers to 7,
5) call the random number generator n-2 times to select pitches from the scale array, and print each pitch to the display screen after it is chosen,
6) print the final, predetermined, pitch (G) to the display screen, then
7) end program execution.

Program Subdivision. All programs can be divided into three sections:

1) Input,
2) Processing, and
3) Output.

It is usually most convenient to begin planning a composition program with the processing section; that is, we normally consider what it is we wish the program to do first, then deal with the form of input and output as secondary considerations. But, for now, we will follow the aforementioned sequence to construct a simple program to transpose an input numeric pitch sequence. In order to establish good programming style, we begin with a short segment which uses REM comments to identify the program variables, and initialize them to zero (0) prior to their first use. Next we add the input stage, then the processing segment, and finally the output section.

PROGRAM #6

```
10   REM**************************************************************
20   REM                        PROGRAM #6                          *
30   REM        PROGRAM TO TRANSPOSE A USER-INPUT PITCH SEQUENCE    *
40   REM             (NON-OCTAVE-MODULAR TRANSPOSITION)             *
50   REM**************************************************************
60   REM****                                                    ****
70   REM****    VARIABLE IDENTIFICATION AND INITIALIZATION      ****
80   REM****                                                    ****
90   REM**************************************************************
100  P1 = 0                         ' stores first pitch number
110  P2 = 0                         ' stores second pitch number
120  P3 = 0                         ' stores third pitch number
130  P4 = 0                         ' stores fourth pitch number
140  P5 = 0                         ' stores fifth pitch number
150  P6 = 0                         ' stores sixth pitch number
160  P7 = 0                         ' stores seventh pitch number
170  P8 = 0                         ' stores eighth pitch number
180  P9 = 0                         ' stores ninth pitch number
190  P10 = 0                        ' stores tenth pitch number
200  T = 0                          ' interval of transposition
210  REM**************************************************************
220  REM****                                                    ****
230  REM****                        INPUT                       ****
240  REM****                                                    ****
250  REM**************************************************************
260  PRINT "Enter a sequence of 10 pitch numbers for melody"
270  PRINT "on 1 line, separated by commas:"
280  INPUT P1,P2,P3,P4,P5,P6,P7,P8,P9,P10
290  INPUT "Enter interval of transposition: ",T
300  REM**************************************************************
310  REM****                                                    ****
320  REM****              (Pitch Transposition)                 ****
340  REM**************************************************************
350  P1 = P1 + T
360  P2 = P2 + T
370  P3 = P3 + T
380  P4 = P4 + T
390  P5 = P5 + T
400  P6 = P6 + T
410  P7 = P7 + T
420  P8 = P8 + T
430  P9 = P9 + T
440  P10 = P10 + T
450  REM**************************************************************
460  REM****                                                    ****
470  REM****                       OUTPUT                       ****
480  REM****                                                    ****
490  REM**************************************************************
500  PRINT "Here is the transposed pitch sequence:"
510  PRINT P1;P2;P3;P4;P5;P6;P7;P8;P9;P10
520  REM**************************************************************
53.0 END
```

Notice that, although Program #6 consists of fifty lines, all the computation is performed in only 10 lines. As pointed out earlier, well designed programs often consume far more space than is necessary for the completion of work. In this case, the actual task requires only 1/5 of the program space - the remainder is devoted to initialization, remarks, input, and output. As you proceed through this chapter, you will learn ways to increase program efficiency and thereby reduce this work/documentation ratio, but it is always advisable to err on the side of clarity rather than economy.

Lines 350-440 produce the transposition of the pitch sequence by performing the addition operation and placing the sum in the original variable (the old value is discarded). The process of user input and program processing can be visualized as:

1:
User inputs pitch 60 (to Variable P1) in Line 280:

$$P1 = 60 \qquad \rightarrow \quad \boxed{60} \longrightarrow \quad (\ 0 \ lost)$$

2:
User inputs transposition interval 5 (to Variable T) in Line 290:

$$T = 5 \qquad \rightarrow \quad \boxed{5} \longrightarrow \quad (\ 0 \ lost)$$

3:
Program transposes pitch and overwrites Variable P1 in Line 350:

$$P1 = P1 + T \qquad \rightarrow \quad \boxed{65} \longrightarrow \quad (60 \ lost)$$
$$(60 + 5)$$

Figure 4-2.

Program Branching

Subroutines. Many programs reflect a liberal use of subroutines, another technique for improving program organization and legibility. This concept centers around a program control center—the Main Routine—which is sometimes also called a Driver Routine. The idea is to create separate routines (subroutines) which are appended to the primary command routine. It is similar in some respects to a large business which maintains a central office for the sole purpose of coordinating the activities of subordinate offices. The Main Routine contains instructions to the computer about which branch office to call for work and where the office is located. A program organized by reference to primary and secondary routines can be visualized as:

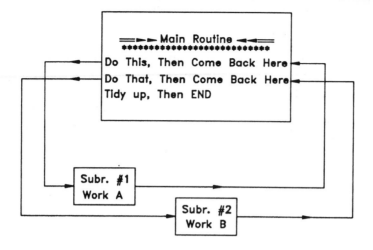

Figure 4-3.

GOSUB Instruction. This command is used in a main routine to direct traffic to subordinate, processing routines. It is called a branch instruction, and is immediately followed by the number to which control must be transferred. For example, the instruction:

100 GOSUB 1000

will cause normal execution by consecutive line numbers to be temporarily suspended; the computer will immediately jump to the line number following the keyword, GOSUB, and will continue execution of line numbers at that point in the program.

RETURN Instruction. After program control is transferred by the GOSUB instruction, the computer will proceed with line-numbered instructions until it encounters GOSUB's companion instruction, RETURN. When the Return instruction is executed, program control returns to the line number immediately following the point of departure.

GOTO Instruction. Beware! This command looks and functions very much like the GOSUB instruction, but it is open-ended; that is, it has no companion instruction to tell the computer when or where to branch back to a logical point in program execution. It is called an unconditional transfer—normal line execution order is interrupted when this statement is encountered, as in:

100 GOTO 1000

The computer shifts its attention to Line 1000 and proceeds until some other branch instruction is reached (or the END command).

Indiscriminate use of GOTOs can cause programmers to spend hours doing maddening detective work, called debugging. Furthermore, it can produce what is called "spaghetti code," a mess so entangled by jumps from line to line, that no one can figure out what the program does.

Once you are familiar with BASIC, you will know ways that are more powerful to manage program control flow. But, for the time being, use of the GOTO instruction is necessary to illustrate some important ideas related to automated data processing. So, we'll just sneak it in here a few times (please try to feel a little guilty about it so it won't become a habit).

Conditional Tests and Branching

IF...THEN Instruction. Often the GOTO command is used in combination with this statement. The IF...THEN instruction performs some kind of test on program data, then prescribes a consequent action which depends upon test results. To illustrate, suppose we wished to ask the program user a "yes-no" question, then branch to a different place in the program corresponding to the reply. In the following program fragment,

```
10 INPUT "Do you wish to run this program? (Enter Y or N): ",A$
20 IF A$ = "N" THEN GOTO 60
30 PRINT "I don't know why you want to use this program."
40 PRINT "It really doesn't do anything except send an"
50 PRINT "apology to the user for not doing any work."
60 PRINT "SO SORRY, BUT I AM TIRED TODAY. GOODBYE."
70 END
```

execution ends if the user enters a negative response to the prompt in Line 10; otherwise it continues in normal line order. There are many different ways to make comparisons and perform conditional branch tests. You will begin to understand the power of the IF...THEN instruction during the course of this chapter.

Relational Operators

Line 20 introduces a new context for the equal sign. Normally it serves as the assignment operator, but when placed within the IF...THEN construct it functions as an relational operator. Relational operators give the computer power to make important decisions in a wide range of situations. They are indispensable in circumstances which require an evaluation of some condition BEFORE further processing action is taken. Moreover, they are commonly used to test the validity of data entered at the keyboard during program execution.

Here is the entire set of relational operators:

```
=  Equal to (not an assignment operator when used to test relationships)
<> Not equal to
>  Greater than
<  Less than
>= Greater than or equal to
<= Less than or equal to
```

Study them carefully and test them out by writing a few simple programs modeled after:

```
10 INPUT "Enter a number larger than 100: ",NUM
20 IF NUM <= 100 THEN PRINT "NUMBER IS TOO LARGE!"
30 END
```

Machine Learning

The computer's ability to compare data is the basis for what is sometimes called machine learning. By storing facts (knowledge) in memory, then asking the computer to perform comparison matching of input data items with memorized information, human learning processes can be simulated. The programs in this book make limited use of the computer's decision-making power to generate compositional structures. By contrast, the field of Artificial Intelligence concentrates almost entirely on the modeling of cognitive systems which rely upon large knowledge bases and complex decision-making processes to perform useful work.

Logical Operators

In addition to relational operators, which allow various types of data comparisons, BASIC provides the logical operators AND and OR for further evaluation of tests.

The AND operator is used to evaluate the tests placed on either side of it. Only if both tests evaluate to true, will further action be taken. If one of the tests evaluates to false, then execution proceeds to the next line. Here is an example:

```
10 IF A = 10 AND B <> C THEN PRINT A
```

You can see that both constants and legal variables are permitted as part of the expressions on either side of the AND operator.

The logical OR operator is also used to evaluate the tests placed on either side of it. However, only one of the tests must evaluate to true for the consequent action to take place. For instance:

10 IF A <= B * C OR A <> D THEN PRINT A

You can gain facility at using these tools by writing a few short programs to test and compare user-input data, as in the following program fragment:

```
10 PRINT "Enter a pitch number within the range of"
20 PRINT "middle C (60) and the next higher octave C (72)."
30 INPUT PITCH
40 IF PITCH >= 60 AND PITCH <=72 THEN PRINT "GOOD!"
50 IF PITCH < 60 THEN PRINT "TOO LOW!"
60 IF PITCH > 72 THEN PRINT "TOO HIGH!"
70 END
```

Pattern Identification

Conditional tests are often employed in situations that require the computer to identify an input datum or pattern of data. For instance, PROGRAM #7 uses the relational equality operator, =, and the logical operator, AND, to "see" the pattern of a major triad, when correctly entered by the program user.

PROGRAM #7

```
10   REM******************************************************
20   REM                      PROGRAM #7                     *
30   REM       PROGRAM TO IDENTIFY USER-INPUT MAJOR TRIAD    *
40   REM                   IN ROOT POSITION                  *
50   REM******************************************************
60   REM****                                            ****
70   REM****    VARIABLE IDENTIFICATION AND INITIALIZATION   ****
80   REM****                                            ****
90   REM******************************************************
100  CT1 = 0                        '<< Stores Triadic Chord Root
110  CT2 = 0                        '<< Stores Triadic Chord  Third
120  CT3 = 0                        '<< Stores Triadic Chord Fifth
210  REM******************************************************
220  REM****                                            ****
230  REM****                    INPUT                   ****
240  REM****                                            ****
250  REM******************************************************
260  PRINT "Enter three numbers on one line having a"
270  PRINT "major triad relationship (e.g., 1,5,8)."
280  PRINT "Separate the numbers with a comma."
290  INPUT CT1,CT2,CT3
```

```
300 REM*******************************************************
310 REM****                                              ****
320 REM****        (Major Triad Pattern Identification)   ****
340 REM*******************************************************
350 IF CT3 - CT2 = 3 AND CT2 - CT1 = 4 THEN PRINT "MAJOR TRIAD"
    ELSE PRINT "NOT A MAJOR TRIAD! - TRY AGAIN." : GOTO 260
360 END
```

Example 4-2.

(Notice the inclusion of the ELSE portion of the IF...THEN instruction. See your BASIC manual for a complete explanation.)

Iterative Processing

Counters. The power of the computer lies in its speed. The machine would be of little use if, in order to perform 1000 arithmetic opera- tions, we had to type in 1000 individual lines of code to perform the work. (You undoubtedly thought about this problem as you studied Program #6.) Most programs involve repetitive processing, called iteration, of some sort, no matter how trivial the particular applica- tion.

A counter does exactly what its name suggests—it counts. What does it count? Well, that depends on the specific situation, but very often counters serve to keep track of how far the program has progressed toward the completion of a task at any given time during the course of data processing. Counters have many other functions, but iteration control is probably the most important one.

To set up an iteration pattern, we create a *de facto* loop structure in the program code; that is, we devise a closed circuit whereby the computer traverses a predetermined number of program lines, then branches back to the first line of the group of lines enclosed in the loop. In musical terms, it is the same as cutting out a segment of recording tape, then splicing the end to the beginning so that it will play endlessly. It looks like this when applied to a pseudocode program segment:

    1 get a pitch (number) from computer keyboard
    2 transpose the pitch by a predetermined value
    3 print the new pitch on the display screen
    4 go back to step 1

In a coded version of this example, the GOTO statement should be positioned in step 4. However, a serious problem would surface during program execution: processing will never end, unless the user exits the program using the Break key. This condition, referred to as an infinite loop, can be rectified through use of a counter and an IF...THEN instruction:

1 determine the TOTAL number of pitches to be processed
2 determine the transposition interval
3 get a pitch (number) from computer keyboard
4 transpose the pitch by a predetermined value
5 print the new pitch on the display screen
6 maintain a COUNT of transposed pitches
7 IF the COUNT does not equal the TOTAL, THEN GOTO 1
8 END execution if TOTAL has been reached

Program Flow Charts

Unlike the Block Diagram encountered earlier in the book, a Flow Chart is a minutely detailed symbolic representation of program steps. A Flow Chart description of the algorithm currently under discussion is:

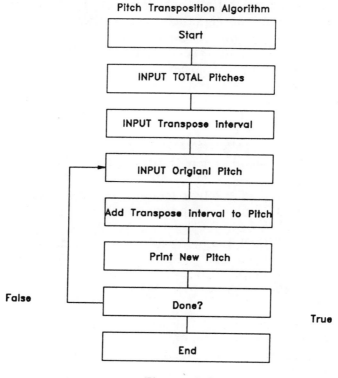

Figure 4-4.

The BASIC implementation of this algorithm is:

```
10    REM ***************************************************
20    REM        Simple Pitch Transposition Program
30    REM ***************************************************
40    COUNTER = 0
50    INPUT "Enter total pitches to be transposed: ",TOTAL
60    INPUT "Enter transposition interval: ",T
70    INPUT "Enter pitch for transposition: ",P
80    P = P + T
90    PRINT P
100   COUNTER = COUNTER + 1
110   IF COUNTER < TOTAL THEN GOTO 70
120   END
```

Line 70 is the start point of the loop and Line 110 the end point. The program terminates only when the COUNTER value reaches the TOTAL value.

Automatic Loops

Earlier in the book, the pitfalls of reliance on the GOTO instruction were pointed out. Fortunately, BASIC offers two sets of automatic looping instructions to eliminate the need for the GOTO statement in many instances. The first set is referred to as a FOR...NEXT loop; the second set is called a WHILE...WEND loop.

FOR...NEXT Loop Instructions. Here is a more efficient way to achieve and clarify the function of the *de facto* loop found in the preceding program fragment:

```
10    REM ***************************************************
20    REM        Simple Pitch Transposition Program
30    REM ***************************************************
40      INPUT "Enter total pitches to be transposed: ",TOTAL
50      INPUT "Enter transposition interval: ",T
60        FOR COUNTER = 1 TO TOTAL
70          INPUT "Enter pitch for transposition: ",P
80          P = P + T
90          PRINT P
100       NEXT COUNTER
110   END
```

The FOR and NEXT instructions have absorbed the individual counting, testing, and branching functions into the visually articulated loop delineated by Lines 60 and 100.

The variable immediately following the FOR instruction is called the control variable, because its value determines when execution of the instructions within the loop will terminate. The first value, which may be an integer or a variable, placed to the right of the assignment operator (=) is the starting value of the control variable, and the second integer or variable is the ending value of the control variable.

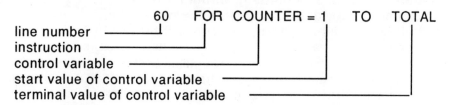

Figure 4-5.

The NEXT instruction demarks the loop and must contain the same variable name as the FOR instruction. Any instructions which occupy the lines lying between the FOR and the NEXT instructions are said to be within the range of the loop.

When the control variable reaches its terminal value, the computer transfers execution to the instruction following the NEXT instruction.

One additional FOR...NEXT loop feature is optionally available: the STEP instruction. Normally the control value contained in the FOR instruction will be advanced in increments of 1. This is called the default condition. However, the control variable can be made to count in multiple increments and it can also be made to count down rather than up. In the next program fragment, the FOR...NEXT loop counts downward from 11 to 1 in steps of 2:

```
60 FOR COUNTER = 11 TO 1 STEP - 2
70 PRINT COUNTER;
80 NEXT COUNTER
```

When this fragment is executed, the screen display will be:

11 9 7 5 3 1

Notice that the control variable may also be used for processing within the loop. Moreover, the initial and terminal values of the control variable may be the result of compound expressions as in the following example:

```
FOR COUNTER = INT(A * B / C) TO INT(E / F + G) STEP H
```

However, you must be certain that the expressions will compute to values that have validity within the FOR instruction, or the loop may not execute at all.

WHILE...WEND Loop Instructions. This pair of instructions functions similarly to the FOR...NEXT automatic loop, but instead of containing the loop counters governing loop range in the initial FOR statement, it simply initiates a potentially infinite loop and relies upon the programmer to provide a switch within the loop to terminate execution. A switch is a variable whose contents will be routinely checked to discover whether a particular value is present. Also called a "flag," the switch variable will assume one of two possible states, such as 0 or 1.

Here is an example of an infinite WHILE...WEND loop which demonstrates IMPROPER use of a switch:

```
                        10 SWITCH = 0
Control Instruction →   20 WHILE SWITCH <> 1
                        30 PRINT "The only pitch we will use is C#"
Loop End Point →        40 WEND
```

Figure 4-6.

When this program fragment is executed, the computer will print the character string in Line 30 until the user manually breaks out of the program:

```
RUN

The only pitch we will use is C#
The only pitch we will use is C#
The only pitch we will use is C#
The only pitch we will use is C#
The only pitch we will use is C#
The only pitch we will use is C#
The only pitch we will use is C#
The only pitch we will use is C#
<CTRL - BREAK>

OK
```

Because the variable SWITCH was initialized to 0 before entering the WHILE...WEND loop, the condition specified within the WHILE instruction will always be met; that is, as long as the value of variable SWITCH is not equal to, the condition for continued loop repetition will be met. We can correct the problem condition in Figure 6-12 by adding a user INPUT statement to force loop termination:

```
                         10 SWITCH = 0
Control Instruction ➤    20 WHILE SWITCH <> 1
                         30 PRINT "The only pitch we will use is C#"
                         35 PRINT "Enter 0 to repeat the loop:"
                         36 PRINT "Enter 1 to end the loop:"
                         37 INPUT SWITCH
Loop End Point ➤         40 WEND
```

Figure 4-7.

Because the WHILE statement does not contain a counter, any required tabulation of data within the loop must be separately provided for. Here is a short program that uses a counter to tally the number of times the user of the preceding program fragment executed the WHILE...WEND loop:

```
REM PROGRAM TO DEMONSTRATE INTERNAL LOOP COUNTER

10      SWITCH = 0
20      COUNTER = 0
30      WHILE SWITCH <> 1
40          PRINT "The only pitch we will use is C#"
50          PRINT "Enter 0 to repeat the loop:"
60          PRINT "Enter 1 to end the loop:"
70          INPUT SWITCH
80          COUNTER = COUNTER + 1
90      WEND
100     PRINT "The loop executed";COUNTER;"times."
100     END
```

Automatic loops may be placed anywhere and in any number in a program, and they may be nested. (See your BASIC manual for an explanation of loop-nesting guidelines.)

ARRAYS

An array is a structure which allows the storage in computer memory of large quantities of related data. It can be viewed as a list of items that have some characteristic in common. One example might be the list of pitches in order of occurrence—first note to last note—in a given melodic line.

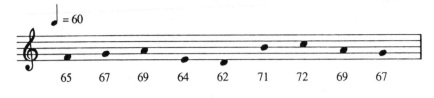

Example 4-3.

Another example might be the list of note dynamics (loudness levels) which are to be attached to a corresponding list of melodic pitches.

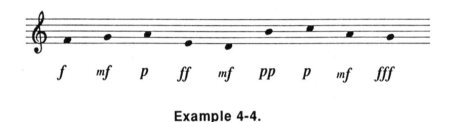

Example 4-4.

SINGLE-DIMENSION ARRAYS

Numeric Arrays.

Numeric arrays store numbers in a collection of memory spaces (called addresses) assigned to a common variable name. For example, the following list of note duration values,

(1) whole-note
(2) half-note
(3) sixteenth-note
(4) sixteenth-note
(5) eighth-note
(6) eighth-note
(7) quarter-note
(8) half-note
(9) whole-note

can be represented numerically as fractions:

(1)	1/1
(2)	1/2
(3)	1/16
(4)	1/16
(5)	1/8
(6)	1/8
(7)	1/4
(8)	1/2
(9)	1/1

However, the fractions contain a string character, "/," and therefore, cannot be stored in this form in a numeric array. The solution is simple in this case. All that we need to place in the array are the fraction denominators; it can be assumed that the numerator of each is the same: 1.

DIM Statement. To store the list of note durations, a legal variable name, such as DURATION, is chosen, then an array dimensioning instruction is entered in the program initialization segment to create memory space for the total number of duration integers we wish to store:

```
10 DIM DURATION(9)
```

Notice that the number of memory slots, called addresses, immediately follows the variable name and is surrounded by parentheses. The number of available array addresses is normally limited only by the amount of Random Access Memory (RAM) supplied with your particular computer; otherwise, you can dimension an array to any reasonable length, for example:

```
20 DIM PITCH(1000)
```

In the preceding statement we have reserved space within the computer to store 1000 separate pitch numbers.

Array Subscripts

It is important to have a clear concept of array organization. The separate array addresses are all grouped under the same variable name used to dimension the array. The individual memory slots are accessed by using what is referred to as a subscript. The array subscript (address) should not be confused with the array contents.

Here is a logical diagram of an array:

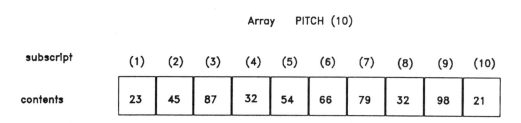

Array   PITCH (10)

subscript	(1)	(2)	(3)	(4)	(5)	(6)	(7)	(8)	(9)	(10)
contents	23	45	87	32	54	66	79	32	98	21

Figure 4-8.

Sometimes, programmers call the integer which corresponds to a particular array address an "offset," and sometimes they call it a "pointer"; both terms can be taken as synonymous with the term "subscript."

Array Initialization

When the computer encounters an array dimension instruction, such as:

10 DIM RHYTHM(10)

it automatically initializes the contents of all addresses to 0. Often, however, the programmer wishes to place some data in an array during the initialization section to prepare it for use as a data table (a list which is used for reference during program execution).

READ...DATA Instruction. This instruction pair allows the storage of data within a program. One of the ways numbers can be entered into arrays designated to hold data tables during program execution is to instruct the computer to load them automatically during the initialization segment of the program. The READ...DATA instruction pair serves this purpose. The READ instruction causes the computer to look within the program code for the companion DATA statement, which simply provides a sequential list of data items to be loaded into the variable name which immediately follows the READ instruction. The following program segment causes ten integers to be placed in array PITCH( ) within a FOR...NEXT loop:

10 DIM PITCH(10)
20 FOR COUNTER = 1 to 10

```
30 READ PITCH(COUNTER)
40 NEXT COUNTER
50 DATA 23,76,12,88,67
60 DATA 54,33,98,97,56
```

Notice that: 1) although the READ statement lies within the loop body, the DATA instruction does not. DATA statements can be placed anywhere in the program code, but it is customary to position them at the physical end of the program so that they will be easy to find if they must be altered at some point in the future; 2) the comma is employed as a data separator; and 3) DATA statements may occupy more than one program line.

RESTORE Instruction. Sometimes the same DATA items will be used repeatedly in different parts of a program. It is not necessary to retype each item several times to satisfy this requirement. The RESTORE instruction is used to reset the DATA "pointer" to a specified line number, or by default to the first DATA line number. The next program segment demonstrates the use of the same set of data in two separate arrays by means of the RESTORE instruction:

```
10      DIM PITCH(10)
20          FOR COUNTER = 1 to 15
30              READ PITCH(COUNTER)
40          NEXT COUNTER
50      RESTORE 100
60          FOR COUNTER = 1 to 5
70              READ VOLUME(COUNTER)
80          NEXT COUNTER
90      DATA 23,76,12,88,67
100     DATA 54,33,98,97,56
110     DATA 44,23,54,76,88
```

In the preceding program segment, the computer first loads all fifteen data items listed in Lines 90-110 into array PITCH( ), then resets the data pointer to the beginning of Line 100 and reads five data items into array VOLUME( ).

Another way to initialize an array is to include an INPUT instruction within the body of a FOR...NEXT loop:

```
10      DIM TIMBRE(10)
20      PRINT "Enter the reference numbers of the instruments"
30      PRINT "you will use (1 per line):"
40          FOR COUNTER = 1 to 15
50              INPUT TIMBRE(COUNTER)
60          NEXT COUNTER
```

Notice that the Loop control variable is used to "point-to" the addresses of the array TIMBRE( ) in ascending order.

Array Printout

The reverse process to array initialization is used to print out the contents of array addresses (subscripts):

```
20 PRINT "Here are the contents of array TIMBRE( ):"
40    FOR COUNTER = 1 to 15
50       PRINT TIMBRE(COUNTER)
60    NEXT COUNTER
```

String Arrays

Character arrays can be thought of as compound string variables. The same operations that are used to manipulate the data contained in single variables can be used to process the data held in multiple addresses of a string array. Each address of a string array can store up to 255 alphanumeric characters; and, the same methods used to initialize numeric arrays are used as well for the loading of character arrays. To illustrate, type in the following program segment, then execute it:

```
10  DIM PITCH$(12)
20  PRINT "First we fill an array with Note Names:"
30     FOR COUNTER = 1 to 12
40        READ PITCH$(COUNTER)
50     NEXT COUNTER
60  PRINT "Then we print the array contents to the screen:"
30     FOR COUNTER = 1 to 12
40        PRINT PITCH$(COUNTER);" ";
50     NEXT COUNTER
60  DATA C,C#,D,D#,E,F,F#,G,G#,A,A#,B
```

Notice: 1) that the character data in the above example is separated by commas; quotation marks are not required unless you wish to pad the front or rear of the character data with white (blank) space; and 2) that a blank space has been added to the printout of the contents of each array address in Line 40; this provides legibility. If you wish to include articulative white space within the string, you must use quotation marks in addition to the commas separating the data items, as follows:

```
10      DIM PITCH$(12)
20      PRINT "First we fill an array with Note Names."
30          FOR COUNTER = 1 to 12
40              READ PITCH$(COUNTER)
50          NEXT COUNTER
60      PRINT "Then we print the array contents to the screen:"
30          FOR COUNTER = 1 to 12
40              PRINT PITCH$(COUNTER);
50          NEXT COUNTER
60      DATA "C ","C# ","D ","D# ","E ","F "
70      DATA,"F# ","G ","G# ","A ","A# ","B "
```

When the program is executed, the computer displays:

First we fill an array with Note Names.
Then we print the array contents to the screen:
C C# D D# E F F# G G# A A# B

Program #8 builds upon the preceding program to load a pitch character array with data to represent the MIDI pitch range (0-127).

PROGRAM #8

```
10 REM:***********************************************************
20 REM                       PROGRAM #8
30 REM: PROGRAM TO LOAD AND PRINT A PITCH-CHARACTER ARRAY
40 REM:***********************************************************
50   DIM PITCH$(128)           'an array to hold pitch characters
60   PRINT "Here is a number/pitch equivalence display:"
70   FOR COUNT = 0 TO 127
80     READ PITCH$(COUNT)      'fill array with pitch characters
90     PRINT COUNT;"=";PITCH$(COUNT),              'send to screen
100    NEXT COUNT
110    PRINT
120    DATA C0,C#0,D0,D#0,E0,F0,F#0,G0,Ab0,A0,Bb0,B0
130    DATA C1,C#1,D1,D#1,E1,F1,F#1,G1,Ab1,A1,Bb1,B1
140    DATA C2,C#2,D2,D#2,E2,F2,F#2,G2,Ab2,A2,Bb2,B2
150    DATA C3,C#3,D3,D#3,E3,F3,F#3,G3,Ab3,A3,Bb3,B3
160    DATA C4,C#4,D4,D#4,E4,F4,F#4,G4,Ab4,A4,Bb4,B4
170    DATA C5,C#5,D5,D#5,E5,F5,F#5,G5,Ab5,A5,Bb5,B5
180    DATA C6,C#6,D6,D#6,E6,F6,F#6,G6,Ab6,A6,Bb6,B6
190    DATA C7,C#7,D7,D#7,E7,F7,F#7,G7,Ab7,A7,Bb7,B7
200    DATA C8,C#8,D8,D#8,E8,F8,F#8,G8,Ab8,A8,Bb8,B8
210    DATA C9,C#9,D9,D#9,E9,F9,F#9,G9,Ab9,A9,Bb9,B9
220    DATA C10,C#10,D10,D#10,E10,F10,F#10,G10
230 END
```

Execution of Program #8:

Here is a number/pitch equivalence display:

0 =C0	1 =C#0	2 =D0	3 =D#0	4 =E0
5 =F0	6 =F#0	7 =G0	8 =Ab0	9 =A0
10 =Bb0	11 =B0	12 =C1	13 =C#1	14 =D1
15 =D#1	16 =E1	17 =F1	18 =F#1	19 =G1
20 =Ab1	21 =A1	22 =Bb1	23 =B1	24 =C2
25 =C#2	26 =D2	27 =D#2	28 =E2	29 =F2
30 =F#2	31 =G2	32 =Ab2	33 =A2	34 =Bb2
35 =B2	36 =C3	37 =C#3	38 =D3	39 =D#3
40 =E3	41 =F3	42 =F#3	43 =G3	44 =Ab3
45 =A3	46 =Bb3	47 =B3	48 =C4	49 =C#4
50 =D4	51 =D#4	52 =E4	53 =F4	54 =F#4
55 =G4	56 =Ab4	57 =A4	58 =Bb4	59 =B4
60 =C5	61 =C#5	62 =D5	63 =D#5	64 =E5
65 =F5	66 =F#5	67 =G5	68 =Ab5	69 =A5
70 =Bb5	71 =B5	72 =C6	73 =C#6	74 =D6
75 =D#6	76 =E6	77 =F6	78 =F#6	79 =G6
80 =Ab6	81 =A6	82 =Bb6	83 =B6	84 =C7
85 =C#7	86 =D7	87 =D#7	88 =E7	89 =F7
90 =F#7	91 =G7	92 =Ab7	93 =A7	94 =Bb7
95 =B7	96 =C8	97 =C#8	98 =D8	99 =D#8
100 =E8	101 =F8	102 =F#8	103 =G8	104 =Ab8
105 =A8	106 =Bb8	107 =B8	108 =C9	109 =C#9
110 =D9	111 =D#9	112 =E9	113 =F9	114 =F#9
115 =G9	116 =Ab9	117 =A9	118 =Bb9	119 =B9
120 =C10	121 =C#10	122 =D10	123 =D#10	124 =E10
125 =F10	126 =F#10	127 =G10		

MULTIPLE-DIMENSION ARRAYS

This data structure provides a means of grouping together data for several musical parameters, such as Pitch and Rhythm. It actually is just a "stacking" of single-dimension arrays, so the same syntax and variable name conventions apply regardless of the number of array dimensions employed. Multiple-dimension arrays, also called matrices, are declared by specifying the amount of memory space to be reserved for each array dimension. For instance, a two-dimensional array for an event-vector (just another name for grouped note parameters) to store data for the pitch and rhythm parameters for a notelist (also called note sequence or melody) is declared as follows:

10 DIM NOTELIST(10,10)

It can be visualized as a rectangle containing 10 squares horizontally and 10 squares vertically, similar to a collection of mailboxes:

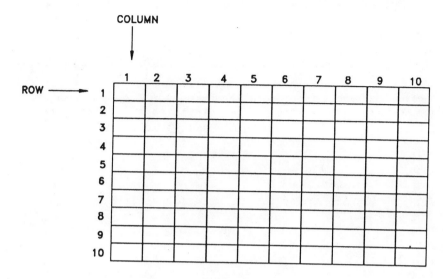

Figure 4-9.

Each "mailbox" is located by reference to its row-column position in the matrix. For example, the first box in the upper left-hand corner is addressed by typing the array name followed by parenthesized row and column numbers:

NOTELIST(1,1)

To enter a number into a specific array address, either the assignment instruction, INPUT instruction, or READ...DATA instruction may be used. The following are all valid ways to put a number into a multidimensional array:

```
LET NOTELIST(5,9) = 23
INPUT NOTELIST(6,2)
READ NOTELIST(ROW,COLUMN)
```

Similarly, the contents of specific array addresses may be copied to other variables or printed:

```
LET PITCH = NOTELIST(5,9)
PRINT NOTELIST(ROW,COLUMN)
```

Notice that array subscripts may take the form of single variables as well as constants.

PROGRAM #9 demonstrates a few of the many data transformation operations that can be performed on multidimensional arrays.

PROGRAM #9

```
100 REM*************************************************************
105 REM                      PROGRAM #9
110 REM        Demonstration of typical matrix operations
190 REM*************************************************************
200 REM                  Variable Descriptions
210 REM        D: full row counter
220 REM        F: flag to print transposed matrix
230 REM        M: scalar multiplication factor
240 REM        X(n,n): matrix 1 to hold primary & multiplied data
250 REM        Y(n,n): matrix 2 to hold transposed data
260 REM        J1: loop index, pointer to matrix rows
270 REM        J2: loop index, pointer to matrix columns
280 REM        K9: subroutine loop index
290 REM        L9: subroutine loop index
300 REM*************************************************************
310 REM                      MAIN ROUTINE
320 REM*************************************************************
330     DIM X(8,8),Y(8,8)
340     D = 0
350     F = 0
360     M = 8
370     PRINT "A 2-DIMENSIONAL MATRIX OF SEQUENTIAL NUMBERS --"
380       FOR J1 = 1 TO 8
390          FOR J2 = 1 TO 8
400             X(J1,J2) = J2 + D
410          NEXT J2
420          D = D + 8
430       NEXT J1
440     GOSUB 1000                        '<< call matrix print
450     PRINT
460     GOSUB 2010              '<< call matrix scalar multiplication
470     PRINT
480     PRINT "MATRIX MULTIPLIED BY 8 --"
490     GOSUB 1000                        '<< call matrix print
500     PRINT
510     GOSUB 3010                    '<< call matrix transposition
520     PRINT
530     PRINT "TRANSPOSED MATRIX (ROWS & COLUMNS EXCHANGED) --"
540     GOSUB 1000                        '<< call matrix print
550     PRINT
560     GOSUB 4000                        '<< call matrix reset
570     PRINT "MATRICES RESET TO ZERO --"
580     GOSUB 1000
```

```
590 END
1000 REM************************************************************
1010 REM          Subroutine to Display Matrix Contents
1020 REM************************************************************
1030      FOR K9 = 1 TO 8
1040          FOR L9 = 1 TO 8
1050              IF F = 0 THEN PRINT TAB(8*(L9-1))X(K9,L9);
ELSE PRINT TAB(8*(L9-1))Y(K9,L9);
1060          NEXT L9
1070          PRINT
1080      NEXT K9
1090 RETURN
2000 REM************************************************************
2010 REM      Subroutine to Multiply Matrix Contents by a Number
2020 REM************************************************************
2030      FOR K9 = 1 TO 8
2040          FOR L9 = 1 TO 8
2050              X(K9,L9) = X(K9,L9) * M
2060          NEXT L9
2070      NEXT K9
2080 RETURN
3000 REM************************************************************
3010 REM   Subroutine to Shift Positions in (transpose) Matrix
3020 REM************************************************************
3030      FOR K9 = 1 TO 8
3040          FOR L9 = 1 TO 8
3050              Y(K9,L9) = X(L9,K9)
3060          NEXT L9
3070      NEXT K9
3080    F = 1
3090 RETURN
4000 REM************************************************************
4010 REM          Subroutine to reset Matrix Contents to Zero
4020 REM************************************************************
4030    FOR K9 = 1 TO 8
4040        FOR L9 = 1 TO 8
4050            X(K9,L9) = 0
4060            Y(K9,L9) = 0
4070        NEXT L9
4080    NEXT K9
4090 RETURN
```

Execution of Program #9:

```
A 2-DIMENSIONAL MATRIX OF SEQUENTIAL NUMBERS --
1        2        3        4        5        6        7        8
9        10       11       12       13       14       15       16
17       18       19       20       21       22       23       24
25       26       27       28       29       30       31       32
33       34       35       36       37       38       39       40
41       42       43       44       45       46       47       48
49       50       51       52       53       54       55       56
57       58       59       60       61       62       63       64
```

```
MATRIX MULTIPLIED BY 8 --
8       16      24      32      40      48      56      64
72      80      88      96      104     112     120     128
136     144     152     160     168     176     184     192
200     208     216     224     232     240     248     256
264     272     280     288     296     304     312     320
328     336     344     352     360     368     376     384
392     400     408     416     424     432     440     448
456     464     472     480     488     496     504     512

TRANSPOSED MATRIX (ROWS & COLUMNS EXCHANGED) --
8       72      136     200     264     328     392     456
16      80      144     208     272     336     400     464
24      88      152     216     280     344     408     472
32      96      160     224     288     352     416     480
40      104     168     232     296     360     424     488
48      112     176     240     304     368     432     496
56      120     184     248     312     376     440     504
64      128     192     256     320     384     448     512

MATRIX RESET TO ZERO --
0       0       0       0       0       0       0       0
0       0       0       0       0       0       0       0
0       0       0       0       0       0       0       0
0       0       0       0       0       0       0       0
0       0       0       0       0       0       0       0
0       0       0       0       0       0       0       0
0       0       0       0       0       0       0       0
0       0       0       0       0       0       0       0
```

SUMMARY

You have learned the rudiments of the BASIC Programming Language, as well as several concepts related to the representation and manipulation of musical data.

Musical Concepts

1. Numeric representation of octave-modular Pitch Classes.
2. Numeric representation of non-octave-modular Pitch Characters.
3. Numeric representation of note duration values (rhythm).
4. Transposition of Pitch Classes (octave-modular) and Pitch Sequences (non-octave-modular).
5. Transposition of rhythmic patterns (duration sequences).

Programming Concepts

1. Primary Data Types
2. Mathematical Operators
3. Relational Operators
4. Logical Operators
5. Automatic Loops
6. Mathematical Functions INT and RND
7. Entering data from the keyboard
8. Reading data contained in the program into variables
9. Interactive programming techniques
10. Conditional Branching
11. Numeric and String Arrays
12. Elementary Matrix Operations
13. Simple Pattern Identification
14. Program Organization: Initialization, Processing, and Output Sections
15. Modular Program Design Concept: GOSUB....RETURN

EXERCISES AND PROGRAMMING PROBLEMS

Before proceeding to the next chapter, test your understanding of the concepts and programming principles presented so far by completing the following exercises. (All programs should be designed for interactive use, and should be organized to clearly show the Initialization, Processing, and Output sections.)

(1) Write a program based on PROGRAM #3 which accepts a sequence of rhythm values (expressed as fraction denominators) from the computer keyboard, then stores them as their decimal equivalents in an array. After the user has entered all rhythm values, the program should report the total length of the sequence (in whole notes).

(2) Write a program based on PROGRAM # 4 which accepts a sequence of rhythm values from the keyboard, then allows the user to alter it by means of rhythmic transposition (augmentation and diminution).

(3) Modify PROGRAM #6 (Pitch Transposition Program) to employ an array to store the user-input pitch sequence.

(4) Write a program based on PROGRAM #7 (Major Triad Identification) to

recognize other types of triadic chords as well as chord inversions.

(5)   Write a program which uses the Number-to-Pitch conversion routine from PROGRAM #8 to translate a user-input number sequence to alphanumeric pitch character form.

(6)   Write a program which uses a multidimensional array to store user-input data for Pitch, Rhythm, Volume, and Timbre parameters.

(7)   Using information you have learned about RND and INT functions, write a program to generate a random-order number sequence which is stored in an array, then printed out as corresponding pitch characters (with octave-register information).

(8)   Modify the program written in exercise (7) to allow the user to determine the range-width and low value of random numbers returned.

(9)   Write a program which accepts a user-input number sequence, then prints out the sequence in pitch characters in forward and reverse (retrograde) forms.

PART II

Computer-Assisted Composition Procedures I:

Deterministic Algorithms

Introduction

Part II covers the range of compositional procedures generally referred to as Deterministic Algorithms. In this category fall all manipulative operations on musical data which do not rely upon probabilities (controlled randomness) to decide the placement and duration of specific note-events over the space-time of the musical canvas. Two examples of deterministic algorithms are pitch sequence transposition and pitch sequence intervallic inversion, as illustrated by Example 5-1.

Example 5-1.

The deterministic algorithms presented herein fall into the following categories:

(1) Mapping
(2) Congruence
(3) Range Rescaling
(4) Range Normalization
(5) Pitch Scale Transforms
(6) Pitch Class Filters
(7) Logical Sieves
(8) Integrative Procedures
(9) Mathematical Algorithms

(10) Motif Transformations
(11) Pattern Recognition and Analysis
(12) Sort and Search
(13) Music from Text (words)
(14) Formal Projection Techniques

It is suggested that the reader become familiar with the conceptual and logical structure of each program before attempting to execute it. In this way, a thorough understanding of some of the most important techniques currently being used by composers will be developed. It is further suggested that the reader exercise the imagination to invent extensions and variations of each program, and then use the results to generate data for short compositions.

Musical Orientation

Much of the American and European music written during the twentieth century is melodically, rather than harmonically, oriented. For this reason, emphasis in the text is placed upon algorithms that "view" the musical texture as a vertical composite of independent melodic sequences.

5

Mapping and Congruence Algorithms

The Composer's Mental Workshop

There are many reasons why composers wish to include the computer among their tools, but perhaps the most powerful ones are:

(1) to avail themselves of its ability to rapidly compute complex data structures impossible for a human to realize;
(2) to collaborate with the computer as a composer's assistant in the working out of compositional details from a master plan; and
(3) to access the computer's decision-making power in the creation of musical texture transition states requiring the rigorous application of the calculus of probabilities (stochastic music).

In the past, composers simply discarded organizational ideas which were too complex to apply by manual methods, or which required an inordinate amount of tedium to accomplish. Unfortunately, this "throwing out the baby with the bath water" had a conceptual side-effect: it delayed the expansion of the composer's aural imagination and awareness of esthetic alternatives, because there was no effective means of simulating and testing hypothetical constructs.

The 1980s have seen the computer assume a compositional role at least equal to that formerly served by the pianoforte. In pre-computer days, composers tested new ideas by sketching and playing at the piano keyboard, whereas many contemporary composers sit at the computer, execute experimental algorithms, and listen immediately to the results on MIDI equipment.

Thought Experiments

The computer has opened the door to an activity long known in the physical sciences: the execution of thought experiments. Thought experiments are hypothetical situations which cannot be modeled outside the brain; that is, they are ideas which, for one reason or another, are physically impossible to perform in a real world context, either because they are too hazardous, or too costly, or too monumental. For example, if a composer wished to implement by hand a concept whose origin was principally philosophical in nature, many problems would arise both in the composition and the testing (performance) of the results. Such an experiment might involve application of the entropy principle, which states that entropy (disorderliness) in nature always increases over time and is irreversible. Realization of this project is not feasible using pencil and paper. But, by programming a computer to apply controlled transition probabilities to the elements of musical textures, the composer can hypothesize and test structures in which various entropic states could symbolize temporal past-present-future reference points, thereby creating a metaphorical environment in which the unidirectionality of time could be circumvented.

The Parameters of Music. Musical parameters are generally synonymous with what are commonly referred to as the elements of music: pitch, rhythm, articulation, dynamics, and tone color (instrument). The term parameter (borrowed from mathematics) has been substituted in recognition of the fact that these dimensions of musical texture can be quantified as scalar values contained within a bounded range and represented numerically for purposes of manipulation.

Pitch Parameter. Composers have many ways of dealing with musical parameters. For example, when referring to the entire collection of equal-tempered pitches available on, say, the pianoforte or a MIDI synthesizer, the term Pitch Element Collection is used. This corresponds to what musicians normally term the Total Chromatic: every note on the keyboard in succession, from low to high. Example 5-2 illustrates this idea.

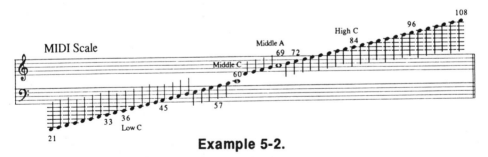

Example 5-2.

When composers wish to acknowledge the octave modularity of the western equal-tempered, semitonal tuning system, they refer to the twelve distinct pitches within the chromatic scale octave as the twelve Pitch Classes. Sometimes we wish to view the Pitch Classes as characters. At other times it is more convenient to represent them by a set of unique integers, 0 - 11. We refer to these integers as the Pitch Class Set. Example 5-3 illustrates this concept.

Example 5-3.

This modular view of pitch intentionally disregards the fact that each pitch of the entire range is actually unique, and focuses attention on the fact that a given Pitch Class played in a specific octave register can be considered by the human ear as identical to the same Pitch Class played in a lower or higher octave register. This modular representation of pitch is important to certain compositional methods, in particular serialism.

Sometimes, instead of simply using the Pitch Classes directly, composers wish to concentrate attention on the distance in semitones between pitches of a melodic sequence. This is the case in music which is intervallically constructed. Measured from an arbitrary start-point in the chromatic scale, for instance middle C, each successive Pitch Class can be referenced in terms of its interval-size distance in semitones away from the start-point, as illustrated in Example 5-4.

Example 5-4.

Notice that, as well as there being 12 distinct Pitch Classes within each octave, there are also 12 distinct interval-sizes.

Rhythm Parameter. The concept of musical rhythm is often misunderstood by nonmusicians. People sometimes refer to anything having a steady beat as "having rhythm." Actually the idea of rhythm is compound, consisting of meter, or a regular accent pattern imposed upon a regular succession of large pulses, called beats, which in turn are subdivided and regrouped into patterns of varying note durations.

Example 5-5 illustrates the relationship between pulse, large beat, note duration, meter, and finally "rhythm."

Example 5-5.

When speaking of the Rhythm Parameter in reference to computer music, normally composers refer to note durations, because note events are often stored inside the computer as individual records, also called event vectors, each of which contains, not entire rhythms, but all necessary parameter information for one note event: its Pitch, Duration, Articulation, Volume, and Timbre. Therefore, by definition, we do not refer to the rhythm of a single note, only its duration.

Articulation Parameter. Articulation is also a compound idea. It refers in general terms to the manner in which a musical note is executed. The outer extremes of articulation can be visualized as accented staccato—a note begun by a hard attack (high volume) and held only for a fraction of the assigned time span—and unaccented legato—a note begun by a soft attack (low volume) and held for its full duration. In actuality, and for convenience, computer music composers normally define the Articulation Parameter as representing only the percentage of the allotted note space that will be used by the tone. Example 5-6 illustrates this concept.

Example 5-6.

Volume Parameter. Sometimes referred to as dynamics or amplitude, the Volume Parameter is represented inside the computer as a scalar range of integer values from soft to loud. In MIDI, this range is from 0 to 127. Volume can be thought of, by analogy to the art of painting, as a kind of musical perspective, or presence. Music played at a low volume level tends to be perceived as "more distant" than music played at a high volume level.

Timbre Parameter. When we listen to various acoustical musical instruments, our brain identifies and classifies the unique character of the source according to many different criteria, but the one most familiar to everyone is known as instrumental color, tone color, or timbre. In the past, change of tone color was available in very limited form and was projected primarily through the craft of orchestration. Today, timbre variation is quite flexible and demands an unusual amount of attention on the part of the composer. It is dealt with in a number of ways in computer music, but in MIDI system work, individual timbres are stored as integers which represent synthesizer "patches" (different tone color settings). These patches can either be imitative of natural acoustical instruments such as the saxophone, or freely invented to provide unique, other-worldy sounding instruments.

Algorithm Formulation

The human brain is quite forgiving. As composers, we often conjure up music from we know not where, relying on intuition and sensitivity to sound materials to provide the necessary stimulus and fodder for subconscious creative activity. Properly fed, the mind rewards us with many gifts, and tolerates imprecision and vagueness, at least in the early stages of working out artistic details. By contrast, the personal computer is merciless. Unless we can clearly define our objectives in machine terms, program output will be useless. Figure 5-1 is a diagram of the complete process of algorithm formulation. You should follow its steps when you begin to write a composition program.

Music Composition Algorithm Formulation Procedure

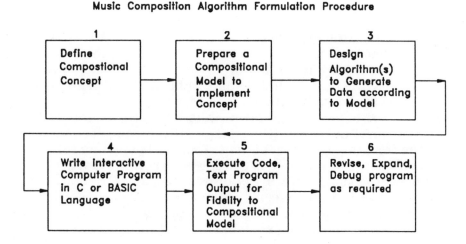

Figure 5-1.

Define Compositional Concept. First, be very clear about the nature of the desired musical result. Be sure you understand in a comprehensive way the style of the composition you wish to generate. To test this, try to describe verbally the salient features of the music you wish to model by computer.

Prepare a Compositional Model. Next, prepare a compositional stylistic model in music notation. If you are unable to write a musical sample that embodies the characteristic you hope to achieve by computer, then you probably won't be able to communicate this style to the machine in program form.

Determine Computer's Role. To successfully interface with the computer, it is necessary to adjust working habits to eliminate ambiguity and fuzziness. The first step is to decide exactly what role the computer will play in the compositional process. That is, we must have a clear idea of the kinds of jobs the machine will be asked to perform. Will it make high- or low-level choices among alternatives? Will it improvise melodic lines from provided (input) source melodies? Will it simply process musical data (pitch series, for instance) and output the results? Will it automatically compose all details of a finished composition? Will it perform analytical functions on preconfigured musical data?

Participation Level. An important step in designing a music composition program is to determine exactly how extensive the role of the computer will be in configuring final musical details. If it will function primarily as a kind of super-calculator, then the program will probably be differently organized than if the computer is to function in a more creative way.

Compositional Strategy. Before we can begin to plan the various segments, routines, and processing orders in a specific program, a rationale or strategy must be formulated which clearly indicates precisely how the desired end result will be achieved. This requires that the composer/programmer decide on the best approach to solving the set of musical problems inherent in the character of the desired musical objective. For example, if the composer wishes to apply the computer solely to the generation and processing of various transformations of a user-input 12-tone pitch series (PC set), then the list of tasks the computer will perform is a good deal simpler than if we were to ask it to make compositional decisions about all of the musical parameters. The strategy in the simpler case will be straightforward; it will consist of determining the logical sequence of operations and the formulation of component algorithms. The second case requires considerably more planning through the consideration of multiple, strategic alternatives for the realization of program goals.

Strategic Focus. Choice of the appropriate problem-solving strategy cannot be over-emphasized. While there are normally many ways to solve a set of problems, usually, after complete familiarity with the compositional materials, one strategy will emerge over others as most fruitful. On the highest level, available strategies often will be selected from the following list of general program types:

(1) utility programs for low-level processing and transformation of parametric data;

(2) procedure-oriented composition programs allowing user-interactive control over formative processes;

(3) automated composition programs which are noninteractive and "black box" oriented;

(4) knowledge-based programs which perform analytical functions to gain information for the generation of fresh musical examples; and

(5) experimental programs which project outcomes which are highly variable (unpredictable) onto the musical canvas.

Algorithm Pseudo-code. After the nature and number of musical tasks to be performed in a specific program is determined, a step-by-step description in natural language should be written for each algorithm. The logical sequence of steps within each algorithm must be ascertained and checked (mentally) to guarantee that the output will be valid. Here is an example of pseudo-code for an algorithm to transpose a user-input pitch sequence in an upward direction by an interval size of four semitones:

(1) get the melodic sequence in integer form from the user (computer keyboard);

(2) add to each pitch number in succession the integer 4;

(3) print out the sum of the original pitch number and the transposition interval after each calculation if performed; and

(4) end the program.

Write Block Pseudo-Code Description after all component algorithms have been written in pseudo-code form, determine the appropriate execution sequence, then place the pseudo-code descriptions in that order in block form, as in Figure 5-2.

Music Composition Program Example Structure
Block Diagram

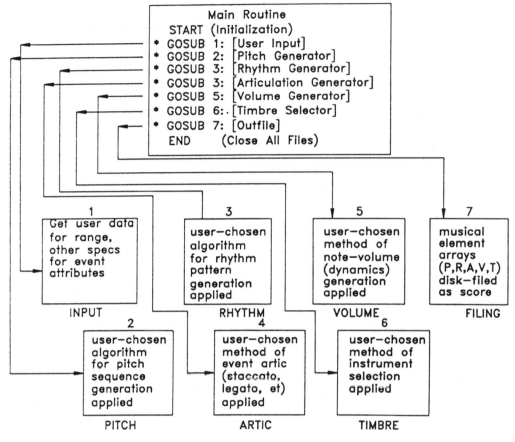

Figure 5-2.

Music from Mathematics

Everyone has heard people say that music has a mathematical basis. When speaking about the music of previous centuries, perhaps it would be more accurate to say that the tools of mathematics can be used to describe and document many of the relationships found in musical structures. Only occasionally can a one-to-one relationship between mathematical concept and musical result be observed. But, when discussing the "classical" music of the twentieth century, it can be shown that the link between the discipline of mathematics and the musical art of composition is fundamental and intimate. In fact, quite often the algorithm applied to the composition of musical data for Pitch, Rhythm, Volume and other parameters will be a mathematical expression, formula, or method borrowed from one of the subdisciplines such as algebra, calculus, or probability theory. Similarly, routines which primarily serve an analytical function owe their existence to one branch or another of mathematics.

BASIC's Built-in Math Functions. BASIC language provides a generous assortment of commonly used mathematical functions. Figure 5-3 is a complete list.

BASIC Library of Mathematical Functions

Function	Intrinsic Function
Absolute Value	ABS(X)
Arctangent	ATN(X)
Cosine	COS(X)
Exponent	EXP(X)
Logarithm (base 2)	LOG(X)
Modulus	MOD(X)
Signum	SGN(X)
Sine	SIN(X)
Square Root	SQR(X)
Tangent	TAN(X)
Random Numbers	RND(X)
Random Function Seed	RANDOMIZE(X)
Integer - truncation; rounds negative numbers, e.g., -6.945 becomes -7.	INT(X)
Integer - rounds both positive and negative numbers.	CINT(X)
Integer - truncation; no rounding of positive or negative numbers.	FIX(X)

Figure 5-3.

User-Defined Math Functions

BASIC allows the user to write a function definition instruction for often-used mathematical functions which are not built into the language.

In the initialization section of the program, you simply write a statement such as:

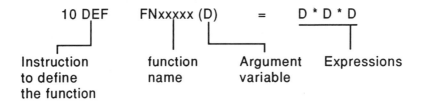

Instruction   function   Argument   Expressions
to define   name   variable
the function

Figure 5-4.

After the function is defined, it is available for use at any point in the program simply by invoking it. The variable you wish to apply the function to is substituted for the argument (dummy) variable of the definition, as follows:

function definition ———— 10 DEF FNCUBE(X) = X * X * X
                            190 A = 2   .
function invocation ———— 200 K = FNCUBE(A)

Figure 5-5.

The variable K will receive the result of the function's operation on the variable A, which will be cubed.

Figure 5-6 is a complete list of instructions for user-defined mathematical functions.

Function	Defined Function
Logarithm to base B	DEF FNLOGB(X) = LOG(X) / LOG(B)
Secant	DEF FNSEC(X) = 1 / COS(X)
Cosecant	DEF FNCSC(X) = 1 / SIN(X)
Cotangent	DEF FNCOT(X) = 1 / TAN(X)
Inverse sine	DEF FNARCSIN(X) = ATN(X) / SQR(1 - X * X))
Inverse cosine	DEF FNARCCOS(X) = 1.570796 - ATN(X / SQR(1 - X * X))
Inverse secant	DEF FNARCSEC(X) = ATN(SQR(X * X - 1)) + (X<0) * 3.141593
Inverse cosecant	DEF FNARCCSC(X) = ATN(1/SQR(X * X - 1)) + (X<0) * 3.141593
Inverse cotangent	DEF FNARCCOT(X) = 1.57096 - ATN(X)
Hyperbolic sine	DEF FNSINH(X) = (EXP(X) - EXP(-X)) / 2
Hyperbolic cosine	DEF FNCOSH(X) = (EXP(X) + EXP(-X)) / 2
Hyperbolic tangent	DEF FNTANH(X) = (EXP(X) = EXP(-X)) / (EXP(X) + EXP(-X))
Hyperbolic secant	DEF FNSECH(X) = 2 / (EXP(X) + EXP(-X))

Hyperbolic cosecant	DEF FNCSCH(X) = 2 / (EXP(X) - EXP(-X))
Hyperbolic cotangent	DEF FNCOTH(X) = (EXP(X) + EXP(-X)) / (EXP(X) - EXP(-X))
Inverse hyperbolic sine	DEF FNARCSINH(X) = LOG(X + SQR(X * X + 1))
Inverse hyperbolic cosine	DEF FNARCCOSH(X) = LOG(X + SQR(X * X - 1))
Inverse hyperbolic tangent	DEF FNARCTANH(X) = LOG((1 + X) / (1 - X)) / 2
Inverse hyperbolic secant	DEF FNARCSECH(X) = LOG((1 + SQR(1 - X * X)) / X)
Inverse hyperbolic cosecant	DEF FNARCCSCH(X) = LOG((1 + SGN(X) * SQR(1 + X * X)) / X)
Inverse hyperbolic cotangent	DEF FNARCCOTH(X) = LOG((X + 1) / (X-1)) / 2

Figure 5-6.

Mapping Concept

The technique of copying a quantifiable characteristic from one phenomenon onto another is called mapping. This concept is fundamental to a full understanding of the procedures used in algorithmic composition.

Iconic Mapping. Musical mapping is accomplished by several means, the most visible of which is iconic, or topological in nature. Iconic mapping is the direct transference of a pattern of numbers to a musical parameter, such as pitch. The number pattern can represent itself or it can be metaphorical, such as a list of heights of adjacent buildings along a city skyline. In any case, the order and magnitude (configuration, shape) of a sequence of numbers can easily be transferred to the element set of any musical parameter. Consider the following ascending number series and its mapping onto the pitch element set consisting of the chromatic scale:

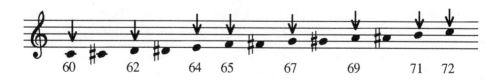

60   62   64 65   67   69   71 72

Example 5-7.

Musicians identify the resulting pattern as the C-Major diatonic scale. Recall that a second method of viewing a sequence of pitches is by measuring the intervallic distance (in semitones) between each member of the sequence. From this perspective, we could characterize the diatonic Major scale pattern as:

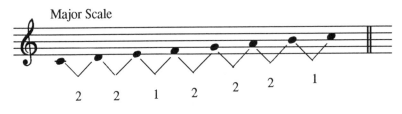

Example 5-8.

Mapping Levels. Program #10 demonstrates the lowest level of iconic mapping along the pitch parameter. MIDI synthesizers accept a range of integer values from 0 to 127, normally distributed in a tuning configuration identical to the acoustic piano keyboard, but of a much broader pitch range. The integers, 0—127, are directly mapped onto the MIDI pitch range, low to high, on a one-to-one basis.

Equal-Temperament Tuning System. The standard tuning system used in Western music is the equal-tempered, semitonal scale. The advent of computerized sound generation devices has opened the door to the easy implementation of other types of tuning systems, the most accessible of which are equal-tempered microtonal scale structures. These scales are octave-modular pitch sequences built, low to high, from a beginning note, using a uniform-size interval between scale steps. The number of steps permissible in the scale is determined by the size of each step. Using the standard semitone, the chromatic scale of 12 steps results. Using the quarter-tone step interval, a 24-step scale results, and so on. To construct a scale containing a given number of tones, the equal temperament coefficient formula must be applied as follows:

$$2 \char94 (1 / octave\ division)$$

(Please see the Variable Description section of Program #10 for details.) This system allows flexible octave-modular microtonal tunings; some MIDI synthesizers are capable of implementing the scales, others must be tuned manually. Program #10 is synthesizer-independent, because it allows the testing and audition of various tuning system results (experimental or not) through application of the personal computer's internal sound chip. While the characteristics of this sound production means are musically quite dull, it provides a quick method of testing algorithm results during program execution.

Sound Instruction. Most IBM-PC compatible computers are supplied with an internal sound-generating chip to provide a primitive, unalterable signal for testing and user warning purposes. This chip can be used to test composition program output by adding an instruction at the appropriate place in program code. After an algorithm has been thoroughly tested and debugged, the SOUND statement can be replaced with an instruction to write the musical data to a MIDI-format file for performance by synthesizer.

The BASIC SOUND instruction requires two pieces of information: (1) the frequency of the tone to be generated in Hertz (cycles per second), and (2) the duration the tone is to sound in computer clock ticks. The statement form is:

SOUND freq, duration

Any value from 37 to 32767 can be used in the frequency position of the instruction; duration is a value determined on the basis of 18.2 ticks per second, within the range 0 to 65535. Therefore, if you wish to sound middle A (on the piano keyboard) for two seconds as a sound chip tone, the instruction will be:

SOUND 440,36.4

If duration is set to 0, any active SOUND statement is turned off. (If no SOUND statement is running, a duration of 0 has no effect.)

To produce rests, use this SOUND Instruction form:

SOUND 32767, duration.

To calculate the duration of one beat, divide beats per minute into the number of clock ticks in a minute (1092). For example, a slow tempo (Largo) of 40-66 M.M. would range from 27.3 to 18.2 ticks per beat.

Execute Program #10 a number of times using progressively smaller scale step sizes; try to determine the point of frequency closeness where it becomes difficult for the ear to distinguish one pitch from the next.

PROGRAM #10

```
10 REM*********************************************************
20 REM                      PROGRAM #10
30 REM     Demonstrate adding Equal-Tempered Tuning Sound
40 REM     Function Routine to Programs for Algorithm Testing
50 REM*********************************************************
60 REM***************     Main Routine     *******************
70 REM*********************************************************
```

```
80   DEFDBL T         'declare TONE() to be double precision array
90   DEFDBL C         'declare COEFF to be double precision variable
100 DIM TONE(128)
110 INPUT "Enter number tones to generate (scale range):",
      NUMTONES
120 INPUT "Enter number of tones in octave: ",OCTDIV
130 INPUT "Enter starting frequency (in cps): ",FREQ1
140   GOSUB 1000                       '<< call tuning compiler
150   FOR J = 1 TO NUMTONES
160       PRINT TONE(J),       '<< send scale frequencies to screen
170       SOUND TONE(J),7       '<< send to internal sound chip
180       SOUND TONE(0),2       '<< send silence to PC sound chip
190   NEXT J
200 END
1000 REM***************************************************************
1030 REM        Equal-Tempered Tunings Compiler Routine
1040 REM***************************************************************
1060 REM                    Variable Descriptions
1070 REM
1080 REM***************************************************************
1090 REM      FREQ1: frequency in Herz (cps) of scale tonic
1100 REM      NUMTONES: number of pitches to compute
1110 REM      OCTDIV: number of equalsize steps within octave
1120 REM   Exiting -
1130 REM      TONE(): array of computed scale frequencies
1140 REM   Local -
1150 REM      COEFF: coefficient for specified octave division
1160 REM      K9: loop index, pointer to array TONE()
1170 REM
1190 COEFF = 2^(1/OCTDIV)
1200 TONE(1) =  FREQ1
1210   FOR K9= 2 TO NUMTONES
1220       TONE(K9) =  TONE(K9-1) * COEFF
1230   NEXT K9
1240 RETURN                                       .
```

Execution of Program #10:

```
Enter number tones to generate (scale range): 128
Enter number of tones in octave: 12
Enter starting frequency (in cps): 8.176
```

8.176	8.66217	9.17725	9.722958	10.30112
10.91365	11.56261	12.25016	12.97859	13.75034
14.56798	15.43424	16.35201	17.32435	18.35451
19.44592	20.60224	21.82732	23.12524	24.50034
25.9572	27.5007	29.13598	30.8685	32.70403
34.64872	36.70904	38.89187	41.20451	43.65466
46.2505	49.0007	51.91443	55.00143	58.27198

61.73702	65.4081	69.29747	73.41811	77.78378
82.40905	87.30935	92.50104	98.00144	103.8289
110.0029	116.544	123.4741	130.8163	138.595
146.8363	155.5677	164.8182	174.6188	185.0022
196.003	207.658	220.006	233.0882	246.9484
261.6327	277.1902	293.6728	311.1355	329.6366
349.2379	370.0046	392.0063	415.3162	440.0122
466.1768	493.8971	523.2658	554.3808	587.346
622.2714	659.2736	698.4761	740.0096	784.0129
830.6328	880.0248	932.3539	987.7946	1046.532
1108.762	1174.693	1244.543	1318.548	1396.953
1480.02	1568.027	1661.267	1760.051	1864.709
1975.591	2093.065	2217.526	2349.387	2489.089
2637.098	2793.908	2960.042	3136.056	3322.535
3520.104	3729.42	3951.183	4186.133	4435.053
4698.775	4978.179	5274.197	5587.817	5920.086
6272.113	6645.073	7040.21	7458.842	7902.369
8372.269	8870.11	9397.555	9956.363	10548.4
11175.64	11840.18	12544.24		

A slightly higher level of iconic mapping results from a narrowing of the elemental pitch repertoire by means of uniform interval (pitch distance between scale degrees) selection, thereby producing a subset of the background repertoire of elements. For instance, Example 5-9 is the scale resulting from the selection and repetition of interval-size 2.

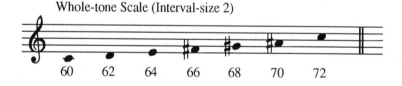

Whole-tone Scale (Interval-size 2)

Example 5-9.

Imagine the pattern created by the number list in Example 5-9 to be transferred to the synthesizer keyboard, which uses the low to high range 0 to 127 (Middle C = 60). When we play the number/pitch pattern, our ear tells us that each note of the sequence is higher in pitch than the last by a constant distance (2 semitones, or major second interval). Our brain identifies this list of pitches as the whole-tone scale, one of many scale patterns based on the elemental semitone pitch scale that has evolved over the centuries to simplify and organize musical pitch material.

The next higher level of iconic mapping is a patterned (structured) narrowing of the background element set to produce a degree of intervallic variety (compared to the uniform-interval chromatic scale) while limiting selectivity of elements of the basic repertoire of pitch frequencies.

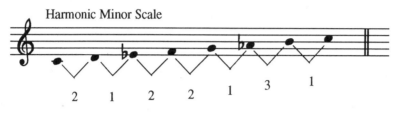

Example 5-10.

This rudimentary mapping of numbers to musical scale can be used as an intermediate-level reduced element set for further mappings of more interesting number distributions. Normally, we do not consider the banal traversal (up and down) of a musical scale to be interesting enough to assume the stature of a melody or theme; therefore, another, higher level of mapping must be employed to add complexity to the rigid linear ascending order of the background scale. This high-level patterning, with recourse to varied interval sizes between notes in the list along with repetitions of scale degrees, is the substance of melodic shape.

2/4	G	E♭	A♭	F	B♭	G	C	A♭	B♭	G	A♭	F	E♭
	8	8	8	8	8	8	8	8	8	8	8	8	1

Example 5-11.

Example 5-11 illustrates a basic condition for the human being's classification of a sequence of pitches as "a melody."

A limited interval-set, in a specific sequence, transposed up and then down on the scale of E-flat major reflects the essence of melodic patterning. Redundancy as well as variety is a precondition to the perception and retention of melodic material. In Western music of the common practice period this patterning had equally balanced vertical and horizontal components: melodic and harmonic. Melodic lines were directly correlated with harmonic (tertian-triadic) content, and subjected to severe constraints with respect to the background harmonic (chordal) progression. Since that period, which ended around the beginning of the twentieth century, Western music has exhibited a preoccupation with principles of order rather than content. This phenomenon is most apparent in the methodology of the serial determinist composers, who use the inherent characteristics of number series to configure most of the details of a musical work.

Example 5-12.

Example 5-12 demonstrates how a number series can determine the rhythmic and melodic details of a theme. The same principle can be similarly extended to the Volume, Articulation, and Timbre parameters of musical events, and it can also be applied to higher levels of the musical texture such as density, phrase structure, length and proportion of musical section, etc. This body of methods, collectively known as Serial Technique, is eminently suited to algorithmic implementation by computer. As you progress through this text you will become familiar with many serial procedures, as well as the more general method used for melodic motif transformation.

Mapping techniques can be used for any event phenomenon which has accessible, scalar dimensions. Temporal events also serve as metaphorical models for musical structures. For example, time intervals between occurrences of a particular natural phenomenon might be scaled within a specific pitch range and mapped onto melodic interval structure. A simple illustration of this application follows:

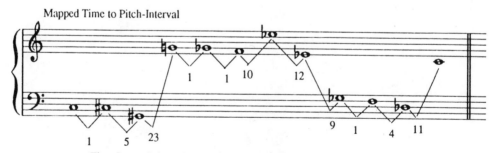

Time Intervals between honking of automobile horns at a city intersection.

Example 5-13.

Mapping techniques frequently require some compression or expansion of scalar data ranges when copying from the source phenomenon to the host phenomenon. Normalization and congruence operations are two frequently used adaptive procedures.

Mapping Programs

Congruence Modulo m. Without some means of transferring data scaled over a particular range to the (probably different) range of a musical parameter, we could accomplish very little. The concept of making data congruent with the requirements of various parametric ranges serves this purpose. BASIC provides a function which automatically converts all input values to the scale of values specified by a modulus value. The MOD function eliminates all multiples of a given integer within a particular modulus, then returns the remainder, called the residual class. For instance, the BASIC instruction,

$$X = Y \text{ MOD } M$$

given the values Y = 23 and M = 5, would evaluate to the residual class, 3, which would be assigned to the variable X.

Program #11 demonstrates this principle in simplified form. Execute the program, then edit the DATA statements at the end to observe the conversion of data scaled over various ranges.

PROGRAM #11

```
20 REM********************************************************
30 REM                      PROGRAM #11
40 REM   Demonstrate Mapping Technique Using Congruence Modulo m
50 REM********************************************************
60 CLS
70 DIM SEQ(40),PIT(12)
80 TOTAL = 40
90 LOW = 30
100 HIGH = 110
110 RANGE = HIGH - LOW + 1
120 PITCHSET = 12
130 PRINT "First, we fill the Pitch Element Table. "
140 PRINT "It will range from 60 (middle C) to 71 (1 octave): "
150 PRINT
160     FOR COUNT = 0 TO PITCHSET-1
170         READ PIT(COUNT)
180         PRINT PIT(COUNT),
190     NEXT COUNT
200 PRINT : PRINT
```

```
210 PRINT "Now, we'll get a random-order number sequence:"
220 PRINT
230      FOR COUNT = 0 TO TOTAL - 1
240         SEQ(COUNT) = INT(RND * RANGE) + LOW
250         PRINT SEQ(COUNT),
260      NEXT COUNT
270 PRINT : PRINT
280 PRINT "Then, using the random sequence as a pointer list,"
290 PRINT "we map each number in the sequence onto the pitch"
300 PRINT "element list using modulus arithmetic."
310 PRINT
320      FOR COUNT = 0 TO TOTAL-1
330         PRINT PIT(SEQ(COUNT) MOD PITCHSET),
340      NEXT COUNT
350 REM ======= DATA FOR PITCH ELEMENT TABLE ==========
360 DATA 60,61,62,63,64,65,66,67,68,69,70,71
370 END
```

Execution of Program #11:

First, we fill the Pitch Element Table.
It will range from 60 (middle C) to 71 (1 octave):

60	61	62	63	64
65	66	67	68	69
70	71			

Now, we'll get a random-order number sequence:

43	44	74	65	45
54	97	96	82	68
31	65	60	84	62
76	65	61	101	70
93	47	107	96	61
101	94	38	64	61
82	81	97	72	71
72	32	73	107	35

Then, using the random sequence as a pointer list,
we map each number in the sequence onto the pitch
element list using modulus arithmetic.

67	68	62	65	69
66	61	60	70	68
67	65	60	60	62
64	65	61	65	70
69	71	71	60	61
65	70	62	64	61
70	69	61	60	71
60	68	61	71	71

Program #12 is an expanded mapping program using the congruence modulo m principle. Run it several times, then write a program of similar structure which allows the user to enter the data for the parameter tables at the keyboard.

PROGRAM #12

```
1   REM*********************************************************
10  REM                     PROGRAM #12
20  REM*********************************************************
30  REM         Demonstrate Mapping of a Number Sequence onto
40  REM         Pitch, Rhythm, Articulation, Volume, & Timbre
50  REM         Parameters, Each of Which Has a Different Length
60  REM         Element List.
70  REM*********************************************************
80  CLS
90  DIM SEQ(100),PIT(12),RHY(6),ART(4),VOL(8),TIM(20)
100 TOTAL = 50
110 LOW = 30
120 HIGH = 110
130 RANGE = HIGH - LOW + 1
140 PITCHSET = 12
150 RHYTHMSET = 5
160 ARTICULATIONSET = 4
170 VOLUMESET = 8
180 TIMBRESET = 9
190 PRINT "First, we fill the Pitch Element Table. "
200 PRINT "It will range from 60 (middle C) to 71 (1 octave): "
210     FOR COUNT = 0 TO PITCHSET-1
220         READ PIT(COUNT)
230         PRINT PIT(COUNT),
240     NEXT COUNT
250 PRINT : PRINT
260 PRINT "Next, we fill the Rhythm Element Table. "
270 PRINT "It will range from a whole-note to a 16th-note:"
280 PRINT
290     FOR COUNT = 0 TO RHYTHMSET-1
300         READ RHY(COUNT)
310         PRINT RHY(COUNT),
320     NEXT COUNT
330 PRINT : PRINT
340 PRINT "Then, we fill the remaining parameter tables."
350 PRINT : PRINT "Articulation Element Table: "
360     FOR COUNT = 0 TO ARTICULATIONSET-1
370         READ ART(COUNT)
380         PRINT ART(COUNT),
390     NEXT COUNT
400 PRINT
410 PRINT : PRINT "Volume Element Table: "
```

```
420      FOR COUNT = 0 TO VOLUMESET-1
430          READ VOL(COUNT)
440          PRINT VOL(COUNT),
450      NEXT COUNT
460 PRINT
470 PRINT : PRINT "Timbre Element Table: "
480      FOR COUNT = 0 TO TIMBRESET-1
490          READ TIM(COUNT)
500          PRINT TIM(COUNT),
510      NEXT COUNT
520 PRINT : PRINT
530 PRINT "--------- PRESS THE SPACEBAR TO CONTINUE ----------"
540 IF INKEY$ <> " " THEN 540
550 CLS
560 PRINT "Now, we'll get a random-order number sequence:"
565 RANDOMIZE
570      FOR COUNT = 0 TO TOTAL - 1
580          SEQ(COUNT) = INT(RND * RANGE) + LOW
590          PRINT SEQ(COUNT),
600      NEXT COUNT
610 PRINT : PRINT
620 '
630 PRINT "--------- PRESS THE SPACEBAR TO CONTINUE ----------"
640 IF INKEY$ <> " " THEN 640
650 PRINT
660 PRINT "Then, using the random sequence as a pointer list,"
670 PRINT "we map each number in the sequence onto the pitch"
680 PRINT "element list using modulus arithmetic."
690 PRINT
700 PRINT "Here are the numbers for the pitch parameter:"
710   FOR COUNT = 0 TO TOTAL-1
720       PRINT PIT(SEQ(COUNT) MOD PITCHSET),
730   NEXT COUNT
735 PRINT : PRINT
740 PRINT "--------- PRESS THE SPACEBAR TO CONTINUE ----------"
750 IF INKEY$ <> " " THEN 750
760 PRINT "Now, we will map the original number sequence to the"
770 PRINT "Rhythm Parameter."
780 PRINT : PRINT "Here are the numbers for the Rhythm Param-
eter:"
790   FOR COUNT = 0 TO TOTAL-1
800       PRINT RHY(SEQ(COUNT) MOD RHYTHMSET),
810   NEXT COUNT
820 PRINT : PRINT
830 PRINT "--------- PRESS THE SPACEBAR TO CONTINUE ----------"
840 IF INKEY$ <> " " THEN 840
850 CLS
860 PRINT "Now, we will map the original number sequence to the"
870 PRINT "Articulation Parameter."
880 PRINT : PRINT "Here is the Articulation Parameter:"
```

```
890    FOR COUNT = 0 TO TOTAL-1
900      PRINT ART(SEQ(COUNT) MOD ARTICULATIONSET),
910    NEXT COUNT
915 PRINT : PRINT
920 PRINT "--------- PRESS THE SPACEBAR TO CONTINUE ----------"
930 IF INKEY$ <> " " THEN 930
940 PRINT "Now, we will map the original number sequence to the"
950 PRINT "Volume Parameter."
960 PRINT : PRINT "Here is the Volume Parameter:"
970    FOR COUNT = 0 TO TOTAL-1
980      PRINT VOL(SEQ(COUNT) MOD VOLUMESET),
990    NEXT COUNT
1000 PRINT "--------- PRESS THE SPACEBAR TO CONTINUE ----------"
1010 IF INKEY$ <> " " THEN 1010
1020 PRINT "Now, we will map the original number sequence to the"
1030 PRINT "Timbre Parameter."
1040 PRINT : PRINT "Here is the Timbre Parameter:"
1050    FOR COUNT = 0 TO TOTAL-1
1060      PRINT TIM(SEQ(COUNT) MOD TIMBRESET),
1070    NEXT COUNT
1130 REM*************** PROGRAM DATA *************************
1140 REM
1150 REM ======= DATA FOR PITCH ELEMENT TABLE =================
1160 DATA 60,61,62,63,64,65,66,67,68,69,70,71
1170 REM ======= DATA FOR RHYTHM ELEMENT TABLE =================
1180 DATA 1,2,3,4,8,16
1190 REM ======= DATA FOR ARTICULATION ELEMENT TABLE =========
1200 DATA 40,50,60,85
1210 REM ======= DATA FOR VOLUME ELEMENT TABLE ===============
1220 DATA 30,40,50,60,70,90,105,120
1230 REM ======= DATA FOR TIMBRE ELEMENT TABLE ===============
1240 DATA 3,13,16,35,50,52,69,78,79,85,88,94,95,98,103,104,106,108,114
1250 REM
1260 REM*************** END OF PROGRAM DATA *******************
1270 REM
1280 REM
1290    END
```

Execution of Program #12:

```
First, we fill the Pitch Element Table.
It will range from 60 (middle C) to 71 (1 octave):
  60            61            62            63            64
  65            66            67            68            69
  70            71

Next, we fill the Rhythm Element Table.
It will range from a whole-note to a 16th-note:

  1             2             3             4             8
```

Then, we fill the remaining parameter tables.

Articulation Element Table:

16	40	50	60

Volume Element Table:

85	30	40	50	60
70	90	105		

Timbre Element Table:

120	3	13	16	35
50	52	69	78	

--------- PRESS THE SPACEBAR TO CONTINUE ----------
Now, we'll get a random-order number sequence:
Random Number Seed (-32768 to 32767)? -1033

96	60	64	58	96
58	106	92	101	65
38	50	94	98	79
90	73	48	97	46
33	61	85	105	44
47	93	44	35	103
96	104	76	66	47
107	37	51	109	52
71	45	105	75	73
85	108	37	44	52

--------- PRESS THE SPACEBAR TO CONTINUE ----------

Then, using the random sequence as a pointer list,
we map each number in the sequence onto the pitch
element list using modulus arithmetic.

Here are the numbers for the pitch parameter:

60	60	64	70	60
70	70	68	65	65
62	62	70	62	67
66	61	60	61	70
69	61	61	69	68
71	69	68	71	67
60	68	64	66	71
71	61	63	61	64
71	69	69	63	61
61	60	61	68	64

--------- PRESS THE SPACEBAR TO CONTINUE ----------
Now, we will map the original number sequence to the
Rhythm Parameter.

Here are the numbers for the Rhythm Parameter:

2	1	8	4	2
4	2	3	2	1
4	1	8	4	8
1	4	4	3	2
4	2	1	1	8
3	4	8	1	4
2	8	2	2	3
3	3	2	8	3
2	1	1	1	4
1	4	3	8	3

--------- PRESS THE SPACEBAR TO CONTINUE ----------
Now, we will map the original number sequence to the
Articulation Parameter.

Here is the Articulation Parameter:

16	16	16	50	16
50	50	16	40	40
50	50	50	50	60
50	40	16	40	50
40	40	40	40	16
60	40	16	60	60
16	16	16	50	60
60	40	60	40	16
60	40	40	60	40
40	16	40	16	16

--------- PRESS THE SPACEBAR TO CONTINUE ----------
Now, we will map the original number sequence to the
Volume Parameter.

Here is the Volume Parameter:

85	60	85	40	85
40	40	60	70	30
90	40	90	40	105
40	30	85	30	90
30	70	70	30	60
105	70	60	50	105
85	85	60	40	105
50	70	50	70	60
105	70	30	50	30
70	60	70	60	60

--------- PRESS THE SPACEBAR TO CONTINUE ----------
Now, we will map the original number sequence to the
Timbre Parameter.

Here is the Timbre Parameter:

52	52	3	35	52
35	69	13	13	13
13	50	35	78	69
120	3	16	69	3
52	69	35	52	78
13	16	78	78	35
52	50	35	16	13
78	3	52	3	69
78	120	52	16	3
35	120	3	78	69

6

Data Rescaling, Normalization, Scale Transforms, Filters, and Sieves

Data Rescaling Procedures

Data rescaling techniques differ from congruence modulo m conversion in that uniform compression or expansion of the data takes place in the former, while a "wrap-around" procedure occurs in the latter. To illustrate this distinction, consider the numerical data 0,1,2,3,4—originally scaled over a five-value range—rescaled to a ten-value range 0,1,2,3,4,5,6,7,8,9.

original values: 0 1 2 3 4

rescaled values: 0 2 4 6 8

Figure 6-8.

By contrast, a ten-value range, 0,1,2,3,4,5,6,7,8,9, converted to a five-value range, (modulo 5) would result in the following sequence of numbers:

original values: 0 1 2 3 4 5 6 7 8 9

congruent values: 0 1 2 3 4 0 1 2 3 4 (modulo 5)

Figure 6-9.

You can see that each method produces quite a different effect; therefore, the consequences of applying one specific method over another must be considered carefully prior to making a final application decision.

Program #13 demonstrates the Data Rescaling procedure. Execute it a number of times using various ranges for original and rescaled data.

PROGRAM #13

```
10  REM***********************************************************
20  REM                     PROGRAM #13
30  REM        Demonstrate Rescaling of Integer Ranges
40  REM***********************************************************
50  DEFDBL F,R          'declare Variables F & RS double precision
60  DIM N(500)                      'array to store original numbers
70  DIM RS(500)                     'array to store rescaled numbers
80    GOSUB 1000           'user input and initialization routine
90  PRINT
100 PRINT "Here is the initial number sequence:"
110   GOSUB 2000  'fill array with random numbers, send to screen
120 PRINT:PRINT
130   GOSUB 3000                             'call scaling routine
140 PRINT:PRINT
150  PRINT "Here is the rescaled sequence:"
160 PRINT "New Low Limit = ";NEWLOW
170 PRINT "New High Limit = ";NEWLOW + SCALE -1
180   FOR COUNT = 1 TO TOTAL
190     PRINT RS(COUNT),         'send rescaled numbers to screen
200   NEXT COUNT
210 END
1000 REM***********************************************************
1010 REM           User Input and Initialization Routine
1020 REM***********************************************************
1030   RANDOMIZE
1040   INPUT "How many random-order integers to return? ",TOTAL
1050   INPUT "Enter Low, High Range Limits: ",LOW,HIGH
1060   RANGE = HIGH-LOW+1
1070   INPUT "Enter Range Width (one number) to Scale values to:",
SCALE
1080   INPUT "Enter new low value for scaled sequence: ",NEWLOW
1090 RETURN
2000 REM***********************************************************
2010 REM            Routine to Load Random Number Array
2020 REM***********************************************************
2030   FOR COUNT = 1 TO TOTAL
2040     N(COUNT) = INT(RND*RANGE)+LOW
2050     PRINT N(COUNT),       'send random number to screen
2060   NEXT COUNT
2070 RETURN
3000 REM***********************************************************
3010 REM                   Range Scaling Routine
3020 REM***********************************************************
3030   MIN = 30000: MAX = -1
3040   FOR COUNT = 1 TO TOTAL
3050     IF N(COUNT) > MAX THEN MAX = N(COUNT)
3060     IF N(COUNT) < MIN THEN MIN = N(COUNT)
3070   NEXT COUNT
```

```
3080   PRINT "Original sequence Minimum =";MIN,"Maximum = ";MAX
3090   FACTOR = SCALE / (RANGE + RANGE / SCALE)
3100   MIN1 = 30000
3110     FOR COUNT = 1 TO TOTAL
3120         NUM = N(COUNT) * FACTOR
3130         IF NUM < MIN1 THEN MIN1 = NUM
3140     NEXT COUNT
3150     FOR COUNT = 1 TO TOTAL
3160         NUM = N(COUNT) * FACTOR - MIN1
3170         RS(COUNT) = INT(NUM + .5) + NEWLOW
3180     NEXT COUNT
3190 RETURN
```

Execution of Program #13:

```
Random Number Seed (-32768 to 32767)? 49
How many random-order integers to return? 20
Enter Low, High Range Limits: 30,50
Enter Range Width (one number) to Scale values to:80
Enter new low value for scaled sequence: 10
```

```
Here is the initial number sequence:
    33          31          49          47          37
    31          49          37          41          33
    43          45          36          43          37
    30          32          37          32          37
```

```
Original sequence Minimum = 30            Maximum =  49
```

```
Here is the rescaled sequence:
New Low Limit =  10
New High Limit =  89
    21          14          81          74          36
    14          81          36          51          21
    59          66          33          59          36
    10          18          36          18          36
```

Program #14 is an expanded variation of Program #13, the rescaling algorithm. A new routine to convert pitch integers to their corresponding alphabetic note-names in various octave registers has been added.

PROGRAM #14

```
10  REM***********************************************************
20  REM                      PROGRAM #14
30  REM              Demonstration of Pitch Scaling
40  REM***********************************************************
50   DEFDBL F,R          'declare Variables F & RS double precision
60   DIM N(500)              'array to store initial number sequence
70   DIM RS(500)            'array to store rescaled number sequence
80   DIM PITCH$(128)          'an array to hold pitch characters
81       ' next line initializes variables for MusicSculptor file
82  NOTEON=0:DURATION=60:VELOCITY=100:ARTDUR=55:CHANNEL=0
85  OPEN "O",#1,"PROG#14.SC"
86  PRINT #1,"File-ID : 2"
87  PRINT #1,"Format : 1"
90     GOSUB 1000               'user input and initialization routine
100   PRINT:PRINT "The original number sequence"
110    GOSUB 4000             'load Pitch Character Element array
120    GOSUB 2000   'fill array with random numbers, send to screen
130  PRINT
140    GOSUB 3000                             'call scaling routine
150  PRINT "Here is the rescaled sequence:"
160  PRINT "New Low Limit = ";NEWLOW
170  PRINT "New High Limit = ";NEWLOW + SCALE - 1
180    FOR COUNT = 1 TO RANGE
190       PRINT RS(COUNT),
191       PITCH=RS(COUNT)
192       ' now file rescaled pitches
193       PRINT #1,NOTEON;PITCH;VELOCITY;ARTDUR;CHANNEL
195       NOTEON=NOTEON+DURATION
200    NEXT COUNT
210  PRINT
220  IF MAX1 <= 127 THEN PRINT
     "Here are the values as Pitch Characters:"
       ELSE PRINT "Values too high for conversion to Pitches."
            :GOTO 270
230  PRINT
240    FOR COUNT = 1 TO RANGE
250       PRINT PITCH$(RS(COUNT)),'send Pitch Characters to screen
260    NEXT COUNT
261  ' write EOF flag
262  PRINT #1,0;-1;0;0;0
265  CLOSE #1
270  END
1000 REM***********************************************************
1010 REM           User Input and Initialization Routine
1020 REM***********************************************************
1025   RANDOMIZE
1030   INPUT "Enter Low, High Range Limits: ",LOW,HIGH
```

```
1040  RANGE = HIGH-LOW+1
1050  INPUT "Enter Range Width (one number) to Scale values to:",
        SCALE
1060  INPUT "Enter New Low Value for scaled sequence: ",NEWLOW
1070 RETURN
2000 REM*********************************************************
2010 REM          Routine to Load Integer Array
2020 REM*********************************************************
2030   FOR COUNT = 1 TO RANGE
2040      N(COUNT) = COUNT + LOW - 1
2050      PRINT N(COUNT),      'send numbers to screen
2055      PITCH=N(COUNT)
2056      PRINT #1,NOTEON;PITCH;VELOCITY;ARTDUR;CHANNEL
2057      NOTEON=NOTEON+DURATION 'advance note start time
2060   NEXT COUNT
2061 ' now insert a rest, then return to main for pitch rescaling
2062      NOTEON=NOTEON + DURATION * 4
2063      PRINT #1,NOTEON;0;0;0;CHANNEL
2070 RETURN
3000 REM*********************************************************
3010 REM                 Scaling Routine
3020 REM*********************************************************
3030   MIN = 30000: MAX = -1
3040   MIN1 = 30000 : MAX1 = -1
3050     FOR COUNT = 1 TO RANGE
3060        IF N(COUNT) > MAX THEN MAX = N(COUNT)
3070        IF N(COUNT) < MIN THEN MIN = N(COUNT)
3080     NEXT COUNT
3090   PRINT "Original sequence Minimum =";MIN,"Maximum = ";MAX
3100 PRINT
3110   FACTOR = SCALE / (RANGE + RANGE / SCALE)
3120   MIN1 = 30000
3130     FOR COUNT = 1 TO RANGE
3140        NUM = N(COUNT) * FACTOR
3150        IF NUM < MIN1 THEN MIN1 = NUM
3160     NEXT COUNT
3170     FOR COUNT = 1 TO RANGE
3180        NUM = N(COUNT) * FACTOR - MIN1
3190        RS(COUNT) = INT(NUM + .5) + NEWLOW
3200        IF RS(COUNT) > MAX1 THEN MAX1 = RS(COUNT)
3210     NEXT COUNT
3220 RETURN
4000 REM:*********************************************************
4010 REM:      Routine to Load Pitch Character Element Array
4020 REM:*********************************************************
4030     FOR COUNT = 0 TO 127
4040        READ PITCH$(COUNT)    'fill array with pitch characters
4050     NEXT COUNT
4060     PRINT
```

```
4070      DATA C0,C#0,D0,D#0,E0,F0,F#0,G0,Ab0,A0,Bb0,B0
4080      DATA C1,C#1,D1,D#1,E1,F1,F#1,G1,Ab1,A1,Bb1,B1
4090      DATA C2,C#2,D2,D#2,E2,F2,F#2,G2,Ab2,A2,Bb2,B2
4100      DATA C3,C#3,D3,D#3,E3,F3,F#3,G3,Ab3,A3,Bb3,B3
4110      DATA C4,C#4,D4,D#4,E4,F4,F#4,G4,Ab4,A4,Bb4,B4
4120      DATA C5,C#5,D5,D#5,E5,F5,F#5,G5,Ab5,A5,Bb5,B5
4130      DATA C6,C#6,D6,D#6,E6,F6,F#6,G6,Ab6,A6,Bb6,B6
4140      DATA C7,C#7,D7,D#7,E7,F7,F#7,G7,Ab7,A7,Bb7,B7
4150      DATA C8,C#8,D8,D#8,E8,F8,F#8,G8,Ab8,A8,Bb8,B8
4160      DATA C9,C#9,D9,D#9,E9,F9,F#9,G9,Ab9,A9,Bb9,B9
4170      DATA C10,C#10,D10,D#10,E10,F10,F#10,G10
4180 RETURN
```

Execution of Program #14:

Random Number Seed (-32768 to 32767)? 6
Enter Low, High Range Limits: 1,50
Enter Range Width (one number) to Scale values to: 35
Enter New Low Value for scaled sequence: 40

Here is the initial sequence:

1	2	3	4	5
6	7	8	9	10
11	12	13	14	15
16	17	18	19	20
21	22	23	24	25
26	27	28	29	30
31	32	33	34	35
36	37	38	39	40
41	42	43	44	45
46	47	48	49	50

Original sequence Minimum = 1   Maximum = 50

Here is the rescaled sequence:
New Low Limit = 40
New High Limit = 74

40	41	41	42	43
43	44	45	45	46
47	47	48	49	50
50	51	52	52	53
54	54	55	56	56
57	58	58	59	60
60	61	62	62	63
64	65	65	66	67
67	68	69	69	70
71	71	72	73	73

Here are the values as Pitch Characters:

E3	F3	F3	F#3	G3
G3	Ab3	A3	A3	Bb3
B3	B3	C4	C#4	D4
D4	D#4	E4	E4	F4
F#4	F#4	G4	Ab4	Ab4
A4	Bb4	Bb4	B4	C5
C5	C#5	D5	D5	D#5
E5	F5	F5	F#5	G5
G5	Ab5	A5	A5	Bb5
B5	B5	C6	C#6	C#6

Data Normalization Procedure. The Data Rescaling operation uniformly expands or compresses integer data, whereas the Data Normalization operation compresses integer data to a range of real numbers between 0 and 1. This conversion is necessary when, for instance, a body of data used for one parameter scaled in integers, must be used in another parameter scaled in real numbers > 0 & < 1, such as when a probability table must be compiled based on information from another parameter.

Program #15 generates a collection of random values, tabulates the number of times a specific value occurs in a frequency table, compresses the data within range 0 to 1, then prints the normalized values along with a histogram of the collection. Notice that this program is noninteractive; it illustrates use of a Driver Program to demonstrate program function while preventing user errors. All constants are hardwired to variables in the program, thereby eliminating the need for keyboard input other than the RUN instruction. This programming technique is useful in classroom and other settings where there is little time to instruct users on the entering of appropriately scaled data.

After running Program #15, modify it to be fully user-interactive. Statements should be added to test the viability of user-entered data and to send error messages to the CRT when input data fails the test for suitability.

PROGRAM #15

```
100 REM*********************************************************
110 REM                        PROGRAM #15
120 REM  Program to Normalize Wide-Range Data and Print Histogram
130 REM*********************************************************
132 REM                      Main Program
134 REM*********************************************************
140    DIM X(20)
```

```
150      RANGE = 20              '<< set random number range 1-20
160      TOTAL = 1000                  '<< return 1000 values
170      RANDOMIZE(222):CLS
180      PRINT "INTEGER VALUE";TAB(20);"NORM. VALUE";TAB(40);"BAR
MAP"
190      GOSUB 1000              '<< generate frequency table
200      GOSUB 2000              '<< call data normalization
210      GOSUB 3000              '<< call bargraph display
220 END
1000 REM********************************************************
1010 REM   Routine to Tabulate Number of Integer Occurrences
1020 REM********************************************************
1030     FOR K9 = 1 TO TOTAL
1040         VALUE = INT(RND * RANGE)+1      '<< gen random value
1050         X(VALUE)=X(VALUE)+1  '<< record occurrence of value
1060     NEXT K9
1070 RETURN
2000 REM********************************************************
2010 REM                Data Normalization Routine
2020 REM********************************************************
2160 REM                Variable Descriptions
2170 REM     Entering -
2180 REM       X(): frequency table to be normalized
2190 REM       RANGE: range of integers in frequency table
2200 REM     Exiting -
2210 REM       X(): normalized frequency table
2220 REM     Local -
2230 REM       SUM: total of values frequency table
2240 REM       K9: loop index,pointer to array X()
2250 REM********************************************************
2260    SUM = 0
2270       FOR K9 = 1 TO RANGE
2280          SUM = SUM + X(K9)
2290       NEXT K9
2300       FOR K9=1 TO RANGE
2310          X(K9) = X(K9)/ SUM
2320       NEXT K9
2330  PRINT
2340  RETURN
3000 REM********************************************************
3010 REM          Routine to Print a Bargraph (Histogram)
3020 REM               of Number Occurrence
3030 REM********************************************************
3040    FOR K9=1 TO RANGE
3050       MAP = INT(100*X(K9)+.5)
3060       PRINT K9;"=";TAB(20);X(K9);TAB(40);STRING$(MAP,">")
3070    NEXT K9
3080 RETURN
```

Execution of Program #15:

```
Random Number Seed (-32768 to 32767)? 222
INTEGER VALUE        NORM. VALUE          BAR MAP

  1 =                   .058              >>>>>>
  2 =                   .064              >>>>>>
  3 =                   .055              >>>>>>
  4 =                   .056              >>>>>>
  5 =                   .049              >>>>>
  6 =                   .058              >>>>>>
  7 =                   .033              >>>
  8 =                   .056              >>>>>>
  9 =                   .051              >>>>>
 10 =                   .046              >>>>>
 11 =                   .046              >>>>>
 12 =                   .047              >>>>>
 13 =                   .037              >>>>
 14 =                   .053              >>>>>
 15 =                   .065              >>>>>>>>
 16 =                   .052              >>>>>
 17 =                   .04               >>>>
 18 =                   .05               >>>>>
 19 =                   .04               >>>>
 20 =                   .044              >>>>
```

Musical Scale Transforms. Transformation procedures differ from congruence modulo m, rescaling, and normalization routines in a radical manner. Instead of uniformly rescaling all input data to a new range, or wrapping one range around another using the modulus function, transform routines significantly alter the structure of input data by reinterpreting it according to a set of criteria.

Program # 16 generates a random number sequence, then allows the user to choose one of several pitch scales to which the data will be transformed. The algorithm leaves pitch order intact, but the result will usually sound quite different from the original sequence, due to the distortion of values by the transform routine.

(Program #16 includes file-writing code for use with the MusicSculptor System.)

Although transforms are usually applied to musical pitch material, they may be applied to other parameters, such as rhythm. Execute Program #16 enough times to try all scale transforms. Add the BASIC SOUND instruction so you can get a clear picture of what is going on in the program. Then, after you are thoroughly familiar with program function, write a program which incorporates the transforms in an interesting way.

PROGRAM #16

```
10  REM*********************************************************
20  REM                    PROGRAM #16
30  REM    Demonstrate Musical Scale Transformation Principles
40  REM*********************************************************
41  DIM N(500)                       ' array to store random numbers
42  DIM TF(500)                  'array to store transformed sequenced
44  DIM PITCH$(128)              'an array to hold pitch characters
45       ' next line initializes variables for MusicSculptor file
46  NOTEON=0:DURATION=60:VELOCITY=100:ARTDUR=55:CHANNEL=0
47  OPEN "O",#1,"PROG#16.SC"
48  PRINT #1,"File-ID : 2"
49  PRINT #1,"Format : 1"
50   GOSUB 1000          'call User Input and Initialization Routine
60   PRINT "Here is the random integer array:"
70   GOSUB 2000     'load array with random numbers, send to screen
80   PRINT
90   PRINT "The array Mapped to Chromatic Scale Pitch Characters:"
100    FOR COUNT = 1 TO TOTAL
110        PRINT PITCH$(N(COUNT)),
111        PITCH=N(COUNT)
112        ' file random-order pitches
113        PRINT #1,NOTEON;PITCH;VELOCITY;ARTDUR;CHANNEL
114        NOTEON=NOTEON+DURATION
120    NEXT COUNT
121  ' put a rest in file before playing rescaled pitches
122  NOTEON=NOTEON+DURATION*4
123        PRINT #1,NOTEON;0;0;0;CHANNEL
130  ON CHOICE GOSUB 3000,4000,5000,6000,7000,8000,9000,10000,
     11000,12000,13000,14000    'call selected transform routine
140  PRINT:PRINT
150  PRINT "The transformed number sequence:"
160    FOR COUNT = 1 TO TOTAL
170        PRINT TF(COUNT),
171        PITCH=TF(COUNT)
172        ' now file rescaled pitches
173        PRINT #1,NOTEON;PITCH;VELOCITY;ARTDUR;CHANNEL
174        NOTEON=NOTEON+DURATION
180    NEXT COUNT
190  PRINT : PRINT
200  PRINT "The sequence as Pitch Characters:"
210    FOR COUNT = 1 TO TOTAL
220        PRINT PITCH$(TF(COUNT)),
230    NEXT COUNT
231  ' write EOF flag
232  PRINT #1,0;-1;0;0;0
233  CLOSE #1
240  END
```

```
1000 REM******************************************************
1010 REM      User Input and Variable Initialization Routine
1020 REM******************************************************
1050 GOSUB 15000                'load Pitch Character Element array
1060 INPUT "How many random-order integers to return? ",TOTAL
1070 INPUT "Enter Low, High Range Limits for Random Numbers: ",
          LOW,HIGH
1080 RANGE = HIGH-LOW+1
1090 PRINT
1100 PRINT "Here are the Musical Pitch Scale Transform Choices:"
1110 PRINT
1120 PRINT "1=Blues,2=Octatonic,3=Pentatonic minor,4=Pentatonic"
1130 PRINT
1140 PRINT "Messiaen Modes:"
1150 PRINT "5=Mode2,6=Mode3,7=Mode4,8=Mode5,9=Mode6,10=Mode7"
1160 PRINT "11=Diatonic Major,12=Harmonic Minor"
1170 PRINT
1180 INPUT "Enter your choice: ",CHOICE
1190 RETURN
2000 REM******************************************************
2010 REM        Random-Order Pitch Generation Routine
2020 REM******************************************************
2030    FOR COUNT = 1 TO TOTAL
2040        N(COUNT) = INT(RND*RANGE)+LOW
2050        PRINT N(COUNT),          'send random number to screen
2060    NEXT COUNT
2070 RETURN
3000 REM******************************************************
3010 REM Blues Scale:    Transform Routine
3020 REM******************************************************
3030 PRINT:PRINT "Blues Scale" : PRINT
3040    FOR COUNT = 1 TO TOTAL
3050        PC = N(COUNT) MOD 12
3060        OCTAVE = INT(N(COUNT) / 12)
3070        IF PC = 1 THEN PC = PC-1
3080        IF PC = 2 THEN PC = PC+1
3090        IF PC = 4 THEN PC = PC-1
3100        IF PC = 8 THEN PC = PC-1
3110        IF PC = 9 THEN PC = PC+1
3120        IF PC = 11 THEN PC = PC+1
3130        IF PC = 11 THEN PC = PC+1
3140        TF(COUNT) = PC + OCTAVE * 12
3150    NEXT COUNT
3160 RETURN
4000 REM******************************************************
4010 REM Octatonic:    Transform Routine
4020 REM******************************************************
4030 PRINT:PRINT "Octatonic Scale:"
4040    FOR COUNT = 1 TO TOTAL
```

```
4050        PC = N(COUNT) MOD 12
4060        OCTAVE = INT(N(COUNT) / 12)
4070        IF PC = 1 THEN PC = PC-1
4080        IF PC = 4 THEN PC = PC-1
4090        IF PC = 7 THEN PC = PC+1
4100        IF PC = 10 THEN PC = PC+1
4110        TF(COUNT) = PC + OCTAVE * 12
4120 NEXT COUNT
4130 RETURN
5000 REM*********************************************************
5010 REM Pentatonic Minor:  Transform Routine
5020 REM*********************************************************
5030 PRINT:PRINT "Pentatonic Minor Scale:"
5040   FOR COUNT = 1 TO TOTAL
5050        PC = N(COUNT) MOD 12
5060        OCTAVE = INT(N(COUNT) / 12)
5070        IF PC = 1 THEN PC = PC-1
5080        IF PC = 4 THEN PC = PC-1
5090        IF PC = 5 THEN PC = PC-2
5100        IF PC = 6 THEN PC = PC+1
5110        IF PC = 8 THEN PC = PC+1
5120        IF PC = 10 THEN PC = PC-1
5130        IF PC = 11 THEN PC = PC+1
5140        TF(COUNT) = PC + OCTAVE * 12
5150 NEXT COUNT
5160 RETURN
6000 REM*********************************************************
6010 REM Pentatonic:  Transform Routine
6020 REM*********************************************************
6030 PRINT:PRINT "Pentatonic Scale:"
6040   FOR COUNT = 1 TO TOTAL
6050        PC = N(COUNT) MOD 12
6060        OCTAVE = INT(N(COUNT) / 12)
6070        IF PC = 1 THEN PC = PC-1
6080        IF PC = 3 THEN PC = PC-1
6090        IF PC = 5 THEN PC = PC+1
6100        IF PC = 6 THEN PC = PC+1
6110        IF PC = 8 THEN PC = PC+1
6120        IF PC = 10 THEN PC = PC-1
6130        IF PC = 11 THEN PC = PC+1
6140        TF(COUNT) = PC + OCTAVE * 12
6150   NEXT COUNT
6160 RETURN
7000 REM*********************************************************
7010 REM Messiaen Mode2: Transform Routine
7020 REM*********************************************************
7030 PRINT:PRINT "Messiaen Mode2:"
7040   FOR COUNT = 1 TO TOTAL
7050        PC = N(COUNT) MOD 12
7060        OCTAVE = INT(N(COUNT) / 12)
```

```
7070        IF PC = 3 THEN PC = PC-1
7080        IF PC = 6 THEN PC = PC+1
7090        IF PC = 9 THEN PC = PC-1
7100        TF(COUNT) = PC + OCTAVE * 12
7110 NEXT COUNT
7120 RETURN
8000 REM************************************************************
8010 REM Messiaen Mode3: Transform  Routine
8020 REM************************************************************
8030 PRINT:PRINT "Messiaen Mode3:"
8040    FOR COUNT = 1 TO TOTAL
8050        PC = N(COUNT) MOD 12
8060        OCTAVE = INT(N(COUNT) / 12)
8070        IF PC = 1 THEN PC = PC-1
8080        IF PC = 5 THEN PC = PC-1
8090        IF PC = 9 THEN PC = PC-1
8100        TF(COUNT) = PC + OCTAVE * 12
8110 NEXT COUNT
8120 RETURN
9000 REM************************************************************
9010 REM Messiaen Mode4: Transform Routine
9020 REM************************************************************
9030 PRINT:PRINT "Messiaen Mode4:"
9040    FOR COUNT = 1 TO TOTAL
9050        PC = N(COUNT) MOD 12
9060        OCTAVE = INT(N(COUNT) / 12)
9070        IF PC = 3 THEN PC = PC-1
9080        IF PC = 4 THEN PC = PC+1
9090        IF PC = 9 THEN PC = PC-1
9100        IF PC = 10 THEN PC = PC+1
9110        TF(COUNT) = PC + OCTAVE * 12
9120 NEXT COUNT
9130 RETURN
10000 REM************************************************************
10010 REM Messiaen Mode5: Transform Routine
10020 REM************************************************************
10030 PRINT:PRINT "Messiaen Mode5:"
10040    FOR COUNT = 1 TO TOTAL
10050        PC = N(COUNT) MOD 12
10060        OCTAVE = INT(N(COUNT) / 12)
10070        IF PC = 2 THEN PC = PC-1
10080        IF PC = 3 THEN PC = PC+2
10090        IF PC = 4 THEN PC = PC+1
10100        IF PC = 8 THEN PC = PC-1
10110        IF PC = 9 THEN PC = PC+2
10120        IF PC = 10 THEN PC = PC+1
10130        TF(COUNT) = PC + OCTAVE * 12
10140 NEXT COUNT
10150 RETURN
```

```
11000 REM*********************************************************
11010 REM Messiaen Mode6: Transform Routine
11020 REM*********************************************************
11030 PRINT:PRINT "Messiaen Mode6:"
11040    FOR COUNT = 1 TO TOTAL
11050       PC = N(COUNT) MOD 12
11060       OCTAVE = INT(N(COUNT) / 12)
11070       IF PC = 1 THEN PC = PC-1
11080       IF PC = 3 THEN PC = PC-1
11090       IF PC = 7 THEN PC = PC+1
11100       IF PC = 9 THEN PC = PC+1
11110       TF(COUNT) = PC + OCTAVE * 12
11120    NEXT COUNT
11130 RETURN
12000 REM*********************************************************
12010 REM Messiaen Mode7: Transform  Routine
12020 REM*********************************************************
12030 PRINT:PRINT "Messiaen Mode7:"
12040    FOR COUNT = 1 TO TOTAL
12050       PC = N(COUNT) MOD 12
12060       OCTAVE = INT(N(COUNT) / 12)
12070       IF PC = 5 THEN PC = PC-1
12080       IF PC = 11 THEN PC = PC+1
12090       TF(COUNT) = PC + OCTAVE * 12
12100 NEXT COUNT
13000 REM*********************************************************
13010 REM Diatonic Major: Tranform Routine
13020 REM*********************************************************
13030 PRINT:PRINT "Diatonic Major:"
13040    FOR COUNT = 1 TO TOTAL
13050       PC = N(COUNT) MOD 12
13060       OCTAVE = INT(N(COUNT) / 12)
13070       IF PC = 1 THEN PC = PC-1
13080       IF PC = 3 THEN PC = PC-1
13090       IF PC = 6 THEN PC = PC+1
13100       IF PC = 8 THEN PC = PC+1
13110       IF PC = 10 THEN PC = PC+1
13120       TF(COUNT) = PC + OCTAVE * 12
13130 NEXT COUNT
13140 RETURN
14000 REM*********************************************************
14010 REM Harmonic Minor: Transform Routine
14020 REM*********************************************************
14030 PRINT:PRINT "Harmonic Minor:"
14040    FOR COUNT = 1 TO TOTAL
14050       PC = N(COUNT) MOD 12
14060       OCTAVE = INT(N(COUNT) / 12)
14070       IF PC = 1 THEN PC = PC-1
14080       IF PC = 4 THEN PC = PC-1
14090       IF PC = 6 THEN PC = PC+1
```

```
14100        IF PC = 9 THEN PC = PC-1
14110        IF PC = 10 THEN PC = PC+1
14120        TF(COUNT) = PC + OCTAVE * 12
14130 NEXT COUNT
14140 RETURN
15000 REM:*************************************************************
15010 REM:    Routine to Load Pitch Element Character Array
15020 REM:*************************************************************
15040        FOR COUNT = 0 TO 127
15050           READ PITCH$(COUNT)   'fill array with pitch characters
15060         NEXT COUNT
15070        PRINT
15080        DATA C0,C#0,D0,D#0,E0,F0,F#0,G0,Ab0,A0,Bb0,B0
15090        DATA C1,C#1,D1,D#1,E1,F1,F#1,G1,Ab1,A1,Bb1,B1
15100        DATA C2,C#2,D2,D#2,E2,F2,F#2,G2,Ab2,A2,Bb2,B2
15110        DATA C3,C#3,D3,D#3,E3,F3,F#3,G3,Ab3,A3,Bb3,B3
15120        DATA C4,C#4,D4,D#4,E4,F4,F#4,G4,Ab4,A4,Bb4,B4
15130        DATA C5,C#5,D5,D#5,E5,F5,F#5,G5,Ab5,A5,Bb5,B5
15140        DATA C6,C#6,D6,D#6,E6,F6,F#6,G6,Ab6,A6,Bb6,B6
15150        DATA C7,C#7,D7,D#7,E7,F7,F#7,G7,Ab7,A7,Bb7,B7
15160        DATA C8,C#8,D8,D#8,E8,F8,F#8,G8,Ab8,A8,Bb8,B8
15170        DATA C9,C#9,D9,D#9,E9,F9,F#9,G9,Ab9,A9,Bb9,B9
15180        DATA C10,C#10,D10,D#10,E10,F10,F#10,G10
15190 RETURN
```

Execution of Program #16:

```
How many random-order integers to return? 50
Enter Low, High Range Limits for Random Numbers: 40,80

Here are the Musical Pitch Scale Transform Choices:

1=Blues,2=Octatonic,3=Pentatonic minor,4=Pentatonic

Messiaen Modes:
5=Mode2,6=Mode3,7=Mode4,8=Mode5,9=Mode6,10=Mode7
11=Diatonic Major,12=Harmonic Minor

Enter your choice: 2
Here is the random integer array:
    46          47          62          58          47
    52          73          73          66          59
    40          58          55          67          56
    63          57          55          76          60
    72          48          79          73          56
    76          72          44          57          55
    66          65          73          61          60
    61          41          61          79          43
    80          42          53          51          60
    55          46          70          64          74
```

The array Mapped to Chromatic Scale Pitch Characters:

Bb3	B3	D5	Bb4	B3
E4	C#6	C#6	F#5	B4
E3	Bb4	G4	G5	Ab4
D#5	A4	G4	E6	C5
C6	C4	G6	C#6	Ab4
E6	C6	Ab3	A4	G4
F#5	F5	C#6	C#5	C5
C#5	F3	C#5	G6	G3
Ab6	F#3	F4	D#4	C5
G4	Bb3	Bb5	E5	D6

Octatonic Scale:

The transformed number sequence:

47	47	62	59	47
51	72	72	66	59
39	59	56	68	56
63	57	56	75	60
72	48	80	72	56
75	72	44	57	56
66	65	72	60	60
60	41	60	80	44
80	42	53	51	60
56	47	71	63	74

The sequence as Pitch Characters:

B3	B3	D5	B4	B3
D#4	C6	C6	F#5	B4
D#3	B4	Ab4	Ab5	Ab4
D#5	A4	Ab4	D#6	C5
C6	C4	Ab6	C6	Ab4
D#6	C6	Ab3	A4	Ab4
F#5	F5	C6	C5	C5
C5	F3	C5	Ab6	Ab3
Ab6	F#3	F4	D#4	C5
Ab4	B3	B5	D#5	D6

Data Filters. Filters are another means of changing input data from one form to another. They are very selective in nature, in that they remove (without transforming) specific values from a collection of data. By contrast to the other methods of changing input data studied so far, filtering has the effect of reducing the number of elements present in the original collection.

Program #17 demonstrates a simple filtering technique, as applied to the twelve pitch classes of the chromatic scale. After you understand its operation, modify the program to be more flexible with regard to manipulation of the filter. For example, instead of a fixed filter, allow the user to request certain types of filter realignment by shifting up or down the filter position over different runs of the program. (Program #17 includes file-writing code for use with the MusicSculptor System.)

PROGRAM #17

```
10  REM***********************************************************
20  REM                      PROGRAM #17
30  REM                   Pitch Class Filter
40  REM***********************************************************
41  DIM N(500)          'array to store original random number list
42  DIM FILTER(12)      'array to store user-input PCs to filter out
43  DIM PC(500)                 'array to store filtered PC list
44  DIM PITCH$(128)             'array to hold pitch characters
45        ' next line initializes variables for MusicSculptor file
46  NOTEON=0:DURATION=60:VELOCITY=100:ARTDUR=55:CHANNEL=0
47  OPEN "O",#1,"PROG#17.SC"
48  PRINT #1,"File-ID : 2"
49  PRINT #1,"Format : 1"
50  PRINT "This program filters Pitch Classes from integer data."
60     GOSUB 1000            'user input and initialization routine
70     GOSUB 4000            'load Pitch Character Element Array
80     GOSUB 2000            'call routine to load random number array
90     GOSUB 3000            'call Pitch Class filtering routine
100 PRINT "Here is the filtered sequence:"
110    FOR COUNT = 1 TO C
120       PRINT PC(COUNT),
121       ' file filtered pitch sequence
122       PITCH=PC(COUNT)
123       PRINT #1,NOTEON;PITCH;VELOCITY;ARTDUR;CHANNEL
124       NOTEON=NOTEON+DURATION
130    NEXT COUNT
140 PRINT : PRINT
150    IF HIGH <= 127 THEN PRINT
       "Here is the sequence as Pitch Characters:" ELSE PRINT
       "Range too high for use as pitches." : GOTO 190
160    FOR COUNT = 1 TO C
170       PRINT PITCH$(PC(COUNT)),
180    NEXT COUNT
181 ' write EOF flag
182 PRINT #1,0;-1;0;0;0
183 CLOSE #1
190 END
1000 REM***********************************************************
1010 REM              User Input & Initialization Routine
1060 INPUT "How many random-order integers to return? ",TOTAL
1070 INPUT "Enter Low, High Range Limits: ",LOW,HIGH
```

```
1080 RANGE = HIGH-LOW+1
1090 PRINT "You may filter out any of the Pitch Classes 0 - 11."
1100 INPUT "How many PCs will you delete? ",TAKEOUT
1110 PRINT "Enter the PC numbers, one per line:"
1120   FOR COUNT = 1 TO TAKEOUT
1130       INPUT FILTER(COUNT)
1140       IF FILTER(COUNT) < 0 OR FILTER(COUNT) > 11 THEN
             PRINT "OUT OF BOUNDS! Use Range 0-11." : GOTO 1130
1150   NEXT COUNT
1160 RETURN
2000 REM*********************************************************
2010 REM          Random-Order Pitch Generation Routine
2020 REM*********************************************************
2030   FOR COUNT = 1 TO TOTAL
2040       N(COUNT) = INT(RND*RANGE)+LOW
2050       PRINT N(COUNT),
2051       PITCH=N(COUNT)
2052       ' file random-order pitches
2053       PRINT #1,NOTEON;PITCH;VELOCITY;ARTDUR;CHANNEL
2054       NOTEON=NOTEON+DURATION
2060   NEXT COUNT
2070 PRINT : PRINT
2071 ' put a rest in file before playing rescaled pitches
2072 NOTEON=NOTEON+DURATION*4
2073 PRINT #1,NOTEON;0;0;0;CHANNEL
2080 RETURN
3000 REM*********************************************************
3010 REM                    Filter  Routine
3020 REM*********************************************************
3030 C = 0
3040   FOR COUNT = 1 TO TOTAL
3050       FOR REMOVE = 1 TO TAKEOUT
3060           IF N(COUNT) MOD 12 = FILTER(REMOVE) THEN 3100
3070       NEXT REMOVE
3080           C = C + 1
3090           PC(C) = N(COUNT)
3100   NEXT COUNT
3110 RETURN
4000 REM:*********************************************************
4010 REM:    Routine to Load Pitch Character Element Array
4020 REM:*********************************************************
4040     FOR COUNT = 0 TO 127
4050       READ PITCH$(COUNT)     'fill array with pitch characters
4060     NEXT COUNT
4070     PRINT
4080     DATA C0,C#0,D0,D#0,E0,F0,F#0,G0,Ab0,A0,Bb0,B0
4090     DATA C1,C#1,D1,D#1,E1,F1,F#1,G1,Ab1,A1,Bb1,B1
4100     DATA C2,C#2,D2,D#2,E2,F2,F#2,G2,Ab2,A2,Bb2,B2
4110     DATA C3,C#3,D3,D#3,E3,F3,F#3,G3,Ab3,A3,Bb3,B3
4120     DATA C4,C#4,D4,D#4,E4,F4,F#4,G4,Ab4,A4,Bb4,B4
```

```
4130      DATA C5,C#5,D5,D#5,E5,F5,F#5,G5,Ab5,A5,Bb5,B5
4140      DATA C6,C#6,D6,D#6,E6,F6,F#6,G6,Ab6,A6,Bb6,B6
4150      DATA C7,C#7,D7,D#7,E7,F7,F#7,G7,Ab7,A7,Bb7,B7
4160      DATA C8,C#8,D8,D#8,E8,F8,F#8,G8,Ab8,A8,Bb8,B8
4170      DATA C9,C#9,D9,D#9,E9,F9,F#9,G9,Ab9,A9,Bb9,B9
4180      DATA C10,C#10,D10,D#10,E10,F10,F#10,G10
4190 RETURN
```

Execution of Program #17

```
This program filters pitch classes from integer data.
How many random-order integers to return? 25
Enter Low, High Range Limits: 20,40
You may filter out any of the pitch classes 0 - 11.
How many PCs will you delete? 3
Enter the PC numbers, one per line:
? 3
? 6
? 9
```

23	23	31	29	23
26	37	37	33	29
20	29	27	34	28
32	29	28	38	30
36	24	40	37	28

```
Here is the filtered sequence:
```

23	23	31	29	23
26	37	37	29	20
29	34	28	32	29
28	38	36	24	40
37	28			

```
Here is the sequence as Pitch Characters:
```

B1	B1	G2	F2	B1
D2	C#3	C#3	F2	Ab1
F2	Bb2	E2	Ab2	F2
E2	D3	C3	C2	E3
C#3	E2			

Logical Sieve Theory. Logical Sieves are somewhat similar to, but are more sophisticated than, data filters. They are relationship-based, rather than target-value based; consequently, they allow greater flexibility with a minimum of alteration in code. In programming situations when many changes in element set characteristics are required, such as referencing various pitch scales or modulating among different scales, logical sieves are most appropriately employed.

Introduced into computer music composition by Iannis Xenakis in his classic book on stochastic music, "Formalized Music," Sieve Theory is derived from the Logic of Classes, wherein relationships are defined by application of various relational criteria and modulus arithmetic to test a value for membership in one logical class or another.

The three operations of logical classes are:

    (1)   Union (disjunction)—OR
    (2)   Intersection (conjunction)—AND
    (3)   Complementation (negation)—NOT

Any imaginable traditional or synthetic pitch scale can be described with this method, although the simplest ones are derived from the semitonal, chromatic, pitch class set. For example, Figure 6-10 presents the algebraic notation for the Major Scale:

$$\text{moduli} \qquad (\overline{3} \wedge 4) \vee (\overline{3} \wedge 4) \vee (3 \wedge 4) \vee (\overline{3} \wedge 4)$$

$$\text{residual classes} \quad 2 \quad\;\; 0 \quad\;\; 1 \quad\;\; 1 \quad\;\; 2 \quad\;\; 2 \quad\;\; 0 \quad\;\; 3$$

    −   means NOT
    ∧   means AND
    ∨   means OR

Figure 6-10.

which, in English, where X represents a value to be tested, is read: "if X mod 3 is not equal to 2 and X mod 4 is equal to 0, or if X mod 3 is not equal to 1 and X mod 4 is equal to 1, or if X mod 3 is equal to 2 and X mod 4 is equal to 2 , or if X mod 3 is not equal to 0 and X mod 4 is equal to 3, then X passes the test."

As values to be tested are sent through the sieve, only those conforming to the logical description of the particular scale are passed. Program #18 performs as a fixed sieve, because the elements to be tested are queued from lowest order to highest order; to obtain a modal scale transposition, the element list must be sent through the sieve, beginning with the integer corresponding to the mode start note. (Program #19 deals with modal transposition using sieves.) Study Program #18, then calculate the logical expressions for two different scale sieves and add them to the program.

(Program #18 includes file-writing code for use with the MusicSculptor System.)

PROGRAM #18

```
10 REM************************************************************
20 REM                      PROGRAM #18
25 REM     Demonstrate Non-transposing Logical Sieve Concept
30 REM************************************************************
40 DIM P$(120)
41          ' next line initializes variables for MusicSculptor file
42 NOTEON=0:DURATION=60:VELOCITY=100:ARTDUR=55:CHANNEL=0
43 OPEN "O",#1,"PROG#18.SC"
44 PRINT #1,"File-ID : 2"
45 PRINT #1,"Format : 1"
50 GOSUB 1000                                '<< initialize pitch table
59 ELEMENTS = 36:LOWP=36
60 PRINT "The number of background scale elements will be";
            ELEMENTS
61 PRINT "beginning on MIDI note number 36)"
70 PRINT "Enter scale type:(1=major,2=harm. minor,3=pentatonic)"
80 INPUT SCALETYPE
90 ON SCALETYPE GOSUB 2000,3000,4000  '<< call sieve routines
95 ' write EOF flag
96 PRINT #1,0;-1;0;0;0
97 CLOSE #1
100 END
1000 REM***********************************************************
1010 REM           Routine to Load a Pitch Character Array
1012 REM                    Using String Functions
1020 REM***********************************************************
1070     NOTE$ = " CC# DD# E FF# GG# AA# B"
1080     OCTAVE$ = "1234567"
1090        FOR K9 = 1 TO 7
1100           FOR L9 = 1 TO 12
1110              P$(L9+(K9-1)*12-1) =
                  MID$(NOTE$,(L9*2-1),2)+MID$(OCTAVE$,K9,1)
1120           NEXT L9
1130        NEXT K9
1140 RETURN
2000 REM***********************************************************
2010 REM           Major Scale Logical Sieve Routine
2020 REM***********************************************************
2030 FOR X = LOWP TO LOWP+ELEMENTS-1
2040 IF X MOD 3 <> 2 AND X MOD 4  = 0 OR  X MOD 3 <> 1 AND
    X MOD 4 =  1 OR  X MOD 3  = 2 AND X MOD 4  = 2 OR
    X MOD 3 <> 0 AND X MOD 4  = 3 THEN PRINT P$(X);" "; ELSE 2050
2045 PRINT #1, NOTEON;X;VELOCITY;ARTDUR;CHANNEL
2046 NOTEON=NOTEON+DURATION
2050 NEXT X
2060 RETURN
3000 REM***********************************************************
3010 REM    Harmonic Minor Scale Logical Sieve Routine
3020 REM***********************************************************
3030 FOR X = LOWP TO LOWP+ELEMENTS-1
```

```
3040 IF X MOD 3 <> 1 AND X MOD 4 = 0 OR X MOD 4 = 3 OR
        X MOD 3 =  2 AND X MOD 4 = 2 OR X MOD 3 = 2 AND
        X MOD 4 =  1 THEN PRINT P$(X);" "; ELSE 3050
3045 PRINT #1, NOTEON;X;VELOCITY;ARTDUR;CHANNEL
3046 NOTEON=NOTEON+DURATION
3050 NEXT X
3060 RETURN
4000 REM*************************************************************
4010 REM         Pentatonic Scale Logical Sieve Routine
4020 REM*************************************************************
4030 FOR X = LOWP TO LOWP+ELEMENTS-1
4040 IF X MOD 3 <> 2 AND X MOD 4 = 0 OR  X MOD 3 = 2  AND
        X MOD 4 = 2  OR  X MOD 3 = 1 AND X MOD 4 = 3  OR
        X MOD 3 = 0  AND X MOD 4 = 1 THEN PRINT P$(X);" ";ELSE
        4050
4045 PRINT #1, NOTEON;X;VELOCITY;ARTDUR;CHANNEL
4046 NOTEON=NOTEON+DURATION
4050 NEXT X
4060 RETURN
```

Execution of Program #18:

```
Enter number of background scale elements: 12
Enter scale type:(1=major,2=harm. minor,3=pentatonic)
? 1
 C1  D1  E1  F1  G1  A1  B1
```

Modal Transposition Using Sieves. Because sieves function on the basis of logical categories, they easily admit modal transposition. All that we need do is to send the element list sequentially through the sieve beginning with the mode tonic note, as in Program #19.

(Program #19 includes file-writing code for use with the MusicSculptor System.)

PROGRAM #19

```
10 REM*************************************************************
20 REM                    PROGRAM #19
35 REM   Demonstrate (Modal) Transposing Logical Sieve Concept
40 REM*************************************************************
41         ' next line initializes variables for MusicSculptor file
42 NOTEON=0:DURATION=60:VELOCITY=100:ARTDUR=55:CHANNEL=0
43 OPEN "O",#1,"PROG#19.SC"
44 PRINT #1,"File-ID : 2"
45 PRINT #1,"Format : 1"
50 DIM P$(120)
60 GOSUB 2000                        '<< initialize pitch table
```

```
70 ELEMENTS = 36                        'set chromatic scale range
80 LOWP=36
90 TRANSINDEX = 2                         'transpose to Dorian Mode
95 TRANSINDEX=TRANSINDEX+LOWP    'bring scale up to range
100 PRINT "This Sieve is Diatonically Transposing (Modal)."
110 GOSUB 1000                          '<< call sieve routine
111 ' write EOF flag
112 PRINT #1,0;-1;0;0;0
113 CLOSE #1
120 END
1000 REM***********************************************************
1020 REM          Major Scale Logical Sieve Routine
1030 REM***********************************************************
1040 FOR X = TRANSINDEX TO TRANSINDEX + ELEMENTS
1050  IF X MOD 3 <> 2 AND X MOD 4=0 OR X MOD 3 <> 1 AND X MOD 4=1
       OR X MOD 3=2 AND X MOD 4=2 OR X MOD 3 <> 0 AND X MOD 4=3
         THEN PRINT P$(X);" ";ELSE 1060
1055   ' file pitches
1056     PRINT#1,NOTEON;X;VELOCITY;ARTDUR;CHANNEL
1057     NOTEON=NOTEON+DURATION
1060 NEXT X
1070 RETURN
2000 REM***********************************************************
2010 REM          Routine to Load a Pitch Character Array
2012 REM                  Using String Functions
2020 REM***********************************************************
2070     NOTE$ = " CC# DD# E FF# GG# AA# B"
2080     OCTAVE$ = "1234567"
2090       FOR K9 = 1 TO 7
2100         FOR L9 = 1 TO 12
2110           P$(L9+(K9-1)*12-1) =
                MID$(NOTE$,(L9*2-1),2)+MID$(OCTAVE$,K9,1)
2120           NEXT L9
2130         NEXT K9
2140 RETURN
```

Execution of Program #19:

```
This Sieve is Diatonically Transposing (Modal).
 D1  E1  F1  G1  A1  B1  C2  D2
```

Tonal Transposition Using Sieves. Index shifting provides the key to tonal transposition of logical sieve data. In this method, the residual class integers are shifted to correspond to the residue index of a particular modulus. In practice, this simply means that the transposition interval is added to the residual class mod modulus.

(Program #20 includes file-writing code for use with the MusicSculptor System.)

PROGRAM #20

```
10 REM*********************************************************
20 REM                      PROGRAM #20
30 REM    Demonstrate (Tonal) Transposing Logical Sieve Concept
40 DIM P$(120)
41        ' next line initializes variables for MusicSculptor file
42 NOTEON=0:DURATION=60:VELOCITY=100:ARTDUR=55:CHANNEL=0
43 OPEN "O",#1,"PROG#20.SC"
44 PRINT #1,"File-ID : 2"
45 PRINT #1,"Format : 1"
50 GOSUB 1000                        '<< initialize pitch table
55 INPUT "Enter T: ",T
56 ELEMENTS=24:LOWP=36
60 PRINT "Number of background scale elements is ";ELEMENTS
70 PRINT "Enter scale type:(1=major,2=harm. minor,3=pentatonic)"
80 INPUT SCALETYPE
90 ON SCALETYPE GOSUB 2000,3000,4000  '<< call sieve routines
91 ' write EOF flag
92 PRINT #1,0;-1;0;0;0
93 CLOSE #1
100 END
1000 REM********************************************************
1010 REM          Routine to Load a Pitch Character Array
1012 REM                  Using String Functions
1020 REM********************************************************
1070     NOTE$ = " CC# DD# E FF# GG# AA# B"
1080     OCTAVE$ = "1234567"
1090        FOR K9 = 1 TO 7
1100           FOR L9 = 1 TO 12
1110              P$(L9+(K9-1)*12-1) =
                  MID$(NOTE$,(L9*2-1),2)+MID$(OCTAVE$,K9,1)
1120           NEXT L9
1130        NEXT K9
1140 RETURN
2000 REM********************************************************
2010 REM          Major Scale Logical Sieve Routine
2020 REM********************************************************
2030 FOR X = LOWP TO LOWP+ELEMENTS - 1
2040 IF X MOD 3<>(T+2) MOD 3 AND X MOD 4=T MOD 4 OR X MOD 3<>(T+1)
 MOD 3 AND X MOD 4=(T+1) MOD 4 OR X MOD 3=(T+2) MOD 3 AND X MOD 4=
 (T+2) MOD 4 OR X MOD 3<>T MOD 3 AND X MOD 4=(T+3) MOD 4
       THEN  PRINT P$(X);" "; ELSE 2050
2045       PRINT #1,NOTEON;X;VELOCITY;ARTDUR;CHANNEL
2046       NOTEON=NOTEON+DURATION
2050 NEXT X
2060 RETURN
3000 REM********************************************************
3010 REM    Harmonic Minor Scale Logical Sieve Routine
3020 REM********************************************************
```

```
3030 FOR X = LOWP TO LOWP+ELEMENTS - 1
3040 IF X MOD 3<>(T+1) MOD 3 AND X MOD 4=T MOD 4 OR X MOD 4=(T+3)
MOD 4 OR X MOD 3=(T+2) MOD 3 AND X MOD 4=(T+2) MOD 4 OR X MOD 3=
(T+2) MOD 3 AND X MOD 4=(T+1) MOD 4 THEN PRINT P$(X);" ";ELSE 3050
3045     PRINT #1,NOTEON;X;VELOCITY;ARTDUR;CHANNEL
3046     NOTEON=NOTEON+DURATION
3050 NEXT X
3060 RETURN
4000 REM*****************************************************
4010 REM         Pentatonic Scale Logical Sieve Routine
4020 REM*****************************************************
4030 FOR X = LOWP TO LOWP+ELEMENTS - 1
4040 IF X MOD 3<>(T+2) MOD 3 AND X MOD 4=T MOD 4 OR X MOD 3=(T+2)
MOD 3 AND X MOD 4=(T+2) MOD 4 OR X MOD 3=(T+1) MOD 3 AND X MOD 4=
(T+3) MOD 4 OR X MOD 3=T MOD 3 AND X MOD 4=(T+1) MOD 4 THEN
   PRINT P$(X);" "; ELSE 4050
4045     PRINT #1,NOTEON;X;VELOCITY;ARTDUR;CHANNEL
4046     NOTEON=NOTEON+DURATION
4050 NEXT X
4060 RETURN
```

Execution of Program #20:

```
Enter T: 2
Enter number of background scale elements: 24
Enter scale type:(1=major,2=harm. minor,3=pentatonic)
? 2
C#1  D1  E1  F1  G1  A1 A#1 C#2  D2  E2  F2  G2  A2 A#2
```

7

Integrative Procedures

Algorithmic composition often requires use of procedures which are integrative. In this category fall all routines which:

(1) accept one or more files, arrays, or other lists of values (sequences) as input material and merge them into an output sequence which in some way combines the characteristics of the source sequences;

(2) process lists of values by simple, non-disruptive element rotation (cycling); or

(3) employ numerical series generators to configure data.

Integrative procedures take a number of different forms. One example is the simple merging of sequences in a straightforward manner, by means of combining the files in an alternating fashion. A more sophisticated example is the use of pattern interpolation routines to integrate several source files into a single sequence in which the original files are interwoven in a complex way.

Pattern Interpolation

The first data interpolation method is demonstrated by Program #21. Two arrays are filled with integers of different ranges, then merged into a single, final array containing interwoven elements of each of the source arrays.

(Program #21 includes file-writing code for use with the MusicSculptor System.)

PROGRAM #21

```
10  REM*********************************************************
20  REM                    PROGRAM #21
30  REM            Demonstrate Data Interpolation Method 1
40  REM
50  REM                   Merge two arrays
60  REM            Array 1 is first value in new array,
70  REM            Array2(1) is second value, etc.
80  REM*********************************************************
82  REM                    Main Routine
84  REM*********************************************************
90     DIM ARRAY1(200),ARRAY2(200),ARRAY3(400)
91         ' next line initializes variables for MusicSculptor file
92  NOTEON=0:DURATION=60:VELOCITY=100:ARTDUR=55:CHANNEL=0
93  OPEN "O",#1,"PROG#21.SC"
94  PRINT #1,"File-ID : 2"
95  PRINT #1,"Format : 1"
100    PRINT "Here is the first array:"
110       FOR J = 1 TO 30    'fill array1 with increasing integers
120          ARRAY1(J) = J+30
130          PRINT ARRAY1(J),
135          PITCH=ARRAY1(J)
136         ' now file array1 pitches
137          PRINT #1,NOTEON;PITCH;VELOCITY;ARTDUR;CHANNEL
138          NOTEON=NOTEON+DURATION
140       NEXT J
141 ' put a rest in file before playing array2 pitches
142    NOTEON=NOTEON+DURATION*4
150    PRINT : PRINT
160    PRINT "Here is the second array:"
170       FOR J = 1 TO 30    'fill array2 with increasing integers
180          ARRAY2(J) = J + 70
190          PRINT ARRAY2(J),
191          PITCH=ARRAY2(J)
192         ' now file array2 pitches
193          PRINT #1,NOTEON;PITCH;VELOCITY;ARTDUR;CHANNEL
194          NOTEON=NOTEON+DURATION
200       NEXT J
201 ' put a rest in file before playing array3 pitches
202    NOTEON=NOTEON+DURATION*4
210    PRINT : PRINT
220    GOSUB 1000                            'call merge routine
230    PRINT "Here is the final, combined array:"
240      FOR FINAL = 1 TO COMBINE - 1
250         PRINT ARRAY3(FINAL),
251         PITCH=ARRAY3(FINAL)
252        ' now file pitches
253         PRINT #1,NOTEON;PITCH;VELOCITY;ARTDUR;CHANNEL
```

```
254         NOTEON=NOTEON+DURATION
260      NEXT FINAL
261 ' write EOF flag
262 PRINT #1,0;-1;0;0;0
263 CLOSE #1
270 END


1000 REM*********************************************************
1010 REM      Subroutine to Combine Two Arrays of Equal Length
1020 REM*********************************************************
1030    COMBINE = 1
1040     FOR COUNT = 1 TO 30
1050         ARRAY3(COMBINE) = ARRAY1(COUNT):COMBINE = COMBINE + 1
1060         ARRAY3(COMBINE) = ARRAY2(COUNT):COMBINE = COMBINE + 1
1070     NEXT COUNT
1080    RETURN
```

Execution of Program #21:

```
Here is the first array:
1             2             3             4             5
6             7             8             9             10
11            12            13            14            15
16            17            18            19            20
21            22            23            24            25
26            27            28            29            30
31            32            33            34            35
36            37            38            39            40
41            42            43            44            45
46            47            48            49            50


Here is the second array:
51            52            53            54            55
56            57            58            59            60
61            62            63            64            65
66            67            68            69            70
71            72            73            74            75
76            77            78            79            80
81            82            83            84            85
86            87            88            89            90
91            92            93            94            95
96            97            98            99            100
```

Here is the final, combined array:

1	51	2	52	3
53	4	54	5	55
6	56	7	57	8
58	9	59	10	60
11	61	12	62	13
63	14	64	15	65
16	66	17	67	18
68	19	69	20	70
21	71	22	72	23
73	24	74	25	75
26	76	27	77	28
78	29	79	30	80
31	81	32	82	33
83	34	84	35	85
36	86	37	87	38
88	39	89	40	90
41	91	42	92	43
93	44	94	45	95
46	96	47	97	48
98	49	99	50	100

Program #22 demonstrates a second data interpolation method. This algorithm allows the selection of the number of elements chosen from each of three source arrays for interpolation in the final, composite array. By changing the values assigned to the variables BACKPATTERN, MIDPATTERN, and FRONTPATTERN, the nature of the final pattern may be controlled over a number of repetitions.

Study Program #22, then modify it to allow complete user interactivity; in addition to control over the number of elements selected from each source array, provide the means for changing the proportion of source array elements from one cycle of the final pattern to the next.

(Program #22 includes file-writing code for use with the MusicSculptor System.)

PROGRAM #22

```
10 REM*********************************************************
20 REM                    PROGRAM #22
30 REM*********************************************************
32 REM          Demonstrate Data Interpolation Method 2
34 REM
40 REM       Subroutine Builds Composite Pattern Pointer List
50 REM       by Regulated Interpolation of Elements from
60 REM       Background, Middleground, and Foreground Arrays.
70 REM
```

```
80 REM      Note:  Although Main Routine is configured to
90 REM      have the fewest elements in the backgroundlevel, any
100 REM     relationship can be set for the ratio of individual
110 REM     array elements in the composite pattern.
120 REM
130 REM          (Pattern ratio in Main Routine is 3:5:7)
140 REM
150 REM*********************************************************
160 REM                    Main Routine
170 REM*********************************************************
180 REM
190     DIM BG(100),MG(100),FG(100),COMP(1000)
191       ' next line initializes variables for MusicSculptor file
192 NOTEON=0:DURATION=60:VELOCITY=100:ARTDUR=55:CHANNEL=0
193 OPEN "O",#1,"PROG#22.SC"
194 PRINT #1,"File-ID : 2"
195 PRINT #1,"Format : 1"
200     BACKSET = 10 : MIDSET = 15 : FRONTSET = 20
210     BACKPATTERN = 3 : MIDPATTERN = 5 : FRONTPATTERN = 7
220     LARGEPATTERN = BACKPATTERN + MIDPATTERN + FRONTPATTERN
230     PATTERNCYCLES = 10
240     TOTAL = LARGEPATTERN * PATTERNCYCLES
250     PRINT "Here is the Background Set: "
260       FOR J1 = 0 TO BACKSET - 1
270         BG(J1) = J1 + 30
280         PRINT BG(J1);
281         PITCH=BG(J1)
282         ' now file Background Set pitches
283         PRINT #1,NOTEON;PITCH;VELOCITY;ARTDUR;CHANNEL
284         NOTEON=NOTEON+DURATION
290       NEXT J1
291 ' put a rest in file
292    NOTEON=NOTEON+DURATION*4
300    PRINT : PRINT
310     PRINT "Here is the Middleground Set: "
320       FOR J1 = 0 TO MIDSET - 1
330         MG(J1) = J1 + 60
340         PRINT MG(J1);
341         PITCH=MG(J1)
342         ' now file Background Set pitches
343         PRINT #1,NOTEON;PITCH;VELOCITY;ARTDUR;CHANNEL
344         NOTEON=NOTEON+DURATION
350       NEXT J1
351 ' put a rest in file
352    NOTEON=NOTEON+DURATION*4
360    PRINT : PRINT
370     PRINT "Here is the Foreground Set: "
380       FOR J1 = 0 TO FRONTSET - 1
390         FG(J1) = J1 + 80
400         PRINT FG(J1);
```

```
401        PITCH = FG(J1)
402        ' now file Background Set pitches
403        PRINT #1,NOTEON;PITCH;VELOCITY;ARTDUR;CHANNEL
404        NOTEON=NOTEON+DURATION
410     NEXT J1
411 ' put a rest in file
412   NOTEON=NOTEON+DURATION*4
420   PRINT : PRINT
421 PRINT "<<<<<<<<<< PRESS THE SPACEBAR TO CONTINUE >>>>>>>>>>
422 IF INKEY$ <> " " THEN 422
430   PRINT "Here are";PATTERNCYCLES;"cycles of the final pattern:"
440   GOSUB 1000                '<< call patterned interpolation
450     FOR J1 = 0 TO TOTAL - 1
460        IF J1 MOD LARGEPATTERN = 0 THEN PRINT : PRINT
470        PRINT COMP(J1);
471        PITCH=COMP(J1)
472        ' now file Composite Pattern pitches
473        PRINT #1,NOTEON;PITCH;VELOCITY;ARTDUR;CHANNEL
474   NOTEON=NOTEON+DURATION
480     NEXT J1
491 ' write EOF flag
492 PRINT #1,0;-1;0;0;0
493 CLOSE #1
500   END
1000 REM*************************************************************
1010 REM          Patterned Interpolation Routine
1020 REM*************************************************************
1030   COUNT = 0 : BACKCOUNT = 0 :MIDCOUNT = 0 : FRONTCOUNT = 0
1040     WHILE COUNT < TOTAL
1050        W = 0
1060        WHILE W < BACKPATTERN
1070           COMP(COUNT) = BG(BACKCOUNT MOD BACKSET)
1080           COUNT = COUNT + 1  : BACKCOUNT = BACKCOUNT + 1
              : W = W + 1
1090        WEND
1100        X=0
1110        WHILE  X < MIDPATTERN
1120           COMP(COUNT) = MG(MIDCOUNT MOD MIDSET)
1130           COUNT = COUNT + 1 : MIDCOUNT = MIDCOUNT + 1
              : X = X + 1
1140        WEND
1150        Y = 0
1160        WHILE Y < FRONTPATTERN
1170           COMP(COUNT) = FG(FRONTCOUNT  MOD FRONTSET)
1180           COUNT = COUNT + 1 : FRONTCOUNT = FRONTCOUNT + 1
              : Y = Y + 1
1190        WEND
1200     WEND
1210   RETURN
```

Execution of Program #22:

```
Here is the Background Set:
 1   2   3   4   5   6   7   8   9   10

Here is the Middleground Set:
 40   41   42   43   44   45   46   47   48   49   50   51   52   53   54

Here is the Foreground Set:
 70   71   72   73   74   75   76   77   78   79   80   81   82   83   84
 85   86   87   88   89
```

Here are 10 cycles of the final pattern:

```
 1    2    3    40   41   42   43   44   70   71   72   73   74   75   76

 4    5    6    45   46   47   48   49   77   78   79   80   81   82   83

 7    8    9    50   51   52   53   54   84   85   86   87   88   89   70

 10   1    2    40   41   42   43   44   71   72   73   74   75   76   77

 3    4    5    45   46   47   48   49   78   79   80   81   82   83   84

 6    7    8    50   51   52   53   54   85   86   87   88   89   70   71

 9    10   1    40   41   42   43   44   72   73   74   75   76   77   78

 2    3    4    45   46   47   48   49   79   80   81   82   83   84   85

 5    6    7    50   51   52   53   54   86   87   88   89   70   71   72

 8    9    10   40   41   42   43   44   73   74   75   76   77   78   79
```

Pattern Cycling

The cyclical rotation of array elements from front to back or back to front is a commonly used compositional device. It differs from merging, or interpolation, in that it operates only on the original, source file rather than combining a number of separate lists of values. It is considered integrative because it generates variations of the original sequence while preserving important characteristics of the original pattern or motif.

Program #23 demonstrates the controllable dimensions of list-element rotation. The user is allowed to decide the rotation start position, and the number of list elements to be shifted with each rotation cycle.

After you become familiar with program function, modify it to allow the user (1) to enter an element array, and (2) to specify whether the rotation will be in a forward or backward direction.
(Program #23 includes file-writing code for use with the MusicSculptor System.)

PROGRAM #23

```
10  REM  ***********************************************************
20  REM                        PROGRAM #23
40  REM     Demonstrate Cyclical Rotation of Parameter Elements
60  REM  ***********************************************************
70    DIM NUMLIST(100)
71        ' next line initializes variables for MusicSculptor file
72  NOTEON=0:DURATION=60:VELOCITY=100:ARTDUR=55:CHANNEL=0
73  OPEN "O",#1,"PROG#23.SC"
74  PRINT #1,"File-ID : 2"
75  PRINT #1,"Format : 1"
76  LOWP=48:ELEMENTS= 12
80    PRINT "List Length=";ELEMENTS
90    INPUT "Enter List Rotation Start Position: ",STARTPOS
100   INPUT "Enter List Rotation Factor: ",ROTFACTOR
130       FOR LISTMEM = 0 TO ELEMENTS-1
140          NUMLIST(LISTMEM)  = LISTMEM+48 'number series to array
141          PITCH=LISTMEM+48:PRINT PITCH;
142          ' now file pitches
143          PRINT #1,NOTEON;PITCH;VELOCITY;ARTDUR;CHANNEL
144          NOTEON=NOTEON+DURATION
150       NEXT LISTMEM
151   ' put a rest in file
153   NOTEON=NOTEON+DURATION*4
154 PRINT:PRINT
180   PRINT "Here are the Element List Rotations:"
210    FOR ROTATION = 0 TO ELEMENTS - 1
230       FOR ROTATE = 0 TO (ELEMENTS-1)
240          OFFSET = (ROTATE + STARTPOS + ROTFACTOR) MOD ELEMENTS
250          PRINT NUMLIST(OFFSET); 'print array address contents
251          PITCH=NUMLIST(OFFSET)
252          ' now file pitches
253          PRINT #1,NOTEON;PITCH;VELOCITY;ARTDUR;CHANNEL
254          NOTEON=NOTEON+DURATION
260       NEXT ROTATE
280       STARTPOS = STARTPOS + ROTFACTOR
281       ' put a rest in file
283       NOTEON=NOTEON+DURATION*4
290       PRINT : PRINT
300       PRINT "---- PRESS SPACEBAR FOR NEXT ROTATION --- "
310       IF INKEY$ <> " " THEN 310
```

```
330     PRINT
350     NEXT ROTATION
351 ' write EOF flag
352 PRINT #1,0;-1;0;0;0
360 END
```

Execution of Program #23:

```
Enter List Length (maximum = 100): 15
Enter List Rotation Start Position: 1
Enter List Rotation Factor: 2
Here is the Element List and its Rotations:
 3   4   5   6   7   8   9   10  11  12  13  14  0   1   2

---- PRESS SPACEBAR FOR NEXT ROTATION ---

 5   6   7   8   9   10  11  12  13  14  0   1   2   3   4

---- PRESS SPACEBAR FOR NEXT ROTATION ---

 7   8   9   10  11  12  13  14  0   1   2   3   4   5   6

---- PRESS SPACEBAR FOR NEXT ROTATION ---

 9   10  11  12  13  14  0   1   2   3   4   5   6   7   8

---- PRESS SPACEBAR FOR NEXT ROTATION ---

 11  12  13  14  0   1   2   3   4   5   6   7   8   9   10

---- PRESS SPACEBAR FOR NEXT ROTATION ---

 13  14  0   1   2   3   4   5   6   7   8   9   10  11  12

---- PRESS SPACEBAR FOR NEXT ROTATION ---

 0   1   2   3   4   5   6   7   8   9   10  11  12  13  14

---- PRESS SPACEBAR FOR NEXT ROTATION ---

 2   3   4   5   6   7   8   9   10  11  12  13  14  0   1

---- PRESS SPACEBAR FOR NEXT ROTATION ---

 4   5   6   7   8   9   10  11  12  13  14  0   1   2   3

---- PRESS SPACEBAR FOR NEXT ROTATION ---

 6   7   8   9   10  11  12  13  14  0   1   2   3   4   5
```

```
---- PRESS SPACEBAR FOR NEXT ROTATION ---

 8  9  10  11  12  13  14  0  1  2  3  4  5  6  7

---- PRESS SPACEBAR FOR NEXT ROTATION ---

 10  11  12  13  14  0  1  2  3  4  5  6  7  8  9


---- PRESS SPACEBAR FOR NEXT ROTATION ---

 12  13  14  0  1  2  3  4  5  6  7  8  9  10  11

---- PRESS SPACEBAR FOR NEXT ROTATION ---

 14  0  1  2  3  4  5  6  7  8  9  10  11  12  13

---- PRESS SPACEBAR FOR NEXT ROTATION

 1  2  3  4  5  6  7  8  9  10  11  12  13  14  0
```

Mathematical Algorithms

Numeric Series Generators. Program #24 demonstrates the application of mathematical curves to the scaling of numbers to be used in musical parameters. Although values scaled in this manner can be used for any of the parameters, they are particularly useful for controlling increase/decrease in tempo, smooth transitions of dynamic levels, and incremental timbre changes.

The curve choices available in Program #21 are linear, exponential, and logarithmic. Program control variables are S (start), E (end), and N (number of values).

Experiment with the application of curves to musical data by writing routines to produce other types of curves in addition to the original ones, then apply them to the Pitch and Rhythm parameters. (Program #24 includes file-writing code for use with the MusicSculptor System.)

PROGRAM #24

```
10 REM****************************************************************
20 REM                    PROGRAM #24
30 REM****************************************************************
40 REM   Demonstrate the Scaling of Music Parameter Values
50 REM   in conformity to continuous mathematical distributions
60 REM****************************************************************
70 REM                    Main Routine
100 REM***************************************************************
```

```
140 REM      Return positive values along three discrete curves:
150 REM      linear, exponential, and logarithmic. Control
160 REM      parameters are starting and ending values, and
170 REM      number of values to be included in the curve.
180 REM*****************************************************
190 REM                    Variable Descriptions
200 REM      MAIN
210 REM        S: starting curve value
220 REM        E: ending curve value
230 REM        N: number of values contained in curve
240 REM        J1: loop index, pointer to subroutines
250 REM        J2: loop index, pointer to array X()
260 REM        X(): array holding curve values
270 REM
280 REM      ROUTINES 1000,2000,3000
290 REM        Entering -
300 REM          S: starting curve value
310 REM          E: ending curve value
320 REM          N: number of values contained in curve
330 REM        Exiting -
340 REM          X(): array holding curve values
350 REM        Local -
360 REM          K9: loop index
370 REM          L9: loop index, pointer to array X()
380 REM*****************************************************
390 REM                    Main Routine
400 REM*****************************************************
410      DIM X(100)
420      S = 35
430      E = 100
440      N = 65
441        ' next line initializes variables for MusicSculptor file
442 NOTEON=0:DURATION=30:VELOCITY=100:ARTDUR=28:CHANNEL=0
443 OPEN "O",#1,"PROG#24.SC"
444 PRINT #1,"File-ID : 2"
445 PRINT #1,"Format : 1"
450          FOR J1 = 1 TO 3
460 REM >> sequentially call LINCURVE, EXPCURVE, LOGCURVE subrs.
470              ON J1 GOSUB 1000,2000,3000
480              FOR J2 = 1 TO N
490                  PRINT X(J2);      '<< send curve values to screen
491                  PITCH=X(J2)
492                ' now file rescaled pitches
493                  PRINT #1,NOTEON;PITCH;VELOCITY;ARTDUR;CHANNEL
494                  NOTEON=NOTEON+DURATION
500              NEXT J2
510              PRINT
511            ' put a rest in file before playing rescaled pitches
512              NOTEON=NOTEON+DURATION*4
```

```
520        NEXT J1
521 ' write EOF flag
522 PRINT #1,0;-1;0;0;0
523 CLOSE #1
530 END
1000 REM**************************************************************
1010 REM                    Linear Curve Routine
1020 REM**************************************************************
1030    PRINT "LINEAR CURVE:"
1040    FOR K9 = 1 TO N STEP 10
1050       FOR L9 = K9 TO K9 + 9
1060 REM >> store current computed curve value
1070          X(L9) = ABS(S + INT((((L9-1)/(N-1)) * (E-S)+.5))
1080          IF L9 = N THEN 1100
1090       NEXT L9
1100    NEXT K9
1110 RETURN
2000 REM**************************************************************
2010 REM           .      Exponential Curve Routine
2020 REM**************************************************************
2030    PRINT "EXPONENTIAL CURVE:"
2040    FOR K9 = 1 TO N STEP 10
2050       FOR L9 = K9 TO K9 + 9
2060 REM >> store current computed curve value
2070          X(L9) = ABS(S+INT(((((L9-1)^2)/((N-1)^2))*(E-S)+.5))
2080          IF L9 = N THEN 2100
2090       NEXT L9
2100    NEXT K9
2110 RETURN
3000 REM**************************************************************
3010 REM                 Logarithmic Curve Routine
3020 REM**************************************************************
3030    PRINT "LOGARITHMIC CURVE:"
3040    FOR K9 = 1 TO N STEP 10
3050       FOR L9 = K9 TO K9 + 9
3060 REM >> store current computed curve value
3070          X(L9)=ABS(S + INT((((LOG(L9))/(LOG(N)))*(E-S)+.5))
3080          IF L9 = N THEN 3100
3090       NEXT L9
3100    NEXT K9
3110 RETURN
```

Execution of Program #24:

```
LINEAR CURVE:
1              2              3              4              5
6              7              8              9              10
11             12             13             14             15
16             17             18             19             20
```

21	22	23	24	25
26	27	28	29	30
31	32	33	34	35
36	37	38	39	40
41	42	43	44	45
46	47	48	49	50
51	52	53	54	55
56	57	58	59	60
61	62	63	64	65
66	67	68	69	70
71	72	73	74	75
76	77	78	79	80
81	82	83	84	85
86	87	88	89	90
91	92	93	94	95
96	97	98	99	100

EXPONENTIAL CURVE:

1	1	1	1	1
1	1	1	2	2
2	2	2	3	3
3	4	4	4	5
5	5	6	6	7
7	8	8	9	9
10	11	11	12	13
13	14	15	16	16
17	18	19	20	21
21	22	23	24	25
26	27	28	29	30
32	33	34	35	36
37	39	40	41	42
44	45	46	48	49
50	52	53	55	56
58	59	61	62	64
66	67	69	71	72
74	76	77	79	81
83	85	86	88	90
92	94	96	98	100

LOGARITHMIC CURVE:

1	16	25	31	36
40	43	46	48	51
53	54	56	58	59
61	62	63	64	65
66	67	68	69	70
71	72	73	73	74
75	76	76	77	77
78	79	79	80	80
81	81	82	82	83

83	84	84	85	85
86	86	86	87	87
88	88	88	89	89
89	90	90	90	91
91	91	92	92	92
93	93	93	94	94
94	94	95	95	95
95	96	96	96	97
97	97	97	97	98
98	98	98	99	99
99	99	100	100	100

Program #25 generates a range-limited list of prime numbers, then measures the intervallic distance between them and creates a secondary list of these intervals. The final array can be used in any situation where it is desirable to map the characteristics of primes onto a musical parameter, such as Pitch or Rhythm.

By editing the variables LOW and HIGH, you can shift the prime number range around to explore characteristic patterns. Interestingly, upward shifting of the prime number range increases the interval size range at the high end while preserving the smallest interval size. In rhythmic applications, this characteristic can be harnessed to create a gradual expansion or contraction of duration patterns by generating prime interval sequences derived from continuous integer ranges.

Execute Program #25, then adapt it to (1) allow the user to enter values for the variables LOW and HIGH, and (2) provide options to scale the returned prime interval array to the range requirements of any musical parameter.
(Program #25 includes file-writing code for use with the MusicSculptor System.)

PROGRAM #25

```
10  REM************************************************************
20  REM                      PROGRAM #25
30  REM      Demonstrate Generation of Prime Numbers and
40  REM      Extraction of Intervals between Them for Use
50  REM      in Musical Parameters.
90  REM************************************************************
100     DIM X(300), Y(300)
101         ' next line initializes variables for MusicSculptor file
102 NOTEON=0:DURATION=60:VELOCITY=100:ARTDUR=55:CHANNEL=0
103 OPEN "O",#1,"PROG#25.SC"
104 PRINT #1,"File-ID : 2"
105 PRINT #1,"Format : 1"
150     LOW = 200
```

```
160     HIGH =1200
170     PRINT "PRIME NUMBERS WITHIN RANGE ";LOW;"TO";HIGH;" --"
180     GOSUB 1000                '<< call prime interval generator
190        FOR J = 1 TO PCNT
200           PRINT X(J);
210        NEXT J
220     PRINT
230     PRINT "NUMERIC INTERVALS BETWEEN PRIMES --"
240        FOR J = 1 TO PCNT-1
250           PRINT Y(J);
260        NEXT J
270     PRINT:PRINT "A Melodic Sequence based on the intervals:"
275     PITCH=60
276     ' file start pitch
277     PRINT #1,NOTEON;PITCH;VELOCITY;ARTDUR;CHANNEL
278     NOTEON=NOTEON+DURATION
279     A = 1
280        FOR J = 1 TO PCNT-1
290           ITVL = Y(J)
291           PITCH=PITCH+ITVL * A
292           PRINT PITCH;
293           ' file pitches
294           PRINT #1,NOTEON;PITCH;VELOCITY;ARTDUR;CHANNEL
295           IF J MOD 3 = 2 THEN A = A * -1   'change interval
direction
296           NOTEON=NOTEON+DURATION
300        NEXT J
301 ' write EOF flag
302 PRINT #1,0;-1;0;0;0
303 CLOSE #1
370 END
1000 REM*********************************************************
1010 REM     Routine to Measure Intervals Between Primes
1020 REM*********************************************************
1030 REM     This subroutine invokes the prime number indicator
1040 REM     subroutine to locate primes, then creates two
1050 REM     array sequences: 1) a list of the primes, and
1060 REM     2) a list of numeric intervals separating primes.
1070 REM     The list can be mapped to various musical parameters,
1080 REM     and can be modified in scale by addition or
1090 REM     subtraction of a numerical constant.
1100 REM ========================================================
1110 REM                 Variable Descriptions
1120 REM     Entering -
1130 REM       LOW: smallest integer within test range
1140 REM       HIGH: largest integer within test range
1150 REM       PRIM: (from SR 2000) prime flag
1160 REM     Exiting -
1170 REM       NUM: (to SR 2000) current integer to be tested
1180 REM       X(): list of prime numbers
```

```
1190 REM       Y(): list of numeric intervals between primes
1200 REM    Local -
1210 REM       PCNT: prime number counter, pointer to X(),Y()
1220 REM ============================================================
1230    PCNT = 0
1240      FOR NUM = LOW TO HIGH
1250         GOSUB 2000            '<< call prime number indicator
1260         IF PRIM <> 1 THEN 1300
1270         PCNT = PCNT + 1
1280         X(PCNT) = NUM
1290         IF PCNT >= 2 THEN Y(PCNT-1) = X(PCNT)-X(PCNT-1)
1300      NEXT NUM
1310 RETURN
2000 REM*********************************************************
2010 REM     Routine to Locate and Return Prime Numbers
2020 REM*********************************************************
2030 REM     Locates and returns prime numbers
2040 REM     from a stream of consecutive numbers within a
2050 REM     specified range. (Prime numbers are integers
2060 REM     which have only themselves or the number 1
2070 REM     as a factor.)
2080 REM*********************************************************
2090 REM               Variable Descriptions
2100 REM    Entering -
2110 REM      NUM: number to be tested for prime
2120 REM    Exiting -
2130 REM      PRIM: flag indicating a  prime number
2140 REM    Local -
2150 REM       DIVISOR: loop index, divisor for prime test
2160 REM ============================================================
2170    PRIM = 1
2180    IF NUM = 1 THEN PRIM = 0 : RETURN
           ELSE IF NUM = 2 OR NUM = 3 THEN RETURN
2190    IF NUM = INT(NUM/2) * 2 THEN PRIM = 0 : RETURN
2200      FOR DIVISOR = 3 TO INT(SQR(NUM)) STEP 2
2210         IF NUM = INT(NUM/DIVISOR) * DIVISOR
               THEN PRIM = 0 : RETURN
2220      NEXT DIVISOR
2230 RETURN
```

Execution of Program #25:

```
PRIME NUMBERS WITHIN RANGE  500 TO 800   --
   503         509         521         523         541
   547         557         563         569         571
   577         587         593         599         601
   607         613    ·    617         619         631
   641         643         647         653         659
   661         673         677         683         691
```

701	709	719	727	733
739	743	751	757	761
769	773	787	797	

NUMERIC INTERVALS BETWEEN PRIMES --

6	12	2	18	6
10	6	6	2	6
10	6	6	2	6
6	4	2	12	10
2	4	6	6	2
12	4	6	8	10
8	10	8	6	6
4	8	6	4	8
4	14	10		

Program #26 demonstrates the computation of a Fibonacci number series for use in any musical parameter. Congruence modulo m is applied to produce compatibility of data with the desired range of parameter values.

Experiment with the effects of a variety of modulus sizes and seed numbers to get a feeling for the character of Fibonacci numbers used in different parameters.

(Program #26 includes file-writing code for use with the MusicSculptor System.)

PROGRAM #26

```
10 REM:*****************************************************************
20 REM                      PROGRAM # 26
30 REM:*****************************************************************
40 REM:  Demonstrate simple numeric series computation for use
50 REM:  in a broad range of musical parameters. Program employs
60 REM:  congruence modulo m concept; the modulus and 2 seeds
70 REM:  to start the series generator are input by the user.
80 REM:*****************************************************************
90 REM:*********** Input and Initialization Section *************
100 REM:*****************************************************************
101        ' next line initializes variables for MusicSculptor file
102 NOTEON=0:DURATION=60:VELOCITY=100:ARTDUR=55:CHANNEL=0
103 OPEN "O",#1,"PROG#26.SC"
104 PRINT #1,"File-ID : 2"
105 PRINT #1,"Format : 1"
106 LOWP=40
110 INPUT "Enter modulus for residual Fibonacci series:",SIZE
120 INPUT "Enter 2 integers (0-32767) to seed the generator: ",
          NUM1,NUM2
130 NUM1 = NUM1 MOD SIZE 'wrap the 1st number around a fixed modulus
140 NUM2 = NUM2 MOD SIZE 'wrap the 2nd number around a fixed modulus
```

```
150 ORIGNUM1 = NUM1     'save seed 1 to check series repetition point
160 ORIGNUM2 = NUM2     'save seed 2 to check series repetition point
170 FLAG = 0   'switch to end While Loop at series repetition point
180 COUNT = 2
190 REM:************************************************************
200 REM:*********** Processing and Output Section ****************
210 REM:************************************************************
220   PRINT NUM1,
230   PRINT NUM2,
240     WHILE FLAG <> 1            'allow for maximum possible loops
250         CURRVAL = (NUM1 + NUM2) MOD SIZE 'add 2 nums to get next
260         NUM1 = NUM2     'shift 2nd number back to first position
270         NUM2 = CURRVAL             'put new term in 2nd position
280           REM:!!!! next line tests for repetition of sequence
290         IF NUM1 = ORIGNUM1 AND NUM2 = ORIGNUM2 THEN FLAG = 1
300         PRINT CURRVAL,      'send current series term to screen
301         PITCH=CURRVAL + LOWP 'bring pitch up to range
302         ' now file pitches
303         PRINT #1,NOTEON;PITCH;VELOCITY;ARTDUR;CHANNEL
304         NOTEON=NOTEON+DURATION
310         COUNT = COUNT + 1
320     WEND
330   PRINT
340   PRINT "The last two numbers mark the series repetition."
350   PRINT COUNT-2;" Member Cycle"
351    ' write EOF flag
352   PRINT #1,0;-1;0;0;0
353 CLOSE #1
360 END
```

Execution of Program #26:

```
Enter modulus for residual Fibonacci series:12
Enter 2 seeds for the generator: 11,83
 11          11          10          9           7
 4           11          3           2           5
 7           0           7           7           2
 9           11          8           7           3
 10          1           11          0           11
 11
The last two numbers mark the series repetition.
 24  Member Cycle
```

Program #27 is an expanded, more universal version of the previous
program. It allows the user to enter more than two seeds, and provides
for cumulative addition of all seeds or addition of only the outer pair of
seeds to produce each successive series term.

(Program #27 includes file-writing code for use with the MusicSculptor System.)

PROGRAM #27

```
10  REM:*********************************************************
20  REM                      PROGRAM #27
30  REM: Compute Fibonacci and other numeric series from a set of
40  REM: seeds entered by the user;employs Congruence Modulo m to
50  REM: adapt the series to a specific musical parameter range.
60  REM
70  REM     Series repetitions are not prevented; therefore, the
80  REM     program can be used to produce ostinato patterns.
90  REM:*********************************************************
100 REM:              Input and Initialization Section
110 REM:*********************************************************
120 DIM SEED(20)            'array to store user-entered seeds
121     ' next line initializes variables for MusicSculptor file
122 NOTEON=0:DURATION=60:VELOCITY=100:ARTDUR=55:CHANNEL=0
123 OPEN "O",#1,"PROG#27.SC"
124 PRINT #1,"File-ID : 2"
125 PRINT #1,"Format : 1"
130 INPUT "how many numbers? ", TOTAL
132 INPUT "Enter lowest Midi pitch number (0-127): ",LOWP
140 INPUT "Enter modulus of residual series:(MAX=97)",SIZE
150 INPUT "How many seeds will you use for the series generator?",
        ORDER
160 IF ORDER < 2 THEN PRINT TAB(15)"!!Enter at least 2 seeds!!"
        : GOTO 150
170 INPUT "Enter 0 for exclusive seed addition, 1 for inclusive ",
        ADDTYPE
180 PRINT "Enter";ORDER;"seeds to start the series generator:"
190    FOR J = 0 TO ORDER - 1
200       INPUT SEED(J)
210       SEED(J) = SEED(J) MOD SIZE
220    NEXT J
230 PRINT
240 REM:*********************************************************
250 REM:              Processing and Output Section
260 REM:*********************************************************
270 FOR J = 0 TO ORDER - 1
280    PRINT SEED(J);
290 NEXT J
300 FOR K = 1 TO 10000          'allow for maximum possible loops
310    FOR L = 0 TO ORDER-1
320       CURRVAL = (CURRVAL + SEED(L)) MOD SIZE
330    NEXT L
340    IF ADDTYPE = 0 THEN CURRVAL = SEED(ORDER-1) + SEED(0)
345    PITCH = CURRVAL MOD SIZE + LOWP
```

```
350      PRINT PITCH; 'send series member to screen
352      ' now file pitches
353      PRINT #1,NOTEON;PITCH;VELOCITY;ARTDUR;CHANNEL
354      NOTEON=NOTEON+DURATION
360      IF K = TOTAL THEN 420
370      FOR L = 0 TO ORDER-2
380         SEED(L) = SEED(L+1)              ' update the seeds
390      NEXT L
400      SEED(ORDER-1) = CURRVAL MOD SIZE
410   NEXT K
420   PRINT
421  ' write EOF flag
422  PRINT #1,0;-1;0;0;0
423  CLOSE #1
430  END
```

Execution of Program #27:

```
How many numbers to be returned? 100
Enter modulus of residual series:(MAX=97)15
How many seeds will you enter to start the series?3
Enter 0 for exclusive seed addition, 1 for inclusive 1
Enter 3 seeds to start the series generator:
? 23
? 2
? 74
```

8	2	14	9	4
1	0	5	11	12
10	13	3	14	14
0	13	10	3	14
11	9	13	1	9
2	14	9	4	1
0	5	11	12	10
13	3	14	14	0
13	10	3	14	11
9	13	1	9	2
14	9	4	1	0
5	11	12	10	13
3	14	14	0	13
10	3	14	11	9
13	1	9	2	14
9	4	1	0	5
11	12	10	13	3
14	14	0	13	10
3	14	11	9	13
1	9	2	14	9
4	1	0	6	

8

Series Transform Procedures

Contemporary composers use a wide range of serial techniques to shape their music. Because the purpose of this book is compositional, not theoretical, the reader is advised to seek further information on Set Theory from one of the following excellent texts:

Rahn, John. *Basic Atonal Theory*. Longman, Inc., New York, 1980.

Forte, Allen. *The Structure of Atonal Music*. Yale University Press, New Haven, Connecticut, 1973.

Wuorinen, Charles. *Simple Composition*. Longman, Inc., New York, 1979.

Program #28 introduces this field by demonstrating the production of a pitch-class matrix containing the four primary forms of a randomly generated pitch-class series and its transpositions.

Study the program and its output, then modify it to accept a user-entered Pitch Class Series.

PROGRAM #28

```
10  REM*********************************************************
20  REM                     PROGRAM #28
30  REM    Demonstrate Twelve-Tone Series Pitch Class Matrix
40  REM*********************************************************
50   DIM P$(12)          'array to store pitch class characters
60   DIM CUM(12)'array to prevent repetition of pitch classes
70   DIM X(12)                 'array to store Prime Series Form
80   DIM Y(12)                'array to store Inverted Series Form
90   RANDOMIZE     'each RUN can produce a unique pitch-class set
100  GOSUB 1000        'call Routine to load Pitch Class Characters
110  GOSUB 2000                           'call set generator
120  GOSUB 3000       'call matrix-format series printout routine
130 END
```

```
1000 REM********************************************************
1010 REM     Routine to load a Pitch Class Character Array
1020 REM********************************************************
1040    FOR J = 0 TO 11
1050       READ P$(J)            'load pitch class character array
1060    NEXT J
1070 REM++++++++++++++++++++++++++++++++++++++++++
1080    DATA "C  ","C# ","D  ","D# ","E  ","F  "
1090    DATA "F# ","G  ","G# ","A  ","A# ","B  "
1100 REM++++++++++++++++++++++++++++++++++++++++++
1110 RETURN
2000 REM********************************************************
2010 REM Routine to Generate a Random-Order Pitch Class Series
2020 REM                 (modified to program specs)
2030 REM********************************************************
2040    FOR K9 = 0 TO 11
2050       F = INT(RND*12)
2060       IF CUM(F) = 1 THEN 2050 'if PC has been used, skip it
2070       CUM(F) = 1 'record the occurrence of a specidic PC
2080       IF K9 = 0 THEN TRANS = F
2090       IF F-TRANS < 0 THEN X(K9) = F-TRANS+ 12
               ELSE X(K9) = F-TRANS
2100       Y(K9) = (12-X(K9)) MOD 12
2110    NEXT K9
2120 RETURN
3000 REM********************************************************
3010 REM     Routine to Compute and Printout a Square Matrix
3020 REM     of Pitch Class Series Forms: Prime, Retrograde,
3030 REM     Inversion, and Retrograde Inversion.
3040 REM********************************************************
3070 REM                 Variable Descriptions
3080 REM     Entering -
3090 REM       X(): original order set array
3100 REM       Y(): inverted order set array
3110 REM       P$(): pitch table array
3120 REM     Exiting -
3130 REM       none  (routine is procedural)
3140 REM     Local -
3150 REM       INTVAL: transposition interval
3160 REM       K9: loop index, pointer to Y()
3170 REM       L9: loop index, pointer to X()
3180 REM =======================================================
3190    CLS
3200    PRINT "    MATRIX OF TRANSPOSITIONS YIELDING O,RO,I,RI   "
3210    PRINT "++++++++++++++++++++++++++++++++++++++++++++++++++++"
3220    PRINT "+                              ORIGINAL --->   +"
3230    PRINT "+ | INVERSION                                 +"
3240    PRINT "+ v                                           +"
3250    FOR K9= 0 TO 11
3260       PRINT "+";TAB(8);
```

```
3270              INTVAL = Y(K9)
3280           FOR L9= 0 TO 11
3290              PRINT P$((X(L9) + INTVAL) MOD 12);
3300           NEXT L9
3310        PRINT TAB(50);"+"
3320     NEXT K9
3330     PRINT "+ ^                                                      +"
3340     PRINT "+ | RETROGRADE INVERSION                                 +"
3350     PRINT "+                                  <--- RETROGRADE        +"
3360     PRINT "++++++++++++++++++++++++++++++++++++++++++++++++++++++++++"
3370 RETURN
```

Execution of Program #28:

MATRIX OF TRANSPOSITIONS YIELDING O,RO,I,RI

```
+++++++++++++++++++++++++++++++++++++++++++++++++++++++++++
+  |                                    ORIGINAL   --->      +
+   v  INVERSION                                             +
+                                                            +
+  C  B    A#  G#   A    E    G    D    D#   F    F#   C#
+
+  C# C    B   A    A#   F    G#   D#   E    F#   G    D
+
+  D  C#   C   A#   B    F#   A    E    F    G    G#   D#
+
+  E  D#   D   C    C#   G#   B    F#   G    A    A#   F
+
+  D# D    C#  B    C    G    A#   F    F#   G#   A    E
+
+  G# G    F#  E    F    C    D#   A#   B    C#   D    A
+
+  F  E    D#  C#   D    A    C    G    G#   A#   B    F#
+
+  A# A    G#  F#   G    D    F    C    C#   D#   E    B
+
+  A  G#   G   F    F#   C#   E    B    C    D    D#   A#
+
+  G  F#   F   D#   E    B    D    A    A#   C    C#   G#
+
+  F# F    E   D    D#   A#   C#   G#   A    B    C    G
+
+  B  A#   A   G    G#   D#   F#   C#   D    E    F    C
+
+ ^                                                          +
+ | RETROGRADE INVERSION                                     +
+                          <--- RETROGRADE                   +
+++++++++++++++++++++++++++++++++++++++++++++++++++++++++++++
```

Program #29 is similar to the previous one, but it is organized into
separate routines for the calculation and output of each series form:

Original, Retrograde, Inversion, and Retrograde Inversion. Transpositions are available in each case.

(Program #29 includes file-writing code for use with the MusicSculptor System.)

PROGRAM #29

```
10 REM******************************************************
20 REM                     PROGRAM #29
30 REM
40 REM   Computes  Prime, Retrograde, Inversion, and Retrograde
50 REM   Inversion Pitch Class Series. A separate routine
60 REM   is employed for the production of each Series Form.
70 REM   The program user enters the source Pitch Class Series.
80 REM******************************************************
100    DIM P$(12)
110    DIM X(12),Y(12)
111        ' next line initializes variables for MusicSculptor file
112 NOTEON=0:DURATION=60:VELOCITY=100:ARTDUR=55:CHANNEL=0
113 OPEN "O",#1,"PROG#29.SC"
114 PRINT #1,"File-ID : 2"
115 PRINT #1,"Format : 1"
120    INTVAL = 4
140    GOSUB 1000                        'load element tables
150    GOSUB 2000                   'call user input routine
160    PRINT
170    PRINT "Here is the Pitch Class Series as characters:"
180      FOR J = 0 TO 11
190         PRINT P$(X(J));" "; 'Pitch Class Series to screen
191              PITCH=X(J) + 60 'bring into range
192              ' now file pitches
193              PRINT #1,NOTEON;PITCH;VELOCITY;ARTDUR;CHANNEL
194              NOTEON=NOTEON+DURATION
200      NEXT J
201         NOTEON=NOTEON+DURATION*4 ' add rest before next form
210    PRINT : PRINT
215    PRINT "Here are the Series Forms in Characters:"
220      FOR J = 1 TO 3
230         ON J GOSUB 3000,4000,5000 'call retro,invrt,trnpz
240            FOR J1 = 0 TO 11
250               PRINT P$(Y(J1));" ";   'series forms to screen
251               PITCH=Y(J1) + 60 'bring into range
252               ' now file pitches
253               PRINT #1,NOTEON;PITCH;VELOCITY;ARTDUR;CHANNEL
254               NOTEON=NOTEON+DURATION
260            NEXT J1
270         PRINT : PRINT
275         NOTEON=NOTEON+DURATION*4 ' add rest before next form
280      NEXT J
```

```
281 ' write EOF flag
282 PRINT #1,0;-1;0;0;0
283 CLOSE #1
290 END
1000 REM************************************************************
1010 REM      Routine to load a Pitch Class Character Array
1020 REM************************************************************
1040    FOR J = 0 TO 11
1050       READ P$(J)              'load pitch class character array
1060    NEXT J
1070 REM++++++++++++++++++++++++++++++++++++++++++++
1080    DATA "C  ","C# ","D  ","D# ","E  ","F  "
1090    DATA "F# ","G  ","G# ","A  ","A# ","B  "
1100 REM++++++++++++++++++++++++++++++++++++++++++++
1110 RETURN
2000 REM************************************************************
2010 REM    Routine to accept User-Input Pitch Class Series
2020 REM************************************************************
2025 PRINT "Enter a Pitch Class Series (0-11), one per line:"
2030    FOR K9 = 0 TO 11
2060       INPUT X(K9)
2080    NEXT K9
2090 RETURN
3000 REM************************************************************
3010 REM      Routine to Compute Retrograde Series Forms
3020 REM************************************************************
3050    PRINT "RETROGRADE ORDER --"
3060       FOR K9 = 0 TO 11
3070          L = (11 - K9) MOD 12
3080          Y(L) = X(K9)
3090       NEXT K9
3100 RETURN
4000 REM************************************************************
4010 REM        Routine to Compute Inverted Series Form
4020 REM************************************************************
4050 PRINT "INVERTED ORDER --"
4060    FOR K9 = 0 TO 11
4070       Y(K9) = (12 - X(K9)) MOD 12
4080    NEXT K9
4090 RETURN
5000 REM************************************************************
5010 REM    Routine to Compute Transpositions of Series Forms
5020 REM************************************************************
5050   PRINT "TRANSPOSED (UP MAJOR 3RD) ORIGINAL (PRIME) FORM --"
5060       FOR K9 = 0 TO 11
5070          Y(K9) = (X(K9) + INTVAL) MOD 12
5080       NEXT K9
5090 RETURN
```

Execution of Program #29:

```
Enter a Pitch-Class Series (0-11), one per line:

?2
?11
?0
?9
?10
?7
?5
?8
?3
?1
?6
?4


Here is the Pitch-Class Series as characters:
D B C A A# G F G# D# C# F# E

Here are the Series Forms in Characters:

RETROGRADE ORDER --
E F# C# D# G# F G A# A C B D

INVERTED ORDER --
A# C# C D# D F G E A B F# G#

TRANSPOSED (UP MAJOR 3RD) PRIME (ORIGINAL) FORM --
F# D# E C# D B A C G F A# G#
```

Series Permutation

Cyclical Rotation. Program #30 deals with the transformation of Pitch Class Series by patterned permutation (reordering) of series members, in this case the cyclical rotation (both partitioned and unpartitioned) of the series.

PROGRAM #30

```
10 REM*********************************************************
20 REM                        PROGRAM #30
30 REM
40 REM    Demonstrate Pitch Class Series Cyclical Permutation
50 REM         Methods: Partitioned-Set & Unpartitioned Set
60 REM*********************************************************
70 REM*****************    Main Routine    *******************
80 REM*********************************************************
```

```
220      DIM SET(12),MAT1(12,12),MAT2(12,12),MAT3(12,12)
240      SET = 12
260      GOSUB 1000 'call routine for user-input pitch class set
265      PRINT "Here is the Pitch Class Series You Entered:"
270         FOR J = 0 TO SET-1
280            PRINT SET(J);" ";
290         NEXT J
300      PRINT
310      PRINT
320      ROTEGROUP = 4
330      PRINT "UNPARTITIONED ARRAY, ELEMENT/GROUP ROTATION -->"
340      PRINT "(";ROTEGROUP;"SET MEMBERS PER CYCLE ROTATED )"
350      GOSUB 5000                        '<< call Euclid's Algorithm
360      PRINT "TOTAL NUMBER OF UNIQUE CYCLES =";CYCLES
370      GOSUB 2000       '<< call unpartitioned set group rotation
380         FOR J1 = 0 TO CYCLES-1
390            FOR J2 = 0 TO SET-1
400               PRINT MAT1(J1,J2);
410            NEXT J2
420            PRINT
430            PRINT
440         NEXT J1
450      PRINT "'0' START POINT TRANSPOSITION -->"
460      GOSUB 3000                          '<< call set transposition
470         FOR J1 = 0 TO CYCLES-1
480            FOR J2 = 0 TO SET-1
490               PRINT MAT2(J1,J2);
500            NEXT J2
510            PRINT
520            PRINT
530         NEXT J1
540      NUMSEGS = 4
550      SEGMEMS = SET/NUMSEGS
560      PRINT "PARTITIONED ARRAY, ROTATION WITHIN SEGMENT -->"
570      PRINT "(DIVIDED INTO";NUMSEGS;"EQUAL SEGMENTS)"
580      GOSUB 4000            '<< call set segment member rotation
590         FOR J1 = 0 TO SEGMEMS - 1
600            PRINT "|";
610            FOR J2 = 0 TO SET - 1
620               PRINT MAT3(J1,J2);
630               IF (J2+1) MOD SEGMEMS = 0 THEN PRINT "|";
640            NEXT J2
650            PRINT
660            PRINT
670         NEXT J1
680 END
1000 REM*********************************************************
1010 REM    Routine to accept User-Input Pitch Class Series
1020 REM*********************************************************
1025 PRINT "Enter a Pitch Class Series (0-11), one per line:"
```

```
1030    FOR K9 = 0 TO 11
1060        INPUT SET(K9)
1080    NEXT K9
1090 RETURN
2000 REM*********************************************************
2010 REM        Routine to Rotate a Variable-Size PC Group
2020 REM        (moves a specified group of notes from the
2030 REM         beginning to the end of the PC series)
2040 REM*********************************************************
2070 REM                    Variable Descriptions
2080 REM        Entering -
2090 REM         SET: length of series
2100 REM         ROTEGROUP: # of contiguous set members to rotate
2110 REM        Exiting -
2120 REM         MAT1: matrix of rotated sets
2130 REM        Local -
2140 REM         R9: rotation factor marker
2150 REM         S9: counter, pointer to MAT1(n,n)
2160 REM         T9: pointer to SET()
2170 REM         K9: loop index
2180 REM         L9: loop index, pointer to MAT(n,n)
2190 REM*********************************************************
2200    ROTEGROUP = ROTEGROUP - 1
2210    R9 = 0
2220    S9 = 0
2230        FOR K9 = ROTEGROUP TO SET-1 + ROTEGROUP
2240            FOR L9 = 1 TO SET
2250                T9 = (K9+L9+R9) MOD SET
2260                MAT1(S9,L9-1) = SET(T9)
2270            NEXT L9
2280            R9 = R9 + ROTEGROUP
2290            S9 = S9 + 1
2295 IF S9 = CYCLES THEN RETURN
2300        NEXT K9
2310 RETURN
3000 REM*********************************************************
3010 REM    Routine to Transpose a Collection of Rotated PC Sets
3020 REM    sets to '0' start point.
3030 REM*********************************************************
3060 REM                    Variable Descriptions
3070 REM        Entering -
3080 REM         MAT1(n,n): matrix of rotated sets
3090 REM         SET: length of series
3100 REM        Exiting -
3110 REM         MAT2(n,n): matrix of transposed sets
3120 REM        Local -
3130 REM         INTVAL: interval of transposition
3140 REM         S9: set member after transposition
3150 REM         K9: loop index, pointer to MAT1(n,n) & MAT2(n,n)
3160 REM         L9: loop index, pointer to MAT1(n,n) & MAT2(n,n)
```

```
3170 REM********************************************************
3180    FOR K9 = 0 TO CYCLES-1
3190       INTVAL = MAT1(K9,0)
3200          FOR L9 = 0 TO SET-1
3210             S9 = MAT1(K9,L9)-INTVAL
3220             IF S9 < 0 THEN S9 = S9 + 12
3230             MAT2(K9,L9) = S9
3240          NEXT L9
3250    NEXT K9
3260 RETURN
4000 REM********************************************************
4010 REM    Routine to Rotate Partitioned-Set Members Within the
4020 REM    Each Segment.
4030 REM********************************************************
4060 REM                  Variable Descriptions
4070 REM     Entering -
4080 REM        SET(): prime set
4090 REM        SET: length of series
4100 REM        NUMSEGS: symmetrical set partitioning
4110 REM     Exiting -
4120 REM        MAT3(n,n): matrix of sets after internal rotation
4130 REM     Local -
4140 REM        SEGMEMS: number of members in each segment
4150 REM        S9: counter, pointer to MAT(n,n)
4160 REM        T9: counter, pointer to MAT(n,n)
4170 REM        K9: loop index
4180 REM        L9: loop index, pointer to SET()
4190 REM        M9: loop index, pointer to SET()
4200 REM********************************************************
4210    S9 = 0
4220    SEGMEMS = SET/NUMSEGS
4230       FOR K9 = 1 TO SEGMEMS
4240          T9 = 0
4250          FOR L9 = 0 TO SET-1 STEP SEGMEMS
4260             FOR M9 = S9 + 1 TO SEGMEMS + S9
4270                MAT3(S9,T9) = SET(M9 MOD SEGMEMS + L9)
4280                T9 = T9 + 1
4290             NEXT M9
4300          NEXT L9
4310          S9 = S9 + 1
4320       NEXT K9
4330 RETURN
5000 REM********************************************************
5010 REM    Routine to Compute Unique Cycles of an Unpartitioned
5020 REM    Set resulting from a Specific Rotation-Group Size.
5030 REM********************************************************
5035 REM Euclid's Algorithm - Greatest Common Divisor
5040    A9 = SET
5050    B9 = ROTEGROUP
5060    IF A9 > B9 THEN SWAP A9,B9
```

```
5070        WHILE A9 > 0
5080            C9 = INT(B9/A9)
5090            D9 = B9-A9*C9
5100            B9 = A9
5110            A9 = D9
5120        WEND
5130     CYCLES = SET/B9
5140 RETURN
```

Execution of Program #30:

```
Enter a Pitch-Class Series (0-11), one per line:
?10
?9
?8
?11
?5
?3
?2
?7
?4
?0
?6
?1

Here is the Pitch-Class Series You Entered:
  10   9   8   11   5   3   2   7   4   0   6   1

UNPARTITIONED ARRAY, ELEMENT/GROUP ROTATION--->
( 4 SET MEMBERS PER CYCLE ROTATED )
TOTAL NUMBER OF UNIQUE CYCLES = 3
  5   3   2   7   4   0   6   1   10   9   8   11

  4   0   6   1   10   9   8   11   5   3   2   7

  10   9   8   11   5   3   2   7   4   0   6   1

'0' START POINT TRANSPOSITION --->
  0   10   9   2   11   7   1   8   5   4   3   6

  0   8   2   9   6   5   4   7   1   11   10   3

  0   11   10   1   7   5   4   9   6   2   8   3

PARTITIONED ARRAY, ROTATION WITHIN SEGMENT--->
(DIVIDED INTO 4 EQUAL SEGMENTS)
| 9   8   10 | 5   3   11 | 7   4   2 | 6   1   0 |

| 8   10   9 | 3   11   5 | 4   2   7 | 1   0   6 |

| 10   9   8 | 11   5   3 | 2   7   4 | 0   6   1 |
```

Multiplicative Operations. Program #31 introduces another common Pitch Class Series transformation: the Multiplicative M5 and M7 operations.

The distinction between a simple, random permutation of a Pitch Class Series and a transformation lies in the orderly propagation of new, related series from a reference series in a manner that preserves some of the original characteristics. The "relatedness" of multiplicative operations is manifest by virtue of the fact that ordered pairs of notes within the series exchange their positions. Moreover, the M5 operation represents a mapping of the chromatic scale onto the cycle of fourths, while the M7 operation is a mapping onto the cycle of fifths. After you are familiar with this program, explore other multiplicative factors, mod 12, to discover what happens to series integrity. Experiment with series length other than 12 and apply the multiplicative operation.

(Program #31 includes file-writing code for use with the MusicSculptor System.)

PROGRAM #31

```
10 REM*********************************************************
20 REM                        PROGRAM # 31
30 REM
40 REM     Demonstration of M5 & M7 PC Set Transformations
50 REM              (Multiplicative Permutations)
60 REM*********************************************************
70 REM****************    Main Routine    *******************
80 REM*********************************************************
140    DIM P$(12)
150    DIM X(12),Y(12)
151    ' next line initializes variables for MusicSculptor file
152    NOTEON=0:DURATION=60:VELOCITY=100:ARTDUR=55:CHANNEL=0
153    OPEN "O",#1,"PROG#31.SC"
154    PRINT #1,"File-ID : 2"
155    PRINT #1,"Format : 1"
156    LOWP=60
170    SET = 12
180    OP = 5                              '<< value for m5 operation
190    GOSUB 1000                    '<< load PC Pitch Character Table
200    GOSUB 2000               '<< call routine for user-input PC Set
210    PRINT
220    PRINT "Here is the Pitch Class Series You Entered:"
230       FOR J = 0 TO SET - 1
240          PRINT P$(X(J));" ";
241          PITCH=X(J) + LOWP
242          ' now file rescaled pitches
243          PRINT #1,NOTEON;PITCH;VELOCITY;ARTDUR;CHANNEL
244          NOTEON=NOTEON+DURATION
```

```
250      NEXT J
251    ' put a rest in file
252    NOTEON=NOTEON+DURATION*4
260    PRINT : PRINT
270      FOR J = 1 TO 2
280        GOSUB 3000                '<< call m5/m7 permutation
290        PRINT "THE PERMUTATION RESULTING FROM ";
                  "M";OP;" OPERATION"
300          FOR J1 = 0 TO SET - 1
310            PRINT P$(Y(J1));" ";        '<< send to screen
311            PITCH=Y(J1) + LOWP
312            ' now file pitches
313            PRINT #1,NOTEON;PITCH;VELOCITY;ARTDUR;CHANNEL
314            NOTEON=NOTEON+DURATION
320          NEXT J1
321        ' put a rest in file
322        NOTEON=NOTEON+DURATION*4
330        PRINT : PRINT
340        OP = 7                        '<< value for m7 operation
350      NEXT J
360 END
1000 REM******************************************************
1010 REM     Routine to load a Pitch Class Character Array
1020 REM******************************************************
1040    FOR J = 0 TO 11
1050       READ P$(J)        '<< load pitch class character array
1060    NEXT J
1070 REM++++++++++++++++++++++++++++++++++++++++++++
1080    DATA "C  ","C# ","D  ","D# ","E  ","F  "
1090    DATA "F# ","G  ","G# ","A  ","A# ","B  "
1100 REM++++++++++++++++++++++++++++++++++++++++++++
1110 RETURN
2000 REM******************************************************
2010 REM   Routine to accept User-Input Pitch Class Series
2020 REM******************************************************
2025 PRINT "Enter a Pitch Class Series (0-11), one PC per line:"
2030    FOR K9 = 0 TO SET - 1
2060       INPUT X(K9)
2080    NEXT K9
2090 RETURN
3000 REM******************************************************
3010 REM   Routine to Apply "M5" or "M7" Set Transforms
3020 REM******************************************************
3060 REM                 Variable Descriptions
3070 REM     Entering -
3080 REM       X(): array holding random 12-tone set
3090 REM       OP: value for m5 or m7 operation
3100 REM     Exiting -
3110 REM       Y(): array holding m5 or m7 permutation
```

```
3120 REM      Local -
3130 REM        K9: loop index, pointer to X(),Y()
3140 REM************************************************************
3150    FOR K9 = 0 TO SET - 1
3160       Y(K9) = (X(K9) * OP) MOD 12
3170    NEXT
3180 RETURN
```

Execution of Program #31:

```
Enter a Pitch-Class Series (0-11), one PC per line:
? 0
? 11
? 4
? 1
? 6
? 3
? 10
? 9
? 2
? 8
? 7
? 5


Here is the Pitch-Class Series You Entered:
C   B   E   C#  F#  D#  A#  A   D   G#  G   F
```

Sampling. The next two routines, Program #32a and 32b are grouped together because they share a common approach to series permutation, that of sampling. Yet, each program achieves its goal in a different way, with a different result.

Program #32a produces numeric series permutations by cyclical set sampling at a selected interval (start at set member n and remove every nth element, looping back through the series until reordered). The algorithm is derived from the classic "Josephus' Problem," which is expressed below in pseudo-code:

> Arrange a group of men in a circle;
> move around the circle;
> shoot and remove every nth man;
> repeat until none remains.

(Program #32a includes file-writing code for use with the MusicSculptor System.)

PROGRAM #32A

```
10  REM******************************************************
20  REM                     PROGRAM #32a
30  REM
40  REM  Demonstrate Cyclical, Reductive Sampling of PC Set
50  REM******************************************************
60  REM***************   Main Routine   *********************
70  REM******************************************************
100     DIM SET(100),A(100),B(100)
101     ' next line initializes variables for MusicSculptor file
102     NOTEON=0:DURATION=60:VELOCITY=100:ARTDUR=55:CHANNEL=0
103     OPEN "O",#1,"PROG#32a.SC"
104     PRINT #1,"File-ID : 2"
105     PRINT #1,"Format : 1"
106     LOWP = 48
150     PERMUT - 5          '<< return 5 Sampled Series Permutations
160     SERIES = 12
170     PRINT "A SEQUENTIAL SET -"
180        FOR J = 1 TO SERIES
190           SET(J) = J - 1:PRINT SET(J)+LOWP;'<< load PC array
191           PITCH=SET(J) + LOWP
192           ' now file pitches
193           PRINT #1,NOTEON;PITCH;VELOCITY;ARTDUR;CHANNEL
194           NOTEON=NOTEON+DURATION
200        NEXT J
201     ' put a rest in file
202     NOTEON=NOTEON+DURATION*4
210     PRINT
220     FACTOR = 2               '<< assign initial sampling interval
230        FOR CYCLE = 1 TO PERMUT
240           PRINT "PERMUTATION ";CYCLE
250           TARGET = 1        '<< assign first set sample position
260           PRINT "SET START POSITION = ";TARGET;"; "
                    "SET TARGET FACTOR= ";FACTOR
270           GOSUB 1000                        '<< call sampling
280           FACTOR = FACTOR + 2  '<< advance sampling interval
281           ' put a rest in file
282           NOTEON=NOTEON+DURATION*4
290        NEXT CYCLE
291  ' write EOF flag
292  PRINT #1,0;-1;0;0;0
293  CLOSE #1
300  END
1000 REM******************************************************
1010 REM  Routine To Perform Reductive Series Sampling
1020 REM******************************************************
1160 REM                     Variable Descriptions
1170 REM     Entering -
1180 REM        SET(): initial value series
```

```
1190 REM         SERIES series length
1200 REM         TARGET: current set sample
1210 REM         FACTOR: sampling interval
1220 REM      Exiting -
1230 REM         none: (subroutine is procedural)
1240 REM      Local -
1250 REM         SETL: current set length (shrinks every iteration)
1270 REM         A(): bounce array 1
1280 REM         B(): bounce array 2
1290 REM         ACNT: pointer to A()
1300 REM         BCNT: pointer to B()
1310 REM         K9: loop index, pointer to A(),B()
1320 REM********************************************************
1330    SETL = SERIES
1340       FOR K9 = 1 TO SETL
1350          A(K9)=SET(K9)
1360       NEXT K9
1370    BCNT = 0
1380       FOR K9 = 1 TO SETL
1390          IF K9 = TARGET THEN PRINT A(K9)+LOWP;:TARGET=TARGET
    +FACTOR:PRINT #1,NOTEON;A(K9)+LOWP;VELOCITY;ARTDUR;CHANNEL
    :NOTEON=NOTEON+DURATION ELSE BCNT = BCNT + 1 :B(BCNT)=A(K9)
1400       NEXT K9
1410    IF BCNT < 1 THEN 1530
1420    TARGET = TARGET - SETL
1430    ACNT = 0
1440    IF TARGET MOD BCNT <> 0
          THEN TARGET = TARGET MOD BCNT
             ELSE TARGET = BCNT
1450       FOR K9 = 1 TO BCNT
1460          IF K9 = TARGET THEN PRINT B(K9)+LOWP;:TARGET=TARGET
    +FACTOR:PRINT #1,NOTEON;B(K9)+LOWP;VELOCITY;ARTDUR;CHANNEL
    :NOTEON=NOTEON+DURATION ELSE ACNT=ACNT + 1 : A(ACNT) = B(K9)
1470       NEXT K9
1480    IF ACNT < 1 THEN 1530
1490    SETL = ACNT
1500    TARGET = TARGET - BCNT
1510    IF TARGET MOD SETL <> 0
          THEN TARGET = TARGET MOD SETL
             ELSE TARGET = SETL
1520    GOTO 1370
1530    PRINT
1540 RETURN
```

Execution of Program #32a:

```
A SEQUENTIAL SET -
 1   2   3   4   5   6   7   8   9   10   11   12
PERMUTATION  1
SET START POSITION =  1 ; SET TARGET FACTOR=  2
 1   3   5   7   9   11   2   6   10   4   12   8
PERMUTATION  2
```

```
SET START POSITION =  1 ; SET TARGET FACTOR=  4
 1   5   9   2   7   12   8   4   3   6   11   10
PERMUTATION  3
SET START POSITION =  1 ; SET TARGET FACTOR=  6
 1   7   2   9   5   3   12   4   8   6   11   10
PERMUTATION  4
SET START POSITION =  1 ; SET TARGET FACTOR=  8
 1   9   6   4   3   5   8   12   11   7   2   10
PERMUTATION  5
SET START POSITION =  1 ; SET TARGET FACTOR=  10
 1   11   10   12   3   6   2   9   5   7   4   8
```

Troping. Program 32b systematically generates permutations of an original Pitch Class Series array by cyclical selection of series elements at uniform position-in-series intervals. In this program, the sampling interval is termed the order; sampling always begins at the first set position. For example, given the following PC set,

$$3\ 6\ 8\ 1\ 4\ 7\ 0\ 11\ 9\ 2\ 10\ 5$$

to calculate a trope, order 2, means to take every other set element-position in rotation,

$$1,3,5,7,9,11,2,4,6,8,10$$

yielding the permutation:

$$3\ 8\ 4\ 0\ 9\ 10\ 6\ 1\ 7\ 11\ 2\ 5.$$

Notice that, for sample-counting purposes, the set size is not reduced by the number of samples taken (as it is in Program #32a). Therefore, this troping method of generating permutations by sampling a PC series produces significantly different results. Compare the different effects of the two programs using identical PC Sets. The output using identical input data for Program #32a is:

$$3\ 8\ 4\ 0\ 9\ 10\ 1\ 11\ 5\ 7\ 6\ 2.$$

(Program #32b includes file-writing code for use with the MusicSculptor System.)

PROGRAM #32B

```
10 REM************************************************************
20 REM                      PROGRAM #32b
30 REM
40 REM  Demonstrate Cyclical, non-Reductive Sampling of PC Set
50 REM            (Sometimes Referred to as TROPING)
60 REM************************************************************
70 REM**************    Main Routine    *********************
80 REM************************************************************
90    DIM SET(12),TROPE(100)
91       ' next line initializes variables for MusicSculptor file
92    NOTEON=0:DURATION=60:VELOCITY=100:ARTDUR=55:CHANNEL=0
93    OPEN "O",#1,"PROG#32b.SC"
94    PRINT #1,"File-ID : 2"
95    PRINT #1,"Format : 1"
96 LOWP=60
100      GOSUB 1010
110      FOR J = 0 TO 11
120         PRINT SET(J);       '<< print user-entered PC Series
121         PITCH=SET(J) + LOWP
122         ' now file pitches
123         PRINT #1,NOTEON;PITCH;VELOCITY;ARTDUR;CHANNEL
124         NOTEON=NOTEON+DURATION
130      NEXT J
131    NOTEON=NOTEON+DURATION*4 ' add a rest
140      PRINT
150      FOR PERMUT = 1 TO 11
160         PRINT "Trope, Order: ";PERMUT
170         GOSUB 2000              '<< call non-reductive sampling
180         GOSUB 3000              '<< print current permutation
190      NEXT PERMUT
191 ' write EOF flag
192 PRINT #1,0;-1;0;0;0
193 CLOSE #1
200 END
1000 REM************************************************************
1010 REM    Routine to accept User-Input Pitch Class Series
1020 REM************************************************************
1030 PRINT "Enter a Pitch-Class Series (0-11), one PC per line:"
1040    FOR K9 = 0 TO 11
1050       INPUT SET(K9)
1060    NEXT K9
1070 RETURN
2000 REM************************************************************
2010 REM      Routine to Generate One Permutation (Trope)
2020 REM************************************************************
2030 COUNT = 0
2040    FOR OFFSET = 0 TO PERMUT - 1
```

```
2050        FOR SAMPLE = OFFSET TO 11 STEP PERMUT
2060            TROPE(COUNT) = SET(SAMPLE)
2070            COUNT = COUNT + 1
2080        NEXT SAMPLE
2090      NEXT OFFSET
2100 RETURN
3000 REM*********************************************************
3010 REM           Routine to Print Current Permutation
3020 REM*********************************************************
3030     FOR COUNT = 0 TO 11
3040        PRINT TROPE(COUNT);
3041        PITCH=TROPE(COUNT) + LOWP
3042        ' now file pitches
3043        PRINT #1,NOTEON;PITCH;VELOCITY;ARTDUR;CHANNEL
3044        NOTEON=NOTEON+DURATION
3050     NEXT COUNT
3055     ' put a rest in file
3056     NOTEON=NOTEON+DURATION*4
3060     PRINT
3070 RETURN
```

Execution of Program #32b:

```
Enter a Pitch-Class Series (0-11), one PC per line:
? 3
? 6
? 8
? 1
? 4
? 7
? 0
? 11
? 9
? 2
? 10
? 5
 3   6   8   1   4   7   0   11   9   2   10   5
Trope, Order: 1
 3   6   8   1   4   7   0   11   9   2   10   5
Trope, Order: 2
 3   8   4   0   9   10   6   1   7   11   2   5
Trope, Order: 3
 3   1   0   2   6   4   11   10   8   7   9   5
Trope, Order: 4
 3   4   9   6   7   2   8   0   10   1   11   5
Trope, Order: 5
 3   7   10   6   0   5   8   11   1   9   4   2
Trope, Order: 6
 3   0   6   11   8   9   1   2   4   10   7   5
```

```
Trope, Order: 7
 3  11  6  9  8  2  1  10  4  5  7  0
Trope, Order: 8
 3  9  6  2  8  10  1  5  4  7  0  11
Trope, Order: 9
 3  2  6  10  8  5  1  4  7  0  11  9
Trope, Order: 10
 3  10  6  5  8  1  4  7  0  11  9  2
Trope, Order: 11
 3  5  6  8  1  4  7  0  11  9  2  10
```

All-Interval Series

Program #33 generates all-interval 12-note series by the sample-test-discard/keep method. Although this "brute force" approach is rather slow, it can produce satisfactory results over short runs. Runs approaching 100 output sets can best be achieved by executing a compiled version of the program.

The routine which begins in Line 3000 performs an identity check on the all-interval series generated by the routine which begins in Line 1000. Each output set is converted to a character string, tested against all previously stored sets for uniqueness, then put in a character string array.

(Program #33 includes file-writing code for use with the MusicSculptor System.)

PROGRAM #33

```
10  REM*********************************************************
20  REM                      PROGRAM #33
30  REM
40  REM  Demonstrate All-Interval Pitch Class Series Concept
50  REM*********************************************************
60  REM***************    Main Routine    ********************
70  REM*********************************************************
80     DIM PCLASS(12),PCUM(12),ICUM(12),TEMP(12),ALSET$(10)
81        ' next line initializes variables for MusicSculptor file
82  NOTEON=0:DURATION=60:VELOCITY=100:ARTDUR=55:CHANNEL=0
83  OPEN "O",#1,"PROG#33.SC"
84  PRINT #1,"File-ID : 2"
85  PRINT #1,"Format : 1"
86  LOWP=60
90     TOTAL = 10
100    SETCOUNT = 0
110    RANDOMIZE(TIMER)
120       FOR J = 1 TO TOTAL
```

```
130            PRINT "COMPUTING -- ALL-INTERVAL 12-TONE SET #";J
140            GOSUB 1000       '<< call all-interval set generator
150            IF FLAG = 1 THEN PRINT ALSET$(SETCOUNT)
                   ELSE GOSUB 1000
160        NEXT J
161 ' write EOF flag
162 PRINT #1,0;-1;0;0;0
163 CLOSE #1
170 END
1000 REM*********************************************************
1010 REM   Routine to Generate All-Interval Pitch Class Series
1020 REM*********************************************************
1110 REM                  Variable Descriptions
1120 REM      Entering -
1130 REM         none
1140 REM      Exiting -
1150 REM         PCLASS(): array holding all-interval series
1160 REM      Local -
1170 REM         PCUM(): array of note redundancy flags
1180 REM         ICUM(): array of interval redundancy flags
1190 REM         TEMP(): array holding temporary trial series
1200 REM         INTSIZE: interval (in 1/2-steps) between notes
1210 REM         R9: random integer for test series
1220 REM         K9: loop index, pointer to TEMP()
1230 REM         L9: loop index, pointer to TEMP(), PCLASS()
1240 REM         M9: loop index, pointer to TEMP(), PCLASS()
1250 REM*********************************************************
1260    PCLASS(1) = 1 : PCLASS(12) = 7
1270       FOR K9 = 2 TO 11
1280          R9 = INT(RND * 11) + 2
1290          IF R9 = 7 THEN 1280
1300          IF PCUM(R9) = 1 THEN 1280
1310          TEMP(K9) = R9
1320          PCUM(R9) = 1
1330       NEXT K9
1340       FOR L9 = 2 TO 12
1350          FOR M9 = 2 TO 11
1360             IF TEMP(M9) > 0
                    THEN INTSIZE = TEMP(M9) - PCLASS(L9-1)
                        ELSE 1390
1370             IF INTSIZE < 0 THEN INTSIZE = 12 + INTSIZE
1380             IF ICUM(INTSIZE) < 1 THEN PCLASS(L9) = TEMP(M9)
                    : TEMP(M9) = 0 : ICUM(INTSIZE) = 1
                        : GOTO 1410 ELSE 1390
1390          NEXT M9
1400          IF PCLASS(L9) = 0 THEN GOSUB 2000 : GOTO 1200
1410       NEXT L9
1420    GOSUB 3000 : GOSUB 2000
1430 RETURN 150
```

```
2000 REM**********************************************************
2010 REM         Routine to Reset Array Contents to Zero
2020 REM**********************************************************
2030    FOR L9 = 1 TO 12
2040        PCUM(L9) = 0 : ICUM(L9) = 0 : PCLASS(L9) = 0
2050    NEXT L9
2060 RETURN
3000 REM**********************************************************
3010 REM    Routine to Store Unique All-Interval PC Sets
3020 REM**********************************************************
3100 REM                    Variable Descriptions
3110 REM      Entering -
3120 REM        PCLASS(): holds current pitchclass (integer) set
3130 REM      Exiting -
3140 REM        ALSET$(): string array holding all unique sets
3150 REM        SETCOUNT: index of unique all-interval sets
3160 REM        FLAG: indicator of set uniqueness
3170 REM      Local -
3180 REM        L9: loop index, pointer to PCLASS()
3190 REM        CURSET$: string buffer holding current set
3200 REM**********************************************************
3210    CURSET$ = ""
3220      FOR L9=1 TO 12
3230          CURSET$ = CURSET$ + STR$(PCLASS(L9)-1)
3231      PITCH=PCLASS(L9) + LOWP
3232      ' now file pitches
3233      PRINT #1,NOTEON;PITCH;VELOCITY;ARTDUR;CHANNEL
3235      NOTEON=NOTEON+DURATION
3240       NEXT L9
3241 ' put a rest in file
3242 NOTEON=NOTEON+DURATION*4
3250    SETCOUNT = SETCOUNT + 1
3260      FOR L9 = 1 TO SETCOUNT - 1
3270      IF ALSET$(L9) = CURSET$ THEN FLAG = 0 : RETURN
3280      NEXT L9
3290    ALSET$(SETCOUNT)=CURSET$
3300    FLAG = 1
3310 RETURN
```

Execution of Program #33:

```
COMPUTING -- ALL-INTERVAL 12-TONE SET # 1
 0 5 7 11 2 3 1 8 4 10 9 6
COMPUTING -- ALL-INTERVAL 12-TONE SET # 2
 0 2 11 4 8 7 1 9 10 5 3 6
COMPUTING -- ALL-INTERVAL 12-TONE SET # 3
 0 5 2 9 1 3 4 10 8 11 7 6
```

```
COMPUTING -- ALL-INTERVAL 12-TONE SET # 4
  0 3 11 10 5 9 2 4 1 7 8 6
COMPUTING -- ALL-INTERVAL 12-TONE SET # 5
  0 9 8 1 7 11 2 10 5 3 4 6
COMPUTING -- ALL-INTERVAL 12-TONE SET # 6
  0 4 10 3 1 9 11 8 7 2 5 6
COMPUTING -- ALL-INTERVAL 12-TONE SET # 7
  0 7 11 4 5 2 10 1 3 9 8 6
COMPUTING -- ALL-INTERVAL 12-TONE SET # 8
  0 2 3 7 5 1 8 11 10 4 9 6
COMPUTING -- ALL-INTERVAL 12-TONE SET # 9
  0 1 10 3 7 2 8 11 9 5 4 6
COMPUTING -- ALL-INTERVAL 12-TONE SET # 10
  0 7 8 2 11 9 1 4 3 5 10 6
```

Serial Time Point System

Program #34 implements the Serial Time Point System to produce rhythm duration values. That is, a sequence of time durations, mod n, is derived from the distance between consecutive set members. The modulus determines the number of metrical pulses contained within one measure.

PROGRAM #34

```
10  REM****************************************************************
20  REM                        PROGRAM #34
30  REM
40  REM       Demonstrate Serial Time-Point System Concept
50  REM****************************************************************
60  REM***************    Main Routine    *********************
70  REM****************************************************************
80    DIM SET(12),CUM(12)
90    DIM P$(12),FRACTION$(12)
100    MDLS = 4                              '<< set modulus to 4
110    MEDIAN = 16
120      GOSUB 1000                     '<< call pitch class table
130      GOSUB 2000           '<< call user-input PC set routine
140    PRINT "The PC character series MOD ";MDLS;"--"
150      FOR J1 =  0 TO 11
160        PRINT P$(SET(J1));" ";   '<< series to screen
170      NEXT J1
180    PRINT
190    PRINT "THE NUMERIC EQUIVALENT --"
200      FOR J1 = 0 TO 11
210        PRINT SET(J1);
220      NEXT J1
230    PRINT
```

```
240    PRINT "DURATIONS REPRESENTING THE DISTANCE";
          " BETWEEN TIME POINTS --"
250        PRINT "(USING A 16TH-NOTE PULSE BASE ";
              "AND A MEASURE OF ";MDLS;"-16THS)"
260     GOSUB 3000              '<< call timepoint generator
270     FOR J1 = 0 TO 11
280        PRINT FRACTION$(J1);  '<< timepoints to screen
290     NEXT J1
300    PRINT "TOTAL OF DURATIONS =";TALLY;
310 END
1000 REM***********************************************************
1010 REM     Routine to load a Pitch Class Character Array
1020 REM***********************************************************
1030      FOR J = 0 TO 11
1040         READ P$(J)         '<< load pitch class character
set
1050      NEXT J
1060 REM++++++++++++++++++++++++++++++++++++
1070    DATA C,C#,D,D#,E,F,F#,G,G#,A,A#,B
1080 REM++++++++++++++++++++++++++++++++++++
1090 RETURN
2000 REM***********************************************************
2010 REM   Routine to accept User-Input Pitch Class Series
2020 REM***********************************************************
2030 PRINT "Enter a Pitch Class Series (0-11), one PC per line:"
2040    FOR K9 = 0 TO 11
2050       INPUT SET(K9)
2060    NEXT K9
2070 RETURN
3000 REM***********************************************************
3010 REM   Routine to Derive Time-Point Series from PC Series
3020 REM***********************************************************
3030 REM                   Variable Descriptions
3040 REM     Entering -
3050 REM       SET(): array of series values
3060 REM       MDLS: modulus for computation
3070 REM       MEDIAN: basic pulse unit
3080 REM     Exiting -
3090 REM       FRACTION$(): character array of time durations
3100 REM       TALLY: total of time durations
3110 REM     Local -
3120 REM       DUR: fraction numerator
3130 REM       K9: loop index, pointer to SET()
3140 REM***********************************************************
3150    TALLY = 0
3160       FOR K9 = 0 TO 10
3170          IF SET(K9+1) <= SET(K9)
                THEN DUR = MDLS - SET(K9) + SET(K9+1)
                   ELSE DUR = SET(K9+1) - SET(K9)
```

```
3180            TALLY = TALLY + DUR
3190            FRACTION$(K9) = STR$(DUR) + "/" + STR$(MEDIAN)
3200        NEXT K9
3210     DUR = MDLS - SET(K9)
3220     TALLY = TALLY + DUR
3230     FRACTION$(11) = STR$(DUR) + "/" + STR$(MEDIAN)
3240 RETURN
```

Execution of Program #34:

```
Enter a Pitch-Class Series (0-11), one PC per line:
? 5
? 7
? 8
? 2
? 9
? 10
? 3
? 6
? 1
? 4
? 11
? 0
The PC character series MOD  4 --
F G G# D A A# D# F# C# E B C
THE NUMERIC EQUIVALENT --
 5  7  8  2  9  10  3  6  1  4  11  0
DURATIONS REPRESENTING THE DISTANCE BETWEEN TIME POINTS --
(USING A 16TH-NOTE PULSE BASE AND A MEASURE OF  4 -16THS)
 2/ 16 1/ 16-2/ 16 7/ 16 1/ 16-3/ 16 3/ 16-1/ 16 3/ 16 7/ 16-7/
16 4/ 16
TOTAL OF DURATIONS = 15
```

9

Melodic Transformation, Analysis, and Sort-Search

Procedures

Motif transformation procedures are related to pitch class series operations, but they differ in two important respects. First, a motive may be of any length, and second, it may have repeated elements within it.

Elementary Transforms. Program #35 demonstrates some fundamental motif transformation techniques. Execute it several times, then adapt the program to an idea of your own for the composition and transformation of melodic material.

(Program #35 includes file-writing code for use with the MusicSculptor System.)

PROGRAM #35

```
10 REM***************************************************************
20 REM                          PROGRAM #35
30 REM
40 REM   Demonstrate Elementary Motive Tranformation Procedures
50 REM***************************************************************
60 REM***************     Main Routine      ********************
70 REM***************************************************************
80    DIM X(15),Y(15),P$(128)
81       ' next line initializes variables for MusicSculptor
file
82 NOTEON=0:DURATION=60:VELOCITY=100:ARTDUR=55:CHANNEL=0
83 OPEN "O",#1,"PROG#35.SC"
84 PRINT #1,"File-ID : 2"
90    GOSUB 6000                              '<< call pitch table
100    INPUT "How many notes in the melody? ",TOTAL
```

```
110     GOSUB 1000 '<< call user-input motif
120     GOSUB 3000                          '<< call retrograde
130     PRINT "THE RETROGRADE MOTIF --"
140     GOSUB 2000                 '<< call motive print routine
150     PRINT
160     GOSUB 4000                      '<< call motif inversion
170     PRINT "THE INVERTED MOTIF --"
180     GOSUB 2000                 '<< call motive print routine
190     PRINT
200     INTVAL = 1              '<<  set transposition interval
210     PRINT "ORIGINAL MOTIF TRANSPOSITIONS"
220        FOR J = 1 TO 11
230           PRINT "NUMBER ";J
240           GOSUB 5000            '<< call motif transposition
250           GOSUB 2000            '<< call motive print routine
260           PRINT
270           INTVAL = INTVAL + 1
280        NEXT J
281 ' write EOF flag
282 PRINT #1,0;-1;0;0;0
283 CLOSE #1
290 END
1000 REM*********************************************************
1010 REM    Routine to accept User-Input Melodic Motive (numeric)
1020 REM*********************************************************
1030 PRINT "Enter a Pitch Motif (range 50-70), one # per line:"
1040    FOR K9 = 1 TO TOTAL
1050        INPUT X(K9)
1051        PITCH=X(K9)
1052        ' now file pitches
1053        PRINT #1,NOTEON;PITCH;VELOCITY;ARTDUR;CHANNEL
1054        NOTEON=NOTEON+DURATION
1060    NEXT K9
1061 ' put a rest in file
1062 NOTEON=NOTEON+DURATION*4
1070 RETURN
2000 REM*********************************************************
2010 REM Routine to Print Motive Transformations
2020 REM*********************************************************
2030        FOR K9 = 1 TO TOTAL
2040           PRINT P$(Y(K9));" ";
2041           PITCH=Y(K9)
2042           ' now file pitches
2043           PRINT #1,NOTEON;PITCH;VELOCITY;ARTDUR;CHANNEL
2044           NOTEON=NOTEON+DURATION
2050        NEXT K9
2051 ' put a rest in file
2052 NOTEON=NOTEON+DURATION*4
2060 RETURN
```

```
3000 REM************************************************************
3010 REM Routine to Compute Retrograde Transform of Motive
3020 REM************************************************************
3030 REM    This subroutine accepts an input pitch sequence
3040 REM    and outputs its retrograde form.
3050 REM************************************************************
3060 REM                Variable Descriptions
3070 REM    Entering -
3080 REM      X(): prime motif array
3090 REM      TOTAL: motif length
3100 REM    Exiting -
3110 REM      Y(): retrograde motif array
3120 REM    Local -
3130 REM      L: pointer to Y()
3140 REM      K9; loop index, pointer to X()
3150 REM************************************************************
3160    FOR K9 = 1 TO TOTAL
3170       L = TOTAL-K9+1
3180        Y(L)=X(K9)
3190    NEXT K9
3200 RETURN
4000 REM************************************************************
4010 REM Routine to Compute Inversion Transform of Motive
4020 REM************************************************************
4030 REM    This subroutine accepts an input pitch sequence
4040 REM    and outputs its inversion (mirror) form.
4050 REM************************************************************
4060 REM                Variable Descriptions
4070 REM    Entering -
4080 REM      X(): prime motif array
4090 REM      TOTAL: motif length
4100 REM    Exiting -
4110 REM      Y(): inverted motif array
4120 REM    Local -
4130 REM      K9: loop index, pointer to X(),Y()
4140 REM =======================================================
4150    Y(1)=X(1)
4160       FOR K9 = 2 TO TOTAL
4170          Y(K9) = Y(K9-1)-(X(K9)-X(K9-1))
4180       NEXT K9
4190 RETURN
5000 REM************************************************************
5010 REM        Routine to Transpose Motive Forms
5020 REM************************************************************
5030 REM    This subroutine transposes an input motif by
5040 REM    a specified number of 1/2 steps. Transposition
5050 REM    direction is determined by the sign of the
5060 REM    transposition interval.
5070 REM************************************************************
```

```
5080 REM              Variable Descriptions
5090 REM      Entering -
5100 REM        X(): array holding random motif
5110 REM        TOTAL: motif length
5120 REM        INTVAL: interval of transposition in 1/2-steps
5130 REM      Exiting -
5140 REM        Y(): array holding transposed motif
5150 REM      Local -
5160 REM        K9: loop index, pointer to Y()
5170 REM ========================================================
5180    FOR K9 = 1 TO TOTAL
5190       Y(K9) = X(K9) + INTVAL
5200    NEXT K9
5210 RETURN
6000 REM:*****************************************************
6010 REM:     Routine to Load Pitch Character Element Array
6020 REM:*****************************************************
6030    FOR COUNT = 1 TO 128
6040       READ P$(COUNT)    'fill array with pitch characters
6050    NEXT COUNT
6060    PRINT
6070    DATA C0,C#0,D0,D#0,E0,F0,F#0,G0,Ab0,A0,Bb0,B0
6080    DATA C1,C#1,D1,D#1,E1,F1,F#1,G1,Ab1,A1,Bb1,B1
6090    DATA C2,C#2,D2,D#2,E2,F2,F#2,G2,Ab2,A2,Bb2,B2
6100    DATA C3,C#3,D3,D#3,E3,F3,F#3,G3,Ab3,A3,Bb3,B3
6110    DATA C4,C#4,D4,D#4,E4,F4,F#4,G4,Ab4,A4,Bb4,B4
6120    DATA C5,C#5,D5,D#5,E5,F5,F#5,G5,Ab5,A5,Bb5,B5
6130    DATA C6,C#6,D6,D#6,E6,F6,F#6,G6,Ab6,A6,Bb6,B6
6140    DATA C7,C#7,D7,D#7,E7,F7,F#7,G7,Ab7,A7,Bb7,B7
6150    DATA C8,C#8,D8,D#8,E8,F8,F#8,G8,Ab8,A8,Bb8,B8
6160    DATA C9,C#9,D9,D#9,E9,F9,F#9,G9,Ab9,A9,Bb9,B9
6170    DATA C10,C#10,D10,D#10,E10,F10,F#10,G10
6180 RETURN
```

Execution of Program #35:

```
How many notes in the melody? 8
Enter a Pitch Motif (range 50-70), one # per line:
? 40
? 41
? 44
? 60
? 63
? 69
? 60
? 62
THE RETROGRADE MOTIF --
C#5 B4 Ab5 D5 B4 G3 E3 D#3
```

```
THE INVERTED MOTIF --
D#3 D3 B2 G1 E1 Bb0 G1 F1
ORIGINAL MOTIF TRANSPOSITIONS
NUMBER  1
E3 F3 Ab3 C5 D#5 A5 C5 D5
NUMBER  2
F3 F#3 A3 C#5 E5 Bb5 C#5 D#5
NUMBER  3
F#3 G3 Bb3 D5 F5 B5 D5 E5
NUMBER  4
G3 Ab3 B3 D#5 F#5 C6 D#5 F5
NUMBER  5
Ab3 A3 C4 E5 G5 C#6 E5 F#5
NUMBER  6
A3 Bb3 C#4 F5 Ab5 D6 F5 G5
NUMBER  7
Bb3 B3 D4 F#5 A5 D#6 F#5 Ab5
NUMBER  8
B3 C4 D#4 G5 Bb5 E6 G5 A5
NUMBER  9
C4 C#4 E4 Ab5 B5 F6 Ab5 Bb5
NUMBER  10
C#4 D4 F4 A5 C6 F#6 A5 B5
NUMBER  11
D4 D#4 F#4 Bb5 C#6 G6 Bb5 C6
```

Interval Alteration. Program #36 does its work on the intervals contained in a melodic sequence, not on the pitch classes. It is similar to writing music on a rubber sheet, then vertically stretching or compressing the sheet to bring the pitches closer together or take them farther apart.

    (Program #36 includes file-writing code for use with the MusicSculptor System.)

PROGRAM #36

```
10  REM*********************************************************
20  REM                      PROGRAM #36
30  REM
40  REM  Demonstrate Expansion/Contraction of a Number Sequence
50  REM*********************************************************
60  REM**************    Main Routine    *********************
70  REM*********************************************************
80      DIM X(12),Y(12)
81        ' next line initializes variables for MusicSculptor file
82      NOTEON=0:DURATION=60:VELOCITY=100:ARTDUR=55:CHANNEL=0
```

```
83      OPEN "O",#1,"PROG#36.SC"
84      PRINT #1,"File-ID : 2"
90      INPUT "How Many Numbers will you enter (range 50-70)? ",
            TOTAL
100     GOSUB 1000              '<< user-input number list routine
110     INTSIZE = 5             '<< expand the sequence intervals
120     PRINT
130     PRINT "The sequence will be expanded by 5 semitones"
140        FOR J = 1 TO 2
150           PRINT "PASS";J
160           PRINT "ALTERATION INTEGER =";INTSIZE"
170           PRINT "ALTERED SEQUENCE --"
180           GOSUB 2000         '<< call sequence alteration routine
190           PRINT "Sequence will be contracted by 5 semitones"
200           FOR J1 = 1 TO TOTAL
210              PRINT Y(J1);   '<< send altered sequence to screen
211              PITCH=Y(J1)
212              ' now file pitches
213              PRINT #1,NOTEON;PITCH;VELOCITY;ARTDUR;CHANNEL
214              NOTEON=NOTEON+DURATION
220           NEXT J1
230           INTSIZE = - 5     '<< contract the sequence intervals
231           ' put a rest in file
232           NOTEON=NOTEON+DURATION*4
240           PRINT
250        NEXT J
251    ' write EOF flag
252    PRINT #1,0;-1;0;0;0
253    CLOSE #1
260 END
1000 REM***************************************************************
1010 REM    Routine to accept User-Input Melodic Motive (numeric)
1020 REM***************************************************************
1030     FOR K9 = 1 TO TOTAL
1040        INPUT X(K9)
1041        PITCH=X(K9)
1042        ' now file pitches
1043        PRINT #1,NOTEON;PITCH;VELOCITY;ARTDUR;CHANNEL
1044        NOTEON=NOTEON+DURATION
1050     NEXT K9
1051     ' put a rest in file
1052     NOTEON=NOTEON+DURATION*4
1060 RETURN
2000 REM***************************************************************
2010 REM  Routine to Intervallically Expand or Contract a list
2020 REM***************************************************************
2030 REM     This subroutine alters a value sequence by interval
2040 REM     expansion or contraction. Positive integers expand
2050 REM     the sequence, negative integers contract it.
```

```
2060 REM      Note that contractions smaller than a semitone are
2070 REM      disallowed.
2080 REM*********************************************************
2090 REM                  Variable Descriptions
2100 REM      Entering -
2110 REM        X(): primary value sequence
2120 REM        TOTAL: length of sequence
2130 REM        INTSIZE: size of alteration interval in units
2140 REM      Exiting -
2150 REM        X(): primary value sequence
2160 REM        Y(): altered value sequence
2170 REM      Local -
2180 REM        INTDIR: direction of alteration
2190 REM        INTVAL: altered interval
2200 REM        K9: loop index, pointer to X(),Y()
2210 REM*********************************************************
2220    Y(1) = X(1)
2230       FOR K9 = 2 TO TOTAL
2240          IF X(K9) <> X(K9-1) THEN 2250
                 ELSE Y(K9) = Y(K9-1) : GOTO 2290
2250          INTDIR = SGN(X(K9)-X(K9-1))
2260          INTVAL=ABS(X(K9)-X(K9-1))+INTSIZE
2270          IF INTVAL <1 THEN INTVAL = 1
2280          Y(K9)=Y(K9-1)+INTDIR * INTVAL
2290       NEXT K9
2300 RETURN
```

Execution of Program #36:

```
How Many Numbers will you enter?12

Enter a number list (range 30-70), one # per line:

?41
?50
?42
?66
?58
?54
?60
?65
?40
?39
?44
?34

PASS 1
ALTERATION INTEGER = 5
ALTERED SEQUENCE --
  41  55  42  71  58  49  60  70  40  34  44  29
```

```
PASS 2
ALTERATION INTEGER =-5
ALTERED SEQUENCE --
 41   45   42   61   58   57   58   59   39   38   39   34
```

Octave Displacement. Program #37 can also expand or contract the intervals of a pitch sequence, but it does so in a radically different manner from Program #36: it adds or subtracts octave multiples of the original value to shift its register around the musical canvas. Called octave-register displacement, this approach preserves the original tonal character of the input array, while creating contrast through the introduction of angularity.

(Program #37 includes file-writing code for use with the MusicSculptor System.)

PROGRAM #37

```
10  REM*********************************************************
20  REM                      PROGRAM #37
30  REM
40  REM     Demonstrate Octave Register Pitch Displacement of
50  REM          Individual Members of a Melodic Motive.
60  REM*********************************************************
70  REM***************    Main Routine    *********************
80  REM*********************************************************
90     DIM P$(108)
100    DIM X(30),Y(30)
110    DIM DISP(30) '<< array to store pitch octave-displacement
111    ' next line initializes variables for MusicSculptor file
112    NOTEON=0:DURATION=60:VELOCITY=100:ARTDUR=55:CHANNEL=0
113    OPEN "O",#1,"PROG#37.SC"
114    PRINT #1,"File-ID : 2"
115    PRINT #1,"Format : 1"
120    RANDOMIZE(TIMER) '<< program will generate random pitches
130    GOSUB 2000                         '<< call pitch table
131 LOWP=25
140    TOTAL = 30                '<< sequence will have 10 notes
150       FOR J= 1 TO TOTAL
160          X(J) = INT(RND * 12) + LOWP '<< load random pitches
161          PITCH=X(J)
162     (    ' now file pitches
163          PRINT #1,NOTEON;PITCH;VELOCITY;ARTDUR;CHANNEL
164          NOTEON=NOTEON+DURATION
170          DISP(J) = INT(RND * 5)+1'<load random octave displ.
180          PRINT P$(X(J));" WILL BE DISPLACED BY ";
                  DISP(J);"OCTAVE(S)"
```

```
190        NEXT J
191      ' put a rest in file
192      NOTEON=NOTEON+DURATION*4
200      GOSUB 1000                    '<< call registral displacement
210        FOR J = 1 TO TOTAL
220            PRINT P$(Y(J));" "; : PITCH=Y(J)
221            ' now file pitches
222            PRINT #1,NOTEON;PITCH;VELOCITY;ARTDUR;CHANNEL
223            NOTEON=NOTEON+DURATION
230        NEXT J
231 ' write EOF flag
232 PRINT #1,0;-1;0;0;0
233 CLOSE #1
240 END
1000 REM*********************************************************
1010 REM    Routine to Displace Individual Melodic Pitches
1020 REM*********************************************************
1030 REM    This subroutine (individually) displaces the pitches
1040 REM    of an input sequence by a specific number of octaves.
1050 REM*********************************************************
1060 REM ·              Variable Descriptions
1070 REM    Entering -
1080 REM      X(): array holding undisplaced pitch sequence
1090 REM      DISP(): array holding individual pitch displacements
1100 REM      TOTAL: sequence length
1110 REM    Exiting -
1120 REM      Y(): array containing octave-displaced pitches
1130 REM    Local -
1140 REM      K9: loop index, pointer to DISP(),X(),Y()
1150 REM ========================================================
1160 REM
1170    FOR K9 = 1 TO TOTAL
1180        Y(K9)=X(K9) + 12 * DISP(K9)
1190    NEXT K9
1200 RETURN
2000 REM*********************************************************
2010 REM          Routine to Load a Pitch Character Array
2020 REM                    Using String Functions
2030 REM*********************************************************
2040    NOTE$ = " CC# DD# E FF# GG# AA# B"
2050    OCTAVE$ = "1234567"
2060       FOR K9 = 1 TO 9
2070          FOR L9 = 1 TO 12
2080             P$(L9+(K9-1)*12-1) =
                 MID$(NOTE$,(L9*2-1),2)+MID$(OCTAVE$,K9,1)
2090          NEXT L9
2100       NEXT K9
2110 RETURN
```

Execution of Program #37:

```
 A1 WILL BE DISPLACED BY  2 OCTAVE(S)
F#1 WILL BE DISPLACED BY  5 OCTAVE(S)
G#1 WILL BE DISPLACED BY  4 OCTAVE(S)
 B1 WILL BE DISPLACED BY  6 OCTAVE(S)
 D1 WILL BE DISPLACED BY  5 OCTAVE(S)
 D1 WILL BE DISPLACED BY  2 OCTAVE(S)
 A1 WILL BE DISPLACED BY  3 OCTAVE(S)
 F1 WILL BE DISPLACED BY  6 OCTAVE(S)
D#1 WILL BE DISPLACED BY  4 OCTAVE(S)
D#1 WILL BE DISPLACED BY  5 OCTAVE(S)
 A3 F#6 G#5  B7  D6  D3  A4  F7 D#5 D#6
```

Statistical Measurement

Sometimes it is desirable to provide analytical information for the purposes of (1) basing further generations of material on characteristics inherent in user-entered sequences, (2) development and testing of algorithms, and (3) analysis of probability distribution functions for conformity to idealized curves.

Program #38 contains a number of statistical routines which serve these goals.

PROGRAM #38

```
10 REM*********************************************************
20 REM                    PROGRAM #38
30 REM
40 REM    Demonstrate Statistical Methods for Music Analysis
50 REM*********************************************************
60 REM***************    Main Routine    ********************
70 REM*********************************************************
80    DIM X(200),Y(15)'<< sequence array, frequency table array
90    RANGE = 15              '<< set random number range 1-15
100   TOTAL = 200                     '<< return 200 values
110   RANDOMIZE(20495)  '<< program will generate random values
120   GOSUB 1000  '<< generate sequence array & frequency table
130   GOSUB 2000                      '<< call bargraph display
140   GOSUB 3000            '<< call statistical mode (maxval)
150   GOSUB 4000            '<< call least frequent (minval)
160   GOSUB 5000                     '<< call arithmetic mean
170   GOSUB 6000               '<< call statistical variance
180   GOSUB 7000               '<< call standard deviation
190 END
1000 REM*********************************************************
1010 REM    Routine to compile an Occurrence Frequency Table
```

```
1020 REM*********************************************************
1030    FOR K9 = 1 TO TOTAL
1040           VALUE = INT(RND * RANGE)+1      '<< gen random value
1050           X(K9) = VALUE                   '<< load sequence array
1060           Y(VALUE)=Y(VALUE)+1  '<< record occurrence of value
1070    NEXT K9
1080 RETURN
2000 REM*********************************************************
2010 REM    Routine to Print a Bargraph of Frequency Table
2020 REM*********************************************************
2030    FOR K9 = 1 TO RANGE
2040       PRINT K9;TAB(10);STRING$(Y(K9),">")
2050    NEXT K9
2060 RETURN
3000 REM*********************************************************
3010 REM    Routine to Find Most Frequent Value in a Dataset
3020 REM*********************************************************
3030 REM     This subroutine finds the statistical mode of
3040 REM     a collection of values. It scans the integer
3050 REM     frequency table, then records the address and
3060 REM     number of occurrence of the most frequent value(s).
3070 REM*********************************************************
3080 REM                 Variable Descriptions
3090 REM     Entering -
3100 REM      Y(): occurrence frequency table
3110 REM      RANGE: range of integer values in table
3120 REM     Exiting -
3130 REM      none   (subroutine is procedural)
3140 REM     Local -
3150 REM      MAX: statistical mode
3160 REM      K9: loop index, pointer to frequency table
3170 REM*********************************************************
3180    MAX = Y(1)
3190       FOR K9 = 2 TO RANGE
3200          IF MAX < Y(K9) THEN MAX = Y(K9)
3210       NEXT K9
3220       FOR K9 = 1 TO RANGE
3230          IF Y(K9) = MAX THEN PRINT "THE INTEGER";K9;
                     "= MODE;";"FREQ =";MAX
3240       NEXT K9
3250 RETURN
4000 REM*********************************************************
4010 REM    Routine to Find Least Frequent Value in a Dataset
4020 REM*********************************************************
4030 REM     This subroutine scans the occurrence frequency
4040 REM     table, then records the address and number of
4050 REM     occurrences of the least frequent value.
4060 REM*********************************************************
4070 REM                 Variable Descriptions
```

```
4080 REM     Entering -
4090 REM       Y(): occurrence frequency table
4100 REM       RANGE: range of integer values in table
4110 REM     Exiting -
4120 REM       none   (subroutine is procedural)
4130 REM     Local -
4140 REM       MIN: least frequent integer
4150 REM       K9: loop index, pointer to array Y()
4160 REM*********************************************************
4170    MIN = Y(1)
4180       FOR K9 = 2 TO RANGE
4190          IF MIN > Y(K9) THEN MIN = Y(K9)
4200       NEXT K9
4210       FOR K9 = 1 TO RANGE
4220          IF Y(K9) = MIN THEN PRINT "THE INTEGER";K9;" =
                 LEAST FREQUENT;";" FREQ =";MIN
4230       NEXT K9
4240 RETURN
5000 REM*********************************************************
5010 REM    Routine to Find Arithmetic Mean of a Dataset
5020 REM*********************************************************
5030 REM                  Variable Descriptions
5040 REM     Entering -
5050 REM       TOTAL: length of sequence
5060 REM     Exiting -
5070 REM       none   (subroutine is procedural)
5080 REM     Local -
5090 REM       SUM: sum of sequence values
5100 REM       MEAN: arithmetic mean of values
5110 REM       K9: loop index, pointer to sequence array X()
5120 REM*********************************************************
5130     SUM = 0
5140       FOR K9 = 1 TO TOTAL
5150          SUM = SUM + X(K9)
5160       NEXT K9
5170     MEAN = SUM / TOTAL
5180     PRINT "MEAN =";MEAN;" ";
5190 RETURN
6000 REM*********************************************************
6010 REM    Routine to Compute Statistical Variance of a Dataset
6020 REM*********************************************************
6030 REM                  Variable Descriptions
6040 REM     Entering -
6050 REM       TOTAL: length of sequence
6060 REM       MEAN: arithmetic mean of sequence values
6070 REM     Exiting -
6080 REM       none   (subroutine is procedural)
6090 REM     Local -
6100 REM       VARIANCE: statistical variance
```

```
6110 REM      TEMP: temporary storage of computation
6120 REM       K9: loop index, pointer to sequence array X()
6130 REM********************************************************
6140    VARIANCE = 0
6150      FOR K9 = 1 TO TOTAL
6160         TEMP = (X(K9) - MEAN) ^ 2
6170           VARIANCE = VARIANCE + TEMP
6180      NEXT K9
6190    VARIANCE = VARIANCE / (TOTAL - 1)
6200    PRINT "VARIANCE = ";VARIANCE
6210 RETURN
7000 REM********************************************************
7010 REM     Routine to Compute Standard Deviation and
7020 REM     Standard Error of the Mean of a Dataset.
7030 REM********************************************************
7040 REM                  Variable Descriptions
7050 REM     Entering -
7060 REM      VARIANCE: statistical variance
7070 REM     Exiting -
7080 REM      none    (subroutine is procedural)
7090 REM     Local -
7100 REM      DEV: standard deviation
7110 REM      STDERR: standard error of the mean
7120 REM********************************************************
7130    DEV = SQR(VARIANCE)
7140    STDERR = DEV / SQR(TOTAL)
7150    PRINT "STANDARD DEVIATION = ";DEV
7160    PRINT "STANDARD ERROR OF THE MEAN = ";STDERR
7170 RETURN
```

Execution of Program #38:

```
1        >>>>>>>>>>>
2        >>>>>>>>>>>>>>>>>>
3        >>>>>>>>>>>>>>>
4        >>>>>>>>>>>>>>>>
5        >>>>>>>>>
6        >>>>>>>>>>>>>>
7        >>>>>>>>>>>>>>
8        >>>>>>>>>>>>>
9        >>>>>>>>>>>>>>>
10       >>>>
11       >>>>>>>>>>>>>>>>>>>
12       >>>>>>>>
13       >>>>>>>>>>>>>>
14       >>>>>>>>>>>>>
15       >>>>>>>>>>>>
```

THE INTEGER 11 = MODE; FREQ = 20
THE INTEGER 10 = LEAST FREQUENT; FREQ = 4
MEAN = 7.7 VARIANCE = 18.96482
STANDARD DEVIATION = 4.354861
STANDARD ERROR OF THE MEAN = .3079352

Sorting, Searching Algorithms

Sorting and searching algorithms are essential to many areas of algorithmic composition, in particular to methods which store production rules and other criteria for generating musical data in voluminous tables (arrays). For instance, a data table containing a variety of solutions to a particular musical problem could be searched by a program routine for the best possible solution under a given set of conditions. Or, a randomly generated collection of values used in one parameter might require linear-ascending sorting prior to use in another parameter.

Quick Sort Algorithm. Program #39 provides one of the most popular sorting routines: the quick sort algorithm.

PROGRAM #39

```
10  REM********************************************************
20  REM                      PROGRAM #39
30  REM
40  REM     Demonstrate Sorting Procedure 1 - Quick Sort
50  REM********************************************************
60  REM***************    Main Routine    ********************
70  REM********************************************************
140     DIM X(60),STACK(40)
150     TOTAL = 60     '<< list to be sorted will have 60 values
160     RANDOMIZE(333) '<< program will generate random numbers
170     PRINT "ARRAY OF RANDOM-ORDER INTEGERS --"
180       FOR J= 1 TO TOTAL
190          X(J) = INT(RND*60)+1
200          PRINT X(J),         '<< send unsorted list to screen
210       NEXT J
220     PRINT
230     PRINT "ARRAY SORTED IN ASCENDING ORDER --"
240     GOSUB 1000    '<< call Quick Sort algorithm
250       FOR J = 1 TO TOTAL
260          PRINT X(J),            '<< send sorted list to screen
270       NEXT J
280 END
1000 REM********************************************************
1010 REM     Routine to Arrange a Table of numbers
1015 REM     into Ascending Order: Quick Sort Algorithm
1020 REM********************************************************
```

```
1120 REM                    Variable Descriptions
1130 REM       Entering -
1140 REM         X(): array of values to be sorted
1150 REM         STACK(): stack to hold array X() pointers
1160 REM         TOTAL: length of array X()
1170 REM       Exiting -
1180 REM         X(): array sorted in ascending order
1190 REM       Local -
1200 REM         FIN : indicator. When zero the sort is done
1210 REM         PTR: stack pointer. PTR+1 points to the top
     of the segment, PTR+2 to bottom of segment
1220 REM         TOPVAL: value at top of segment
1230 REM         BOTTOMVAL: value at bottom of segment
1240 REM         SEGTOP: pointer to top of segment
1250 REM         SEGBOTTOM: pointer to bottom of segment
1260 REM         COMPVAL: value being compared against current X()
1270 REM*********************************************************
1280    FIN = 1
1290    PTR = 0
1300    STACK(PTR+1)=1
1310    STACK(PTR+2)=TOTAL
1320       WHILE FIN <> 0
1330          FIN=FIN-1
1340          PTR=FIN+FIN
1350          TOPVAL=STACK(PTR+1)
1360          BOTTOMVAL=STACK(PTR+2)
1370          COMPVAL=X(TOPVAL)
1380          SEGTOP=TOPVAL
1390          SEGBOTTOM=BOTTOMVAL+1
1400             WHILE SEGBOTTOM-1 <> SEGTOP
1410                SEGBOTTOM=SEGBOTTOM-1
1420                IF COMPVAL <=X(SEGBOTTOM) THEN 1450
                         ELSE X(SEGTOP) = X(SEGBOTTOM)
1430                SEGTOP=SEGTOP+1
1440                IF SEGBOTTOM = SEGTOP THEN 1460
                      ELSE IF COMPVAL >= X(SEGTOP)
                         THEN 1430 ELSE X(SEGBOTTOM) = X(SEGTOP)
1450             WEND
1460          X(SEGTOP)=COMPVAL
1470          IF BOTTOMVAL-SEGTOP < 2   THEN 1520
1480          PTR=FIN+FIN
1490          STACK(PTR+1)=SEGTOP+1
1500          STACK(PTR+2)=BOTTOMVAL
1510          FIN=FIN+1
1520          IF SEGBOTTOM - TOPVAL < 2 THEN 1570
1530          PTR=FIN+FIN
1540          STACK(PTR+1)=TOPVAL
1550          STACK(PTR+2)=SEGBOTTOM-1
1560          FIN=FIN+1
1570       WEND
1580 RETURN
```

Execution of Program #39:

```
ARRAY OF RANDOM-ORDER INTEGERS --
   37            31            39            56            29
   22            1             17            13            55
   17            59            60            16            30
   50            9             55            26            41
   59            33            21            42            46
   56            16            60            59            9
   14            27            53            3             3
   43            12            56            6             39
   14            31            35            51            3
   7             47            26            3             10
   47            11            41            50            23
   52            29            2             8             47


ARRAY SORTED IN ASCENDING ORDER --
   1             2             3             3             3
   3             6             7             8             9
   9             10            11            12            13
   14            14            16            16            17
   17            21            22            23            26
   26            27            29            29            30
   31            31            33            35            37
   39            39            41            41            42
   43            46            47            47            47
   50            50            51            52            53
   55            55            56            56            56
   59            59            59            60            60
```

Unsorted Table Search. Program #40 is a linear unsorted table search routine. It scans a value sequence (list) for occurrences of keyed values. In this implementation, the search is for array positions where the low and high boundaries of the random generator range are stored. If the values are not found to be present at all, a message to that effect is printed. Although not strictly a part of the searching algorithm, a value occurrence counter (the variable, ITEMCOUNT) has been included. If this algorithm is to be applied to pitch, then the indicated key positions would be used to reference the appropriate addresses in the pitch character string array (table).

PROGRAM #40

```
10 REM**********************************************************
20 REM                      PROGRAM #40
30 REM
40 REM          Demonstrate Unsorted Table Searching
50 REM               Procedure 1: Linear Method
60 REM**********************************************************
```

```
70 REM*************** Main Routine ********************
80 REM*******************************************************
90    DIM X(200)
100   TOTAL = 200           '<< length of table to be searched
110   LOW = 1               '<< least potential value in table
120   HIGH = 60             '<< greatest potential value in table
130   RANGE = HIGH - LOW + 1
140   RANDOMIZE(-2044)  '<< program will generate random values
150   PRINT "ARRAY OF RANDOM-ORDER NUMBERS (RANGE 1-";RANGE;")"
160     FOR J = 1 TO TOTAL
170        X(J) = INT(RND * RANGE)+1
180        PRINT X(J),        '<< send unsorted list to screen
190     NEXT J
200   PRINT
210   PRINT
220   TABLKEY = LOW '<< first search for position of least value
230   PRINT "LOWEST VALUE -";LOW
240   GOSUB 1000            '<< call linear unsorted table search
250   TABLKEY = HIGH  '<< search for position of greatest number
260   PRINT "HIGHEST VALUE -";HIGH
270   GOSUB 1000            '<< call linear unsorted table search
280 END
1000 REM*******************************************************
1010 REM       Linear Unsorted Table Search Roution
1020 REM*******************************************************
1030 REM                  Variable Descriptions
1040 REM     Entering -
1050 REM       X(): array of bounded random integers
1060 REM       TOTAL: length of sequence
1070 REM       TABLKEY: search argument (key to search for)
1080 REM     Exiting -
1090 REM       none  (subroutine is procedural)
1100 REM     Local -
1110 REM       ITEMCOUNT: occurrence frequency tabulator
1120 REM       K9: loop index, pointer to X(),
1130 REM           key position indicator
1140 REM*******************************************************
1150   ITEMCOUNT = 0
1160     FOR K9 = 1 TO TOTAL
1170        IF TABLKEY = X(K9) THEN PRINT "FOUND AT POSITION ";
                  K9 ELSE 1190
1180        ITEMCOUNT = ITEMCOUNT + 1
1190     NEXT K9
1200   PRINT "KEY ITEM OCCURRED";ITEMCOUNT;"TIME(S)"
1210   PRINT
1220 RETURN
```

Execution of Program #40:

```
ARRAY OF RANDOM-ORDER NUMBERS (RANGE 1- 60 )
    20          32          5           11          5
    27          59          42          6           56
    15          6           29          12          24
    55          31          1           37          39
    25          12          37          12          24
    44          50          19          53          53
    47          35          4           40          41
    22          37          35          22          11
    47          33          27          18          33
    4           40          34          15          45
    33          26          17          56          19
    21          8           45          59          19
    40          13          46          41          34
    43          47          16          13          47
    49          41          37          57          36
    53          41          58          4           2
    47          21          8           31          29
    56          29          23          34          59
    42          47          17          17          48
    56          53          36          40          4
    25          27          8           53          38
    60          59          2           25          19
    24          58          9           43          39
    4           33          37          53          55
    42          21          19          53          16
    29          38          59          3           12
    38          55          44          59          5
    26          53          39          52          52
    17          30          27          2           22
    46          23          14          60          21
    19          37          35          45          .4
    46          9           15          4           29
    5           26          56          57          42
    47          26          58          24          46
    34          35          49          56          58
    54          28          24          36          11
    23          35          33          9           13
    5           16          35          28          59
    53          7           1           12          53
    21          52          17          60          9
```

```
LOWEST VALUE - 1
FOUND AT POSITION   18
FOUND AT POSITION   193
KEY ITEM OCCURRED 2 TIME(S)
```

```
HIGHEST VALUE - 60
FOUND AT POSITION  106
FOUND AT POSITION  149
FOUND AT POSITION  199
KEY ITEM OCCURRED 3 TIME(S)
```

Sorted Table Search. Program #41 is a binary search routine which requires a sorted table with unique entry keys. It is the fastest algorithm in common use, and has a variety of compositional applications—from simple boundary searches to test condition retrieval.

PROGRAM #41

```
10  REM*********************************************************
20  REM                         PROGRAM #41
30  REM
40  REM          Demonstrate Sorted Table Searching
50  REM               Procedure 2: Linear Method
60  REM*********************************************************
70  REM***************    Main Routine    *********************
80  REM*********************************************************
90     DIM X(50)
100    TOTAL = 50                '<< length of table to search
110    PRINT "A SORTED ARRAY OF INTEGERS (RANGE 1-100) --"
120       FOR J = 1 TO TOTAL
130          X(J) = J  * 2  '<< create an ordered (sorted) list
140          PRINT X(J),                '<< send list to screen
150       NEXT J
160    PRINT
170    PRINT
180    ARG = 58                  '<< choose a value to search for
190    PRINT "THE INTEGER";ARG;"WILL BE THE ITEM TO SEARCH FOR"
200    GOSUB 1000            '<< call sorted table search routine
210    IF KPOS = 0 THEN PRINT "NOT FOUND"
                 ELSE PRINT  "KEY ";ARG;"= POS"KPOS;
220 END
1000 REM*********************************************************
1010 REM    Routine Search a Sorted Table for Location of Values
1020 REM*********************************************************
1030 REM                  Variable Descriptions
1040 REM      Entering -
1050 REM       X() array of sorted items (keys)
1060 REM       TOTAL: length of array X()
1070 REM       ARG: search argument (item to look for)
1080 REM      Exiting -
1090 REM       KPOS: location (address) of item if found,
1100 REM              0 if not found
1110 REM      Local -
```

```
1120 REM         LL: lower limit for current search portion
1130 REM         UL: upper limit for current search portion
1140 REM         KVAL: computed value of key
1150 REM         MP: computed halfway point
1160 REM***********************************************************
1170    LL=0
1180    UL=TOTAL+1
1190    KPOS=0
1200    IF ARG < X(1) OR ARG > X(TOTAL) THEN RETURN
1210    IF UL >=LL THEN MP=INT((UL+LL)/2) : KV=X(MP):IF KV <> ARG
           THEN IF KV >= ARG THEN UL=MP-1:GOTO 1210 ELSE LL=MP+1
             : GOTO 1210 ELSE KPOS=MP ELSE KPOS=UL
1220    IF ARG <> X(KPOS) THEN KPOS = 0
1230 RETURN
```

Execution of Program #41:

```
A SORTED ARRAY OF INTEGERS (RANGE 1-100) --
  2          4          6          8         10
 12         14         16         18         20
 22         24         26         28         30
 32         34         36         38         40
 42         44         46         48         50
 52         54         56         58         60
 62         64         66         68         70
 72         74         76         78         80
 82         84         86         88         90
 92         94         96         98        100

THE INTEGER 58 WILL BE THE ITEM TO SEARCH FOR
KEY  58 = POS 29
```

Proximity Table Search. Program #42 is a Proximity Search routine which requires a sorted list of unique keys (elements). It is quite powerful in that it returns a subset of the array on either side of the key (even if the requested item is missing from the list). This method may be preferable for compositional applications which require searching of rule-groups for prioritized solutions to compositional problems, an approach gaining popularity as an alternative to the Monte Carlo method of random number parameter generation.

PROGRAM #42

```
10 REM************************************************************
20 REM                  PROGRAM #42
30 REM
40 REM          Demonstrate Sorted Table Searching
50 REM              Procedure 3: Proximity Method
60 REM************************************************************
```

```
70 REM**************   Main Routine   *********************
80 REM****************************************************
90    DIM X(52)
100   TOTAL = 50               '<< length of list to be searched
110   PRINT "A SORTED ARRAY OF INTEGERS (RANGE 1-100) --"
120     FOR J = 1 TO TOTAL
130        X(J) = J  * 2                  '<< create ordered table
140        PRINT X(J),                    '<< send table to screen
150     NEXT J
160   PRINT
170   PRINT
180   ARG = 42                  '<< choose a value to search for
190   SWIDTH = 5       '<< choose a surrounding range to return
200   PRINT "THE INTEGER";ARG; "WILL BE THE ITEM TO SEARCH
FOR"
210   GOSUB 1000                          '<< call proximity search
220     FOR J =LLL TO LUL
230        PRINT X(J)      '<< send returned segment to screen
240     NEXT J
250 END
1000 REM******************************************************
1010 REM          Proximity Method Table Search Routine
1020 REM******************************************************
1030 REM                 Variable Descriptions
1040 REM     Entering -
1050 REM       X(): array of sorted items (keys)
1060 REM       TOTAL: length of array X()
1070 REM       ARG: search argument (item to look for)
1080 REM       SWIDTH: width of search below & above item
1090 REM     Exiting -
1100 REM       LUL: upper limit of list of items returned
1110 REM       LLL: lower limit of list of items returned
1120 REM     Local -
1130 REM       K9: loop index, pointer to array X()
1140 REM******************************************************
1150   FOR K9=1 TO TOTAL
1160      IF ARG <= X(K9) THEN 1190
1170   NEXT K9
1180   K9=TOTAL+1
1190   IF ARG=X(K9) THEN LUL=K9+SWIDTH ELSE LUL=K9+SWIDTH-1
1200   LLL=K9-SWIDTH
1210   IF LUL > TOTAL THEN LUL=TOTAL
1220   IF LLL < 1 THEN LLL=1
1230 RETURN
```

Execution of Program #42:

```
A SORTED ARRAY OF INTEGERS (RANGE 1-100) --
  2           4           6           8          10
 12          14          16          18          20
 22          24          26          28          30
 32          34          36          38          40
 42          44          46          48          50
 52          54          56          58          60
 62          64          66          68          70
 72          74          76          78          80
 82          84          86          88          90
 92          94          96          98         100

THE INTEGER 42 WILL BE THE ITEM TO SEARCH FOR
 32
 34
 36
 38
 40
 42
 44
 46
 48
 50
 52
```

Music From Text

Composers in the twentieth century have exhibited a keen interest in the relationship between speech and music. This has taken many forms, among them the propensity for deriving musical elements from the characteristics of various kinds of written texts. This kind of mapping requires the use of the BASIC library of string handling functions, which is presented in Figure 9-1.

BASIC Library Text-Handling Functions

Instruction	Purpose
LEFT$(A$,n)	Extracts substring of leftmost n characters of A$.
RIGHT$(A$,n)	Extracts substring of rightmost n characters of A$.
MID$(A$,n,n)	Replace a part of one string with another string; also used to extract a substring.

ASC(A$)	Return the ASCII code number for the first character of A$.
CHR$(P)	Return the equivalent character for the ASCII code number.
INSTR(A$,"c") or INSTR(A$,B$)	Return the position of first occurrence of string A$ in B$.
LEN(A$)	Returns the number of characters in A$.
VAL(A$)	Numerical value of A$.
STRING$(n,j) or STRING$(n,A$)	Return a string of length containing ASCII code j.
STR$(n)	String representation of n.
SPACE$(n)	String of n spaces
+	String concatenation (A$+B$).

Figure 9-1.

Sound-Text Relationships. Program #43 demonstrates some procedures for mapping pitches onto characters and characters onto pitches, by means of their ASCII code values.

PROGRAM #43

```
10 REM********************************************************
20 REM                    PROGRAM #43
30 REM                 Text/Sound Composition
40 REM          Demonstrate Numbers-to-Characters and
50 REM          Characters-to-Numbers Mapping Principle.
60 REM********************************************************
70 CLS
80 PRINT "The BASIC function, ASC(), returns the ASCII code"
90 PRINT "representation of a specific character."
100 PRINT
110 PRINT"For example, the ASCII code for Alphabet Letter 'A'is"
120 PRINT ASC("A")
130 PRINT
140 PRINT "The BASIC function, CHR$(), returns the character"
150 PRINT "represented by a specific ASCII code integer value."
160 PRINT
170 PRINT "For example,number 90 is the ASCII code for character"
180 PRINT CHR$(90)
190 PRINT "Using these two functions, we can transform text into"
200 PRINT "musical pitches and pitches into text."
210 PRINT
220 PRINT "Press the Space Bar to continue:"
230 IF INKEY$ = "" THEN 230
240 CLS
```

```
250 PRINT "NOTE: NOT ALL ASCII CODES REPRESENT ALPHABET LETTERS."
260 PRINT
270 PRINT "ASCII codes 65-90 are the 26 upper case letters."
280 PRINT "ASCII codes 97-122 are the 26 lower case letters."
290 PRINT
300 PRINT "Use BASIC to discover some of the other characters"
310 PRINT "that are represented by numbers."
320 PRINT
330 PRINT "See the ASCII code Table in your BASIC manual for"
340 PRINT "a complete listing of number-character correspondence."
350 PRINT
360 PRINT "Modulus arithmetic and range/register shifting are"
370 PRINT "techniques used in dealin with sound/text operations."
380 PRINT
390 PRINT "Can you think of some different ways to apply them?
400 END
```

Program #44 is a practical demonstration of routines commonly used in the sound-text conversion process. The routine which begins in Line 1000 converts integers to their corresponding character representation using the CHR$ function. It also adds blanks randomly to simulate the appearance of normal text. It may be adapted to a number of applications which correlate text and musical parameters in some fashion. For example, a sequence of pitch values, transposed to the appropriate ASCII code range, can be converted to alphabetic characters whose codes represent the mapping of pitch onto text. The result, however, will probably not conform to any known language because of the absence of syntactical rules.

The routine which begins in Line 2000 is a character-to-number conversion algorithm. Text strings may be input and translated to integers, which in turn may be assigned to pitch, rhythm, volume, or any musical parameter.

PROGRAM #44

```
10  REM************************************************************
20  REM                     PROGRAM #44
30  REM
40  REM          Practical Demonstration of Bi-directional
50  REM          Number/Character Mapping Procedures
60  REM************************************************************
70  REM**************    Main Routine    ********************
80  REM************************************************************
90     DIM X(51),Y(100)
100     TOTAL = 50                        '<< length of sequence
110     RANGE = 26                        '<< letters of alphabet
120     BLANKS = 10 '<< additional codes to be filtered as blanks
```

(Program #45 includes file-writing code for use with the MusicSculptor System.)

PROGRAM #45

```
10 REM*********************************************************
20 REM                      PROGRAM #45
30 REM
40 REM          Program to Create Simple Haiku-like Poems
50 REM
60 REM        Demonstrate Linguistic Model for the Generation
70 REM*********************************************************
80 REM*********************************************************
90 REM****************     Main Routine     ********************
100 REM*********************************************************
110    DIM P$(84),VOCAB$(300),W(15),SET(300)
120 REM >>> assign parts of speech totals (see DATA categories)
121       ' next line initializes variables for MusicSculptor file
122 NOTEON=0:DURATION=60:VELOCITY=100:ARTDUR=55:CHANNEL=0
123 OPEN "O",#1,"PROG#45.SC"
124 PRINT #1,"File-ID : 2"
125 PRINT #1,"Format : 1"
126 LOWP=25
130    AR = 2                        '<< articles
140    AD = 72                       '<< adjectives
150    NO = 103                          '<< nouns
160    VE = 55                        '<< verbs
170    PR = 15                        '<< prepositions
180    WORDTOT = AR + AD + NO + VE + PR    '<< program vocabulary
190    GOSUB 4000              '<< initialize pitch data table
200    RANDOMIZE(TIMER)  '<< poems will vary with different seeds
210    PRINT "EACH LINE OF EACH POEM WILL BE PRINTED, THEN "
       : PRINT "CONVERTED TO CORRESPONDING PITCH SEQUENCE"
220       FOR J = 1 TO 4
230          PRINT "POEM ";J
240          GOSUB 1000                    '<< call poem generator
250          PRINT:PRINT
260       NEXT J
261 ' write EOF flag
262 PRINT #1,0;-1;0;0;0
263 CLOSE #1
270 END
1000 REM*********************************************************
1010 REM          Routine to Generate 3-line Poems
1020 REM*********************************************************
1030 REM                 Variable Descriptions
1040 REM     Entering -
1050 REM      J: flag from DRIVER to load program vocabulary
1060 REM      WORDTOT: vocabulary size
```

```
1070 REM      AR: number of articles in vocabulary
1080 REM      AD: number of adjectives in vocabulary
1090 REM      NO: number of nouns in vocabulary
1100 REM      VE: number of verbs in vocabulary
1110 REM      PR: number of prepositions in vocabulary
1120 REM   Exiting -
1130 REM      LIN$: full poem line
1140 REM   Local -
1150 REM      VOCAB$(): array of program vocabulary
1160 REM      SET(): flag array to prevent word repetition
1170 REM      W(): array storing current poem formal structure
1180 REM      W: current part of speech, or blank space
1190 REM      L: low end vocabulary delimiter
1200 REM      S: range span for parts of speech categories
1210 REM      RNDWRD: randomly selected word
1220 REM      K9: loop index, pointer to W()
1230 REM*****************************************************************
1240    LIN$ = ""
1250    IF J > 1 THEN 1290
1260       FOR K9 = 1 TO WORDTOT
1270          READ VOCAB$(K9)                    '<< load vocabulary
1280       NEXT K9
1290       FOR K9 = 1 TO 15
1300          READ W(K9)        '<< load 1 of 4 unique poem forms
1310       NEXT K9
1320       FOR K9 = 1 TO 15
1330          W = W(K9)
1340 REM << if end-of-text (W=-1) or end-of-line (W=0), call   >>
1350 REM << article-checking subroutine, print line of text,   >>
1360 REM << call text-to-pitch conversion subroutine to print  >>
1370 REM << resulting pitch sequence.                          >>
1380          IF W = -1 THEN GOSUB 2000 : PRINT LIN$ : GOSUB 3000
                 : RETURN
1390          IF W =  0 THEN GOSUB 2000 : PRINT LIN$ : GOSUB 3000
                 : LIN$= "" : GOTO 1470
1400 REM >>>  locate vocab range for selected part of speech
1410          IF W=1 THEN L=1:S=AR ELSE IF W=2 THEN L=AR+1:S=AD
                 ELSE IF W=3 THEN L=AR+AD+1:S=NO ELSE IF W=4
                 THEN L=AR+AD+NO+1:S=VE ELSE L=AR+AD+NO+VE+1:S=PR
1420          RNDWRD = INT(RND * S) + L
1430          IF RNDWRD <= AR THEN 1460 '<<permit article repetit.
1440          IF SET(RNDWRD) = 1 THEN 1420 '<<prevent word repetit.
1450          SET(RNDWRD) = 1
1460          LIN$ = LIN$ + " " + VOCAB$(RNDWRD) '<< build a line
1470       NEXT K9
1480 RETURN
2000 REM*****************************************************************
2010 REM   Routine to Check for Article-Adjective Agreement
2020 REM*****************************************************************
```

```
2030 REM    Scans the line of text most recently created by
2040 REM    poem-generating routine. If it finds the article A
2050 REM    before a vowel, it changes it to the article AN.
2060 REM*********************************************************
2070 REM                    Variable Descriptions
2080 REM     Entering -
2090 REM       LIN$: uncorrected line of text
2100 REM     Exiting -
2110 REM       LIN$: text line after article checking/correction
2120 REM     Local -
2130 REM       B$: stores indicator to add letter N to article
2140 REM       I: loop index, pointer to LIN$ substring
2150 REM*********************************************************
2160    FOR I = 1 TO LEN(LIN$) - 2
2170       IF MID$(LIN$,I,3) = " A " THEN B$ = MID$(LIN$,I+3,1)
              ELSE 2190
2180       IF B$="A" OR B$="E" OR B$="I" OR B$="O" OR B$="U"
              THEN LIN$ = LEFT$(LIN$,I+1) + "N" + MID$(LIN$,I+2)
2190      NEXT I
2200 RETURN
3000 REM*********************************************************
3010 REM     Routine to Convert Characters to Numbers
3020 REM*********************************************************
3030    LINELENGTH = LEN(LIN$)
3040      FOR M9 = 1 TO LINELENGTH
3050         NOTENUM = ASC(MID$(LIN$,M9,1))-32 '<<convert to int
3060         PRINT P$(NOTENUM);" ";            '<< convert to pitch
3061      PITCH=NOTENUM:IF PITCH=0 THEN VEL1=0 ELSE VEL1=VELOCITY
3062      ' now file pitches
3063      PRINT #1,NOTEON;PITCH+LOWP;VEL1;ARTDUR;CHANNEL
3064      NOTEON=NOTEON+DURATION
3065         IF M9 MOD 15 = 0 THEN PRINT
3070      NEXT M9
3080      PRINT
3090 RETURN
4000 REM*********************************************************
4010 REM     Routine to Load a Pitch Character Array
4020 REM               Using String Functions
4030 REM*********************************************************
4040    P$(0) = " R "        '<< blank spaces will print as rests
4050    NOTE$ = " CC# DD# E FF# GG# AA# B"
4060    OCTAVE$ = "1234567"
4070      FOR K9 = 1 TO 7
4080        FOR L9 = 1 TO 12
4090           P$(L9+(K9-1) * 12) =
                MID$(NOTE$,(L9*2-1),2) + MID$(OCTAVE$,K9,1)
4100         NEXT L9
4110       NEXT K9
4120 RETURN
5000 REM*********************************************************
```

```
5010 REM +++++++++++++++++++++++++++++++++++++++++++++++++++++++++++++
5020 REM                      PROGRAM VOCABULARY
5030 REM                      ++++++++++++++++++
5040 REM
5050 REM                      ARTICLES
5060 REM +++++++++++++++++++
5070 DATA A,THE
5080 REM +++++++++++++++++++
5090 REM                      ADJECTIVES
5100 REM +++++++++++++++++++
5110 DATA AUTUMN,HIDDEN,BITTER, MISTY,SILENT,EMPTY,VERDANT
5120 DATA DRY,DARK,SUMMER,ICY,DELICATE,QUIET,BEMUSED,DIMPLED
5130 DATA WHITE,COOL,SPRING,WINTER,DAPPLED,MOLTEN,FLORAL,DAMP
5140 DATA TWILIGHT,DAWN,CRIMSON,WISPY,AZURE,FRIGID,ASHEN,WHITE
5150 DATA BLUE,BILLOWING,BROKEN,COLD,DAMP,FALLING,INDIGO,SILKEN
5160 DATA FROSTY,GREEN,LONG,LATE,LINGERING,LIMPID,DUSTY,MIDNIGHT
5170 DATA LITTLE,EVENING,MUDDY,OLD,RED,ROUGH,TRANQUILL,WISTFUL
5180 DATA STILL,SMALL,SPARKLING,THROBBING,VERMILION,SOUR,LEMON
5190 DATA WANDERING,WITHERED,WILD,BLACK,YOUNG,STRICKEN,FLEECY
5200 DATA RADIANT,TENDER,DARK
5210 REM +++++++++++++++++++
5220 REM                      NOUNS
5230 REM +++++++++++++++++++
5240 DATA WATERFALL,RIVER,BREEZE,MOON,CAVE,MOON,DREAMSCAPE,DEER
5250 DATA RAIN,WIND,SEA,TABLEAU,SNOWFLAKE,LAKE,SUNSET,SAND-GRAIN
5260 DATA PINE,SHADOW,LEAF,DAWN,GROTTO,FOREST,TROUT,POOL,WIND,ASH
5270 DATA HILL,CLOUD,MEADOW,SUN,GLADE,BIRD,BROOK,MILKWEED,WILLOW
5280 DATA BUTTERFLY,BUSH,DEW,STORMCLOUD,FIELD,FIR,BRANCH,FLAME
5290 DATA FLOWER,FIREFLY,FEATHER,GRASSBED,HAZE,MOUNTAIN,HONEYDEW
5300 DATA NIGHT,POND,SHADE,SNOWFLAKE,DRAGONFLY,LAUREL,COMET,STAR
5310 DATA SILENCE,SOUND,SKY,SHAPE,SURF,THUNDERCLAP,MEADOW,GLOW
5320 DATA VIOLET,PLUME,WILDFLOWER,WAVE,SPIRIT,TWILIGHT,HALO,OWL
5330 DATA SPIDER WEB,LONLINESS,MIST,IVY,DREAM,LIGHT,WOOD,SEASHELL
5340 DATA SWAN,CEDAR,ICE,ROSE,THORN,SUNBEAM,BLOSSOM,GULL,PETAL
5350 DATA STONE,BEE,LEAF,HORIZON,SHOWER,AIR,ROOT,LILAC,HEART
5360 DATA WHISPER,BREATH,SCENT
5370 REM +++++++++++++++++++
5380 REM                      VERBS
5390 REM +++++++++++++++++++
5400 DATA SHAKES,DRIFTS,HAS STOPPED,STRUGGLES,IS DEPARTING
5410 DATA HAS FALLEN,HAS PASSED,SLEEPS,CREEPS,RECLINES,SIGHS
5420 DATA FLUTTERS,HAS RISEN,IS FALLING,IS TRICKLING,DAMPENS
5430 DATA DRINKS IN,TREMBLES,SWALLOWS,TRANSCENDS,MOCKS,LINGERS
5440 DATA MURMURS,IS FLOATING,DREAMS,RETURNS,WAS GLEAMING,RESTS
5450 DATA IS SWEETENING,FLICKERS,SHIVERS,VANISHES,SPARKS,WEAVES
5460 DATA IS GLOWING,HAS EMBARKED,IS PLUNGING,SHINES,IS PRAYING
5470 DATA HAS HIDDEN,DROWNS,BEAMS DOWN,TWITTERS,HAS DANCED,GLIDES
5480 DATA IS WHISPERING,HAS BURNT,BREATHES,EMBRACES,DRONES
5490 DATA DESCENDS,LIFTS,CREEPS,DWELLS,FLICKERS
```

```
5500 REM +++++++++++++++++
5510 REM                       PREPOSITIONS
5520 REM +++++++++++++++++
5530 DATA ON,IN,FROM,UNDER,OVER,NEAR,BENEATH,ATOP,WITH,ACROSS
5540 DATA BESIDE,ASTRIDE,IMMERSED IN,INSIDE,THROUGH
6000 REM*********************************************************
6010 REM                       FORMAL STRUCTURES
6020 REM*********************************************************
6030 DATA 1,2,3,0,1,3,4,5,1,3,0,2,2,3,-1
6040 DATA 3,5,1,3,0,1,2,3,5,1,3,0,2,3,-1
6050 DATA 1,2,3,0,5,1,2,3,0,1,3,4,-1,-1,-1
6060 DATA 1,2,3,4,0,1,2,2,3,0,5,1,2,3,-1
```

Execution of Program #45:

Random Number Seed (-32768 to 32767)? -1033
EACH LINE OF EACH POEM WILL BE PRINTED, THEN
CONVERTED TO CORRESPONDING PITCH SEQUENCE

POEM 1
 THE AZURE FLOWER
 R   D#5 D#4 C4 R G#3 A5 E5 C#5 C4 R C#4 G4 A#4 F#5
 C4 C#5
 A CEDAR TRANSCENDS THROUGH THE PETAL
 R   G#3 R A#3 C4 B3 G#3 C#5 R D#5 C#5 G#3 A4 D5 A#3
 C4 A4 B3 D5 R D#5 D#4 C#5 A#4 E5 D4 D#4 R D#5 D#4
 C4 R   B4 C4 D#5 G#3 G4
 BLUE DRY HILL
 R   A3 G4 E5 C4 R   B3 C#5 G#5 R D#4 E4 G4 G4

POEM 2
 SEASHELL IMMERSED IN THE MIST
 R   D5 C4 G#3 D5 D#4 C4 G4 G4 R   E4 G#4 G#4 C4 C#5
 D5 C4 B3 R   E4 A4 R D#5 D#4 C4 R G#4 E4 D5 D#5

 THE COOL ROSE UNDER A FIELD
 R   D#5 D#4 C4 R A#3 A#4 A#4 G4 R C#5 A#4 D5 C4 R
 E5 A4 B3 C4 C#5 R G#3 R C#4 E4 C4 G4 B3
 MUDDY AIR
 R   G#4 E5 B3 B3 G#5 R G#3 E4 C#5

POEM 3
 A WHITE LEAF
 R   G#3 R F#5 D#4 E4 D#5 C4 R   G4 C4 G#3 C#4
 ON THE VERMILION HORIZON
 R   A#4 A4 R D#5 D#4 C4 R   F5 C4 C#5 G#4 E4 G4 E4
 A#4 A4 R D#4 A#4 C#5 E4 A5 A#4 A4
 THE GRASSBED FLUTTERS
 R   D#5 D#4 C4 R   D4 C#5 G#3 D5 D5 A3 C4 B3 R C#4
 G4 E5 D#5 D#5 C4 C#5   D5
```
```

```
POEM  4
THE VERDANT CLOUD FLICKERS
R  D#5  D#4  C4  R   F5  C4  C#5  B3  G#3  A4  D#5  R  A#3  G4
A#4  E5  B3  R  C#4  G4  E4  A#3  F#4  C4  C#5  D5
A FALLING BEMUSED SHOWER
R  G#3  R  C#4  G#3  G4  G4  E4  A4  D4  R   A3  C4  G#4  E5
D5  C4  B3  R  D5  D#4  A#4  F#5  C4  C#5
WITH THE EVENING WHISPER
R  F#5  E4  D#5  D#4  R  D#5  D#4  C4  R   C4  F5  C4  A4  E4
A4  D4  R  F#5  D#4  E4  D5  B4  C4  C#5
```

Motivic Cell Program. Program #46 is organized to produce musical output with a cell-structure orientation.

PROGRAM #46

```
10 REM*********************************************************
20 REM                    PROGRAM #46
30 REM
40 REM     Demonstrate Cell-Form Structural Approach to
50 REM              Organizing a Composition
60 REM*********************************************************
70 REM**************    Main Routine    *********************
80 REM*********************************************************
90 DIM A$(255)
100 DIM SEED(20)          'array to store user-entered seeds
110 PRINT "This Program generates 'Cells' into which you"
120 PRINT "can insert alphanumeric (character) data for"
130 PRINT "assignment in Pitch, Rhythm, Volume, or other"
140 PRINT "Musical Parameter."
150 PRINT
160 PRINT "Note, however, that data in alphanumeric form"
170 PRINT "is not directly useable by MIDI synthesizers."
180 PRINT
190 PRINT "The output of this program is intended for use"
200 PRINT "in music where the output will be transcribed"
210 PRINT "by hand to conventional music notation."
220 PRINT
230 PRINT "After you input the data into the basic cells,"
240 PRINT "a number series generator will decide the order"
250 PRINT "in which to return the requested number of cell"
260 PRINT "copies."
270    GOSUB 1000    'call user-input and initialization routine
280    GOSUB 2000     'call series generator to distrubute cells
290 END
1000 REM*********************************************************
1010 REM           User-Input and Initialization Routine
1020 REM*********************************************************
```

```
1030 PRINT "Enter the number of distinct Cells you wish to use:"
1040 INPUT CELLNUM
1050 SIZE = CELLNUM 'modulus for series Generator
1060 PRINT "Enter all alphanumeric characters for each cell"
1070 PRINT "on separate lines, use spaces to separate data:"
1080    FOR COUNT = 0 TO CELLNUM-1
1090        PRINT "Enter Cell";COUNT;"Data:"
1100        INPUT A$(COUNT)
1110    NEXT COUNT
1120 PRINT "Enter the number of Cell copies you wish returned:"
1130 INPUT TOTAL
1140 INPUT "How many seeds will you enter?", ORDER
1150 IF ORDER < 2 THEN
            PRINT TAB(15)"!!You must enter at least 2 seeds!!"
               : GOTO 1140
1160 INPUT "Enter 0 for exclusive seed addition, 1 for incl. ",
            ADDTYPE
1170 PRINT "Enter";ORDER;"seeds to start the series generator:"
1180    FOR J = 0 TO ORDER - 1
1190        INPUT SEED(J)
1200        SEED(J) = SEED(J) MOD SIZE
1210    NEXT J
1220 RETURN
2000 REM*****************************************************
2010 REM     Routine to Generate Cell Copy Series
2020 REM*****************************************************
2030  FOR K = 1 TO 10000      'allow for maximum possible loops
2040     FOR L = 0 TO ORDER-1
2050        CURRVAL = (CURRVAL + SEED(L)) MOD SIZE
2060     NEXT L
2070     IF ADDTYPE = 0 THEN CURRVAL = SEED(ORDER-1) + SEED(0)
2080     CELLCHOICE = CURRVAL MOD SIZE  'send series  to screen
2090     PRINT A$(CELLCHOICE),
2100     IF K = TOTAL THEN 2160
2110     FOR L = 0 TO ORDER-2
2120        SEED(L) = SEED(L+1) MOD SIZE   ' update the seeds
2130     NEXT L
2140     SEED(ORDER-1) = CURRVAL MOD SIZE
2150  NEXT K
2160 RETURN
```

Execution of Program #46:

This Program generates 'Cells' into which you
can insert alphanumeric (character) data for
assignment in Pitch, Rhythm, Volume, or other
Musical Parameter.

Note, however, that data in alphanumeric form
is not directly useable by MIDI synthesizers.

The output of this program is intended for use
in music where the output will be transcribed
by hand to conventional music notation.

After you input the data into the basic cells,
a number series generator will decide the order
in which to return the requested number of cell
copies.
Enter the number of distinct Cells you wish to use:
? 4
Enter all alphanumeric characters for each cell
on separate lines, use spaces to separate data:
Enter Cell 0 Data:
? Cell0: 65 8 44 8 76 16 76 16
Enter Cell 1 Data:
? Cell1: 32 3 54 3 65 3 66 4 66 8 67 8 55 16
Enter Cell 2 Data:
? Cell2: 87 16 87 16 88 8 65 8 34 4 35 4
Enter Cell 3 Data:
? Cell3: 55 1 55 1 55 2 55 4 55 8
Enter the number of Cell copies you wish returned:
? 40
How many seeds will you enter to start the series generator?3
Enter 0 for exclusive seed addition, 1 for inclusive 32
Enter 3 seeds to start the series generator:
? 45
? 6
? 1

Cell0: 65 8 44 8 76 16 76 16
Cell3: 55 1 55 1 55 2 55 4 55 8
Cell3: 55 1 55 1 55 2 55 4 55 8
Cell1: 32 3 54 3 65 3 66 4 66 8 67 8 55 16
Cell0: 65 8 44 8 76 16 76 16
Cell0: 65 8 44 8 76 16 76 16
Cell1: 32 3 54 3 65 3 66 4 66 8 67 8 55 16
Cell3: 55 1 55 1 55 2 55 4 55 8
Cell1: 32 3 54 3 65 3 66 4 66 8 67 8 55 16
Cell1: 32 3 54 3 65 3 66 4 66 8 67 8 55 16
Cell1: 32 3 54 3 65 3 66 4 66 8 67 8 55 16
Cell0: 65 8 44 8 76 16 76 16
Cell2: 87 16 87 16 88 8 65 8 34 4 35 4
Cell1: 32 3 54 3 65 3 66 4 66 8 67 8 55 16
Cell0: 65 8 44 8 76 16 76 16
Cell3: 55 1 55 1 55 2 55 4 55 8
Cell3: 55 1 55 1 55 2 55 4 55 8

```
Cell1: 32 3 54 3 65 3 66 4 66 8 67 8 55 16
Cell0: 65 8 44 8 76 16 76 16
Cell0: 65 8 44 8 76 16 76 16
Cell1: 32 3 54 3 65 3 66 4 66 8 67 8 55 16
Cell2: 87 16 87 16 88 8 65 8 34 4 35 4
Cell1: 32 3 54 3 65 3 66 4 66 8 67 8 55 16
Cell1: 32 3 54 3 65 3 66 4 66 8 67 8 55 16
Cell1: 32 3 54 3 65 3 66 4 66 8 67 8 55 16
Cell0: 65 8 44 8 76 16 76 16
Cell2: 87 16 87 16 88 8 65 8 34 4 35 4
Cell1: 32 3 54 3 65 3 66 4 66 8 67 8 55 16
Cell0: 65 8 44 8 76 16 76 16
Cell3: 55 1 55 1 55 2 55 4 55 8
Cell3: 55 1 55 1 55 2 55 4 55 8
Cell1: 32 3 54 3 65 3 66 4 66 8 67 8 55 16
Cell0: 65 8 44 8 76 16 76 16
Cell0: 65 8 44 8 76 16 76 16
Cell1: 32 3 54 3 65 3 66 4 66 8 67 8 55 16
Cell2: 87 16 87 16 88 8 65 8 34 4 35 4
Cell1: 32 3 54 3 65 3 66 4 66 8 67 8 55 16
Cell1: 32 3 54 3 65 3 66 4 66 8 67 8 55 16
Cell1: 32 3 54 3 65 3 66 4 66 8 67 8 55 16
Cell0: 65 8 44 8 76 16 76 16
```

A Simple Artificial Intelligence Program. Program #47 is a result of combining Program #45 and Program #46 to arrive at a linguistic model for generating compositions.

PROGRAM #47

```
10  REM*************************************************************
20  REM                        PROGRAM #47
30  REM    Artificial Intelligence Composition Program  Model
40  REM*************************************************************
50  REM                       Main Routine
60  REM*************************************************************
80      DIM CELL$(300),W(15)
90      REM >>> assign syntactical categories (see DATA)
100     INTR = 3 : ANT = 4 : CONS = 6 : ALINK = 7 : PLINK = 3
150     REPERTOIRE = INTR + ANT + CONS + ALINK + PLINK
160     SIZE = 1000      '<< initial modulus for series generator
170     INPUT "Enter 2 seeds for the series generator: ",NUM1,NUM2
180     NUM1 = NUM1 MOD SIZE                    '<<apply modulus
190     NUM2 = NUM2 MOD SIZE                    '<< apply modulus
200     PRINT "EACH CELL OF MUSICAL PHRASE-GROUP WILL BE PRINTED"
210     PRINT "ON A SEPARATE LINE."
220       FOR J = 1 TO 4
230         PRINT  TAB(20)"====PRESS SPACEBAR TO CONTINUE===="
```

```
240              IF INKEY$ <> " " THEN 240
250              PRINT "MUSICAL PHRASE-GROUP STRUCTURE NUMBER ";J
260              GOSUB 1000          '<< call music generator
270              PRINT
280          NEXT J
290 END
1000 REM***************************************************************
1010 REM          Routine to Generate Phrase-Groups
1020 REM***************************************************************
1030 REM                    Variable Descriptions
1040 REM     Entering -
1050 REM       J: flag from Main Routine to load cell repertoire
1060 REM       REPERTOIRE: total Number of Cells
1070 REM       INTR: number of articles in repertoire
1080 REM       ANT: number of adjectives in repertoire
1090 REM       CONS: number of nouns in repertoire
1100 REM       ALINK: number of verbs in repertoire
1110 REM       PLINK: number of prepositions in repertoire
1120 REM     Exiting -
1130 REM       LIN$: full musical phrase (line)
1140 REM     Local -
1150 REM       CELL$(): array of Elemental Musical Cells
1160 REM       W(): array storing current poem formal structure
1170 REM       W: current syntactical category, or blank space
1180 REM       L: low end repertoire delimiter
1190 REM       S: range span for parts of syntactical categories
1200 REM       K9: loop index, pointer to W()
1210 REM***************************************************************
1220    LIN$ = ""
1230    IF J > 1 THEN 1270
1240       FOR K9 = 1 TO REPERTOIRE
1250          READ CELL$(K9)            '<< load cells repertoire
1260       NEXT K9
1270       FOR K9 = 1 TO 15
1280          READ W(K9)      '<< load 1 of 4 unique phrase forms
1290       NEXT K9
1300       FOR K9 = 1 TO 15
1310          W = W(K9)
1320          IF W = -1 THEN RETURN
1330 IF W=1 THEN L=1:S=INTR ELSE IF W=2 THEN L=INTR+1:S=ANT ELSE
     IF W=3 THEN L=INTR+ANT+1:S=CONS ELSE IF W=4 THEN L=
   INTR+ANT+CONS+1:S=ALINK ELSE L=INTR+ANT+CONS+ALINK+1:S=PLINK
1340          CURRVAL = (NUM1 + NUM2) MOD SIZE '<< get next term
1350          NUM1 = NUM2
1360          NUM2 = CURRVAL
1370          CURRVAL = CURRVAL MOD S  + L
1380          PRINT CELL$(CURRVAL)            '<< print one cell
1390       NEXT K9
1400 RETURN
2000 REM***************************************************************
```

```
2010 REM +++++++++++++++++++++++++++++++++++++++++++++++++++++++
2020 REM              PROGRAM CELL REPERTOIRE
2030 REM                 +++++++++++++++++++
2040 REM
2050 REM                 INTR(oductory) Cells
2060 REM ++++++++++++++++++
2070 DATA   (Int1)Ab0 32   A0 32
2071 DATA   (Int2)G4 16   Ab4 16
2072 DATA   (Int3)F#3 16   Bb3 16
2080 REM ++++++++++++++++++
2090 REM                 ANT(ecedent) Cells
2100 REM ++++++++++++++++++
2110 DATA   (Ant1)F#1 8   G1 8   A4 8
2112 DATA   (Ant2)Ab4 16   F#3 16   Bb3 8
2114 DATA   (Ant3)G4 8   Ab4 4
2120 DATA   (Ant4)Bb3 8   G4 8   Ab4 4   Bb3 8
2130 REM ++++++++++++++++++
2140 REM                 CON(sequent) Cells
2150 REM ++++++++++++++++++
2160 DATA   (Con1)Bb3 2   B3 2   G5 3   Ab5 3   A5 3
2162 DATA   (Con2)Bb5 4   B5 4   G3 2
2170 DATA   (Con3)F#3 8   Bb3 2   B3 1   G5 4
2172 DATA   (Con4)A3 4   G4 4   Ab4 2   Bb3 1
2180 DATA   (Con5)Bb3 4   G5 4   B5 4   D#5 1
2182 DATA   (Con6)F#3 2   Bb3 2   B3 2
2190 REM ++++++++++++++++++
2200 REM                 ALI(nk) Cells
2210 REM ++++++++++++++++++
2220 DATA   (Ali1)Bb4 16   B4 16   F#3 8
2222 DATA   (Ali2)Bb3 4   Bb4 8   B4 1   F#3 16
2230 DATA   (Ali3)G3 2   Ab3 16   A3 16   G4 8   Ab4 4   Bb3 8
2240 DATA   (Ali4)F#5 3   Ab4 3   Bb3 3   G5 16   B5 16
2242 DATA   (Ali)D#5 8   E5 4   F5 4
2250 DATA   (Ali5)G4 2   Ab4 16   F#3 16   Bb3 4   B3 3
2252 DATA   (Ali)G5 3   G3 16   Ab3 16
2260 REM ++++++++++++++++++
2270 REM                 PLI(nk) Cells
2280 REM +++++++++++++++++++++++
2290 DATA   (Pli1)E1 16   F1 16   F#1 16   G1 16
2292 DATA   (Pli2)A4 8   Bb4 8   B4 16   F4 16
2300 DATA   (Pli3)F#4 4   G4 8   B3 4   Ab4 8
2310 REM+++++++++++++++++++++++++++++++++++++++++++++++++++++++++++
2320 REM              PHRASE-FORM STRUCTURES
2330 REM+++++++++++++++++++++++++++++++++++++++++++++++++++++++++++
2340 DATA 1,2,3,0,1,3,4,5,1,3,0,2,2,3,-1
2350 DATA 3,5,1,3,0,1,2,3,5,1,3,0,2,3,-1
2360 DATA 1,2,3,0,5,1,2,3,0,1,3,4,-1,-1,-1
2370 DATA 1,2,3,4,0,1,2,2,3,0,5,1,2,3,-1
```

Execution of Program #47:

```
Enter 2 seeds for the series generator: 103,645
EACH CELL OF MUSICAL PHRASE-GROUP WILL BE PRINTED
ON A SEPARATE LINE.
                        ====PRESS SPACEBAR TO CONTINUE====
MUSICAL PHRASE-GROUP STRUCTURE NUMBER   1
(Int2)G4 16   Ab4 16
(Ant2)Ab4 16   F#3 16   Bb3 8
(Con4)A3 4   G4 4   Ab4 2   Bb3 1
(Pli1)E1 16   F1 16   F#1 16   G1 16
(Int1)Ab0 32   A0 32
(Con6)F#3 2   Bb3 2   B3 2
(Ali3)G3 2   Ab3 16   A3 16   G4 8   Ab4 4   Bb3 8
(Pli1)E1 16   F1 16   F#1 16   G1 16
(Int3)F#3 16   Bb3 16
(Con5)Bb3 4   G5 4   B5 4   D#5 1
(Pli3)F#4 4   G4 8   B3 4   Ab4 8
(Ant2)Ab4 16   F#3 16   Bb3 8
(Ant1)F#1 8   G1 8   A4 8
(Con6)F#3 2   Bb3 2   B3 2


                        ====PRESS SPACEBAR TO CONTINUE====
MUSICAL PHRASE-GROUP STRUCTURE NUMBER   2
(Con2)Bb5 4   B5 4   G3 2
(Pli1)E1 16   F1 16   F#1 16   G1 16
(Int1)Ab0 32   A0 32
(Con4)A3 4   G4 4   Ab4 2   Bb3 1
(Pli3)F#4 4   G4 8   B3 4   Ab4 8
(Int3)F#3 16   Bb3 16
(Ant2)Ab4 16   F#3 16   Bb3 8
(Con3)F#3 8   Bb3 2   B3 1   G5 4
(Pli2)A4 8   Bb4 8   B4 16   F4 16
(Int3)F#3 16   Bb3 16
(Con1)Bb3 2   B3 2   G5 3   Ab5 3   A5 3
(Pli3)F#4 4   G4 8   B3 4   Ab4 8
(Ant2)Ab4 16   F#3 16   Bb3 8
(Con5)Bb3 4   G5 4   B5 4   D#5 1


                        ====PRESS SPACEBAR TO CONTINUE====
MUSICAL PHRASE-GROUP STRUCTURE NUMBER   3
(Int1)Ab0 32   A0 32
(Ant2)Ab4 16   F#3 16   Bb3 8
(Con1)Bb3 2   B3 2   G5 3   Ab5 3   A5 3
(Pli2)A4 8   Bb4 8   B4 16   F4 16
(Pli2)A4 8   Bb4 8   B4 16   F4 16
(Int2)G4 16   Ab4 16
(Ant4)Bb3 8   G4 8   Ab4 4   Bb3 8
(Con6)F#3 2   Bb3 2   B3 2
```

```
(Pli1)E1 16   F1 16   F#1 16   G1 16
(Int3)F#3 16   Bb3 16
(Con6)F#3 2   Bb3 2   B3 2
(Ali1)Bb4 16   B4 16   F#3 8


                    ====PRESS SPACEBAR TO CONTINUE====
MUSICAL PHRASE-GROUP STRUCTURE NUMBER   4
(Int3)F#3 16   Bb3 16
(Ant2)Ab4 16   F#3 16   Bb3 8
(Con5)Bb3 4   G5 4   B5 4   D#5 1
(Ali3)G3 2   Ab3 16   A3 16   G4 8   Ab4 4   Bb3 8
(Pli1)E1 16   F1 16   F#1 16   G1 16
(Int2)G4 16   Ab4 16
(Ant4)Bb3 8   G4 8   Ab4 4   Bb3 8
(Ant2)Ab4 16   F#3 16   Bb3 8
(Con5)Bb3 4   G5 4   B5 4   D#5 1
(Pli3)F#4 4   G4 8   B3 4   Ab4 8
(Pli1)E1 16   F1 16   F#1 16   G1 16
(Int3)F#3 16   Bb3 16
(Ant4)Bb3 8   G4 8   Ab4 4   Bb3 8
(Con6)F#3 2   Bb3 2   B3 2
```

PART III

Computer-Assisted
Composition Procedures II

Probabilistic Algorithms

10

Uniform and Non-uniform
Probability Distributions

STOCHASTIC PROCESSES

The Computer as Composer/Performer

Human performers of contemporary music are commonly required to assume a larger role in the playing of a composition than that of simple interpretation. Many scores instruct the performer to improvise musical patterns from variously constrained, skeletal information provided by the composer. This filling-in of musical details amounts to a limited participation in the compositional process, and an entire set of notational conventions dealing with control over the performer-participation process has evolved over the past fifty years. For instance, a musical score may ask the performer to play, in random order, a group of pitches supplied by the composer. Or, a musician may be allowed to determine the sequential order of placement of a collection of musical phrases or section fragments.

Similarly, a BASIC program can be viewed as a "score" which the computer performs. During the performance, the machine may be asked to apply various stochastic (controlled, random) processes to the organization of material on a low or high level of participation. In concept, this collaboration of the composer and computer is analogous to the relationship between composer and human performer. The primary difference is that the human performer can not improvise randomness as the direct product of a mathematical function, as does the computer. On the contrary, subjective factors within the performer influence the degree of true "randomness": the performer's sense of melodic contour, idiomatic nature of the instrument in use, and personal preferences. Moreover, in concert environments, it may be of no consequence to the audience whether or not a played pattern is rigorously produced; randomness is a perceived quality in this context, and it reduces to apparent patternlessness.

The crudest stochastic process—the uniform random number generator, available as the BASIC RND function—can be said to produce stochastic music only in the most general definition of the term. Stochastic music composition, as exemplified by the work of two algorithmic composition pioneers, Lejaren Hiller in the USA and Iannis Xenakis in France, goes far beyond the low-level generation of discrete, randomly ordered data into the domain of comprehensive structural methods.

Lejaren Hiller's early work, detailed in his book entitled *Experimental Music*, deals with complex musical grammars based on historical style models. In fact, many of Hiller's experiments seem to test the programmer's ability to extract, enumerate, and encode myriad interdependent rules for recreating specific musical rhetorics, resulting in sonic structures more computer-composed than computer-assisted. His pioneering studies laid much of the groundwork for the current explorations of Expert Systems, designed to compose particular musical styles in a masterful way.

By contrast, the work of Iannis Xenakis in stochastic music, as documented in his book called *Formalized Music*, is speculative, forward-looking, and visionary in nature. The programs contained herein are presented in the spirit of Xenakis' approach to musical structure—the projection of original material as opposed to the recreation of compositional precedents.

Stochastic processes, in the service of compositional intention, provide new models for the organization of musical events. In the past, composers often improvised or pecked exploringly at the piano keyboard in search of fresh ideas; today, the personal computer has found its place alongside traditional musical instruments as a creative tool, ready to project hypothetical structures for the composer's scrutiny in ways previously impossible. For example, probability distributions and other shaping controls can be applied to musical parameters, then tested, discarded, reshaped, or "tweaked" until the concept at hand is realized to the artist's satisfaction.

Probability Experiments

The study of games of chance, such as cards, craps, and roulette, gave rise to the body of laws called probability theory, which is the study of random or nondeterministic experiments. The simplest kinds of probability experiments can be carried out using an ordinary coin, for example counting the number of "heads" and "tails" occurring over a given number of tosses of the coin. When carried out by hand, this technique is much too slow to be of use in compositional situations. However, when implemented by computer, it becomes one of a growing number of probabilistic tools for the control of musical structures.

Uniform Probability Distributions

Random experiments in which all possible outcomes are equally likely to occur are said to be representative of the uniform probability distribution. Tossing an unweighted coin or an unloaded die, or dealing cards from a thoroughly shuffled deck, are a few examples, as is the RND function provided by the BASIC programming language.

Shuffle Algorithms. The Monte Carlo method is fundamental to many stochastic processes. Developed by mathematicians for the analysis of data structures and simulation of mathematical models, this method is used synthetically rather than analytically in music composition. That is, instead of working backward from a group of data toward a set of observations about that data, the method is applied via a pseudo-random number algorithm coupled with sets of constraints to process fresh data for the control of musical parameters. Also known as the sample-test-discard/keep method, Monte Carlo randomly samples elements contained in a finite sample space, tests them to see whether they meet certain conditions, then keeps or discards them.

Program #48 contains a Monte Carlo shuffle routine, which is used to randomly reorder the contents of an array. It works by calling the random number generator to select array addresses for the swapping of contents. For this reason, it is called a disruptive shuffle routine. It is applied in situations where random-order variations on a pre-existent set of values is desired. For example, the pitches of a melodic line could be rearranged by calls to this routine. Or, rhythm parameter values might be varied in sequence while the pitches remain in original order.

Expand Program #48 to allow the user to randomize the contents of arrays for four parameters—Pitch, Rhythm, Articulation, and Volume. There are several ways to accomplish this, but the most straightforward is to first fill the parameter element tables with integers within a user-determined range, then call the shuffle routine to reorder the array contents.

A second programming idea is to figure out a way to prompt the user to enter data for a melodic sequence, then make a second, randomly shuffled version of the sequence while leaving the original sequence intact. (The procedure to be used is termed a nondisruptive shuffle.)

(Program #48 includes file-writing code for use with the MusicSculptor System.)

PROGRAM #48

```
10  REM*************************************************************
20  REM                      PROGRAM #48
30  REM       Demonstrate Monte Carlo Shuffle Procedure
40  REM*************************************************************
50  REM                     Main Routine
60  REM*************************************************************
70    DIM X(20)
80    RANDOMIZE(TIMER)
90       ' next line initializes variables for MusicSculptor file
100   NOTEON=0:DURATION=60:VELOCITY=100:ARTDUR=55:CHANNEL=0
110   OPEN "O",#1,"PROG#48.SC"
120   PRINT #1,"File-ID : 2"
130   PRINT #1,"Format : 1"
150   TOTAL = 20
151   LOWP=60
155   PRINT "INTEGER SEQUENCE ARRAY -- "
160      FOR J = 1 TO TOTAL
170         X(J) = J + LOWP   '<< fill array with number sequence
175         PRINT X(J),
176         PITCH=X(J)
177         ' now file pitches
178         PRINT #1,NOTEON;PITCH;VELOCITY;ARTDUR;CHANNEL
179         NOTEON=NOTEON+DURATION
180      NEXT J
181   ' put a rest in file
182   NOTEON=NOTEON+DURATION*4
190   GOSUB 1000
195   PRINT "SHUFFLED ARRAY --"
200      FOR J = 1 TO TOTAL
210         PRINT X(J),            '<< send shuffled array to screen
211         PITCH=X(J)
212         ' now file pitches
213         PRINT #1,NOTEON;PITCH;VELOCITY;ARTDUR;CHANNEL
214         NOTEON=NOTEON+DURATION
220      NEXT J
221   ' write EOF flag
222   PRINT #1,0;-1;0;0;0
223   CLOSE #1
230 END
1000 REM*************************************************************
1010 REM                 Disruptive Shuffle Routine
1020 REM*************************************************************
1100 REM                  Variable Descriptions
1110 REM    Entering -
```

```
1120 REM      X(): array of sequential values
1130 REM      TOTAL: length of list (array)
1140 REM   Exiting -
1150 REM      X(): randomized array of values
1160 REM   Local -
1170 REM      R9: random number
1180 REM      S9: temporary storage variable
1190 REM      K9: loop index, pointer to array X()
1200 REM*********************************************************
1220         FOR K9 = 1 TO TOTAL
1230             R9 = INT(RND * TOTAL) + 1
1300             S9 = X(K9)
1310             X(K9) = X(R9)
1320             X(R9) = S9
1330         NEXT K9
1340 RETURN
```

Execution of Program #48:

INTEGER SEQUENCE ARRAY --

1	2	3	4	5
6	7	8	9	10
11	12	13	14	15
16	17	18	19	20

SHUFFLED ARRAY --

20	12	3	18	8
11	19	9	13	15
1	7	14	16	5
2	4	10	6	17

Program #49 is an algorithm which controls the proportion of repeated values to unique values in a randomly generated sequence. It works by preventing repetition of values which fall within a specified "window" of predetermined size. For instance, if 100 values are to be returned, a window of 10 is specified, and a random number value range of 1-10 is entered, then the sequence which is generated will consist of ten 10-note series (sets). However, if a smaller window is entered, then only the values falling within the sliding "window" will be prevented from containing repetitions.

Modify the Main Routine to allow the user to control the total number of values to be returned, the size of the repetition prevention window, and the range of permissible values (integers).

(Program #49 includes file-writing code for use with the MusicSculptor System.)

PROGRAM #49

```
10  REM************************************************************
20  REM                     PROGRAM #49
30  REM       Demonstrate Run-Time Value Repetition Control
40  REM************************************************************
50  REM                     Main Routine
60  REM************************************************************
130     DIM P(12),X(100)
140     RANDOMIZE(-29312)
141     ' next line initializes variables for MusicSculptor file
142     NOTEON=0:DURATION=60:VELOCITY=100:ARTDUR=55:CHANNEL=0
143     OPEN "O",#1,"PROG#49.SC"
144     PRINT #1,"File-ID : 2"
145     PRINT #1,"Format : 1"
146     LOWP=60
150     TOTAL = 100
160     RANGE = 12                      '<< range of random integers
170     WINDO = 4           ' << size of repetition prevent window
180     GOSUB 1000                       '<< call value ratio control
185     PRINT "SIZE OF VALUE WINDOW IS ";WINDO
190        FOR J = 1 TO 100
200           PRINT X(J) + LOWP;
201           PITCH=X(J) + LOWP
202           ' now file pitches
203           PRINT #1,NOTEON;PITCH;VELOCITY;ARTDUR;CHANNEL
204           NOTEON=NOTEON+DURATION
210        NEXT J
211     ' write EOF flag
212     PRINT #1,0;-1;0;0;0
213     CLOSE #1
220 END
1000 REM************************************************************
1010 REM       Run-Time Value Repetition Control Routine
1020 REM************************************************************
1140 REM                 Variable Descriptions
1150 REM
1160 REM    Entering -
1170 REM      TOTAL: number of values to be returned
1180 REM      RANGE: 1-n inclusive limits for random numbers
1190 REM      WINDO: size of window for repetition prevention
1200 REM    Exiting -
1210 REM      X(): array holding sequence of values
1220 REM    Local -
1230 REM      U: random number, pointer to array P()
1240 REM      P(): array which records value occurrence
1250 REM      K9: loop index, pointer to array X()
1260 REM
1270 REM************************************************************
```

```
1280        FOR K9 = 1 TO TOTAL
1290            U = INT(RND * RANGE)+1
1300            IF P(U) = 1 THEN 1290
1310            P(U) = 1
1320            X(K9) = U
1330            IF K9 <= WINDO THEN 1350
1340            P(X(K9-WINDO)) = 0
1350        NEXT K9
1360 RETURN
```

Execution of Program #49:

```
SIZE OF VALUE WINDOW IS   4
   7             2             8             3            11
   4            12            10             2             1
   4             3             5             2            11
   1             7             3             4            12
   9             8            11             4             1
   6             3            11             4             9
   2             7            10            12             1
   6            11             4             2             3
   5            12             6             8            10
   1             2             4             7             8
  10             5             4            11             9
   1            12             5             8            10
   6             2             4             1             5
   6            11             7            12             9
   3             5            10             2             7
   1             5            10             8            12
   2             4            11             3             1
   8             6             9            12             5
   7             8             9             2             1
   6            11             7             4             9
```

The segment of Program #49 which prevents repetition of previously generated values, Line 1300, is useful in a number of other programming contexts, in particular for the random-order generation of numeric series. It works as follows:

(1) when an integer is generated, a flag value, 1, is placed in a secondary array at the address corresponding to the integer's magnitude;

(2) as subsequent integers are randomly generated, their corresponding addresses in the secondary array are checked to ascertain whether a flag (for previous generation) is present;

(3) if a flag is present, the integer under consideration has already been returned, and the program loops back to the random

number generator to get another integer; and

(4) if no flag is present in the secondary array, the current integer is added to the list.

Program #50 demonstrates the use of the repetition-prevention algorithm to generate random-order, 12-tone series. This routine is appropriately used in certain situations where a shuffle routine cannot be applied.

(Program #50 includes file-writing code for use with the MusicSculptor System.)

PROGRAM #50

```
10  REM***********************************************************
20  REM                        PROGRAM #50
30  REM       Demonstrate 12-Tone Random-Order Set Generator
40  REM***********************************************************
50  REM                       Main Routine
60  REM***********************************************************
130     DIM SET(12),CUM(12)
140     RANDOMIZE(TIMER)
141     ' next line initializes variables for MusicSculptor file
142     NOTEON=0:DURATION=60:VELOCITY=100:ARTDUR=55:CHANNEL=0
143     OPEN "O",#1,"PROG#50.SC"
144     PRINT #1,"File-ID : 2"
145     PRINT #1,"Format : 1"
146     LOWP=60
150     TOTAL = 12
160     LOW = 0
170     HIGH = 11
180     RANGE = HIGH-LOW+1
190     GOSUB 1000
200        FOR J = 0 TO TOTAL-1
210           PRINT  SET(J);" ";        '<< send series to screen
211           PITCH=SET(J) + LOWP
212           ' now file rescaled pitches
213           PRINT #1,NOTEON;PITCH;VELOCITY;ARTDUR;CHANNEL
214           NOTEON=NOTEON+DURATION
220        NEXT J
221 ' write EOF flag
222 PRINT #1,0;-1;0;0;0
223 CLOSE #1
230 END
1000 REM***********************************************************
1010 REM          Routine to Generate Nonrepeating Series
1020 REM***********************************************************
1130 REM                   Variable Descriptions
```

```
1140 REM       Entering -
1150 REM        TOTAL: length of set
1160 REM        LOW: lowest value
1170 REM        RANGE: set value range
1180 REM       Exiting -
1190 REM        SET(): final set of values
1200 REM       Local -
1210 REM        CUM(): array holding occurrence flags
1220 REM        R9: random value to be tested for occurrence
1230 REM        K9: loop index, pointer to array SET()
1240 REM =======================================================
1250      FOR K9 = 0 TO TOTAL-1
1260          R9 = INT(RND * RANGE) + LOW
1270          IF CUM(R9) = 1 THEN 1260
1280          CUM(R9) = 1
1290          SET(K9) = R9
1300      NEXT K9
1310 RETURN
```

Random Walks. Program #51 demonstrates the Random Walk concept. In this program, a coin is tossed to determine the direction of steps taken by an imaginary walker, up or down a scale of values. In this version of the algorithm, the walker is not allowed to step in place because Line 1200 forces a move of one position. Repeated values can be obtained by filling an array with integers distributed according to compositional plan, then walking through the array using the output of Program #51 as pointers to the array addresses.

Modify Program #51 to allow the user to specify the start-point for the walk (variable LASTLOC) and the number of steps to be taken. Add the BASIC SOUND instruction at Line 185 and listen to the effects of random walks using different random number generator seeds.

(Program #51 includes file-writing code for use with the MusicSculptor System.)

PROGRAM #51

```
10 REM*********************************************************
20 REM                     PROGRAM #51
30 REM       Demonstrate Simple Random Walk Procedure
40 REM*********************************************************
50 REM                    Main Routine
60 REM*********************************************************
130     RANDOMIZE(timer)
131     ' next line initializes variables for MusicSculptor file
132     NOTEON=0:DURATION=60:VELOCITY=100:ARTDUR=55:CHANNEL=0
133     OPEN "O",#1,"PROG#51.SC"
```

```
134    PRINT #1,"File-ID : 2"
135    PRINT #1,"Format : 1"
140    LASTLOC = 7
141    LOWP=60
150    PRINT "START POSITION = ";LASTLOC
160       FOR J = 1 TO 40
170          GOSUB 1000                    '<< call random walk
180          PRINT CURRLOC;        '<< send current step to screen
181          PITCH=CURRLOC + LOWP
182          ' now file pitches
183          PRINT #1,NOTEON;PITCH;VELOCITY;ARTDUR;CHANNEL
184          NOTEON=NOTEON+DURATION
190          LASTLOC = CURRLOC
200    NEXT J
201    ' write EOF flag
202    PRINT #1,0;-1;0;0;0
203    CLOSE #1
210 END
1000 REM*******************************************************
1010 REM                   Random Walk Routine
1020 REM*******************************************************
1030 REM    This subroutine simulates a simple, bi-directional
1040 REM    random walk which is restricted at both ends.
1050 REM*******************************************************
1060 REM                 Variable Descriptions
1070 REM
1080 REM    Entering -
1090 REM      LASTLOC: previous location of walker
1100 REM    Exiting -
1110 REM      CURRLOC: present location of walker
1120 REM    Local -
1130 REM      D: step direction storage
1140 REM      U: random number determining step direction
1150 REM      S: next step value after computation
1160 REM
1170 REM*******************************************************
1180    D=1
1190    U=RND
1200    IF U < .5 THEN D = -1
1210    S = LASTLOC + D
1220    IF S > 15 THEN S = 14     '<< upper boundary test & reset
1230    IF S < 1 THEN S = 2       '<< lower boundary test & reset
1240    CURRLOC = S
1250 RETURN
```

Execution of Program #51:

```
START POSITION =   7
   6            7          6          5          4
   5            6          5          4          3
   2            3          4          5          6
   5            6          7          6          5
   4            5          6          7          6
   5            6          7          6          7
   8            9          8          9         10
   9            8          7          6          7
```

Matrix Random Walk. Program #52 is a two-dimensional matrix random walk algorithm. It differs from the previous program in that the walker is free to step up, down, sideways, diagonally, or in-place around a rectangular surface. The vertical/horizontal proportions of the matrix are determined in Line 160, and the walker's start position coordinates are set in Line 170. The character of the number sequence produced by the random walk can be changed by reshaping the matrix in various proportions (variables ROWS and COLUMNS). For example, when values generated are to be interpreted as pointers to a registered pitch element array, matrix configuration determines the interval content of the resulting sequence. Figure 10-1 illustrates the consequences of matrices shaped in two different ways.

========= 15 x 6 matrix =========

1	2	3	4	5	6	7	8	9	10	11	12	13	14	15
16	17	18	19	20	21	22	23	24	25	26	27	28	29	30
31	32	33	34	35	36	37	38	39	40	41	42	43	44	45
46	47	48	49	50	51	52	53	54	55	56	57	58	59	60
61	62	63	64	65	66	67	68	69	70	71	72	73	74	75
76	77	78	79	80	81	82	83	84	85	86	87	88	89	90

(Random Walk produces melodic interval-sizes of + or - 1, 14, 15, and 16 exclusively.)

========= 4 x 9 matrix =========

1	2	3	4
5	6	7	8
9	10	11	12
13	14	15	16
17	18	19	20
21	22	23	24
25	26	27	28
29	30	31	32
33	34	35	36

(Random Walk produces melodic interval-sizes of + or - 1, 3, 4, and 5 exclusively.)

Figure 10-1.

Modify Program #52 to allow application of the random walk to any or all of four musical parameters (user must be able to specify range of elements for each parameter).

(Program #52 includes file-writing code for use with the MusicSculptor System.)

PROGRAM #52

```
10  REM*********************************************************
20  REM                       PROGRAM #52
30  REM          Demonstrate Matrix Random Walk Procedure
40  REM*********************************************************
50  REM                     Main Routine
60  REM*********************************************************
130     DIM W(10,10)
131     ' next line initializes variables for MusicSculptor file
132     NOTEON=0:DURATION=60:VELOCITY=100:ARTDUR=55:CHANNEL=0
133     OPEN "O",#1,"PROG#52.SC"
134     PRINT #1,"File-ID : 2"
135     PRINT #1,"Format : 1"
140     COUNT = 0
141     LOWP=30
150     TOTAL = 40
160     XLOC = 5 : YLOC = 5              '<< matrix start coordinates
170     ROWS = 8 : COLS = 8
180     PRINT "THE MATRIX FOR THIS RANDOM WALK -"
190         FOR J1 = 1 TO ROWS
200            FOR J2 = 1 TO COLS
210                W(J1,J2)=((J1-1) * COLS) + J2
220                COUNT = COUNT + 1
230                IF (COUNT/COLS) = J1 THEN PRINT W(J1,J2)
                        ELSE PRINT W(J1,J2);
240                IF COUNT < 9 THEN PRINT " ";
250            NEXT J2
260         NEXT J1
270     PRINT "START COORDINATES ARE: ROW ";XLOC;"COLUMN ";YLOC
275     PRINT : RANDOMIZE(TIMER)
290     GOSUB 1000                            '<< call matrix walk
291     ' write EOF flag
292     PRINT #1,0;-1;0;0;0
293     CLOSE #1
300  END
1000 REM*********************************************************
1030 REM          Two-Dimensional Random Walk Routine
1110 REM*********************************************************
1120 REM                  Variable Descriptions
1130 REM     Entering -
1140 REM       W(n,n): random walk matrix
1150 REM       TOTAL: number of random steps to be taken
1160 REM       XLOC: stores current location on horizontal
```

```
1170 REM      YLOC: stores current location on vertical
1180 REM      ROWS: length of matrix
1190 REM      COLS: width of matrix
1200 REM  Exiting -
1210 REM    none (subroutine is procedural)
1220 REM  Local -
1230 REM      XSTEP: random number -1, 0, or + 1
1240 REM      YSTEP: random number -1. 0, or + 1
1250 REM      K9: loop index
1260 REM***************************************************
1270      FOR K9 = 1 TO TOTAL
1280          PRINT W(XLOC,YLOC);
1281          PITCH=W(XLOC,YLOC) + LOWP
1282          ' now file pitches
1283          PRINT #1,NOTEON;PITCH;VELOCITY;ARTDUR;CHANNEL
1284          NOTEON=NOTEON+DURATION
1290          XSTEP = INT(RND * 3) - 1
1300          YSTEP = INT(RND * 3) - 1
1310          XLOC = XLOC + XSTEP
1320          YLOC = YLOC + YSTEP
1330          IF XLOC <= 0 THEN XLOC = 2 ELSE IF XLOC > ROWS
                        THEN XLOC = ROWS - 1
1340          IF YLOC <= 0 THEN YLOC = 2 ELSE IF YLOC > COLS
                        THEN YLOC = COLS - 1
1350      NEXT K9
1360 RETURN
```

Execution of Program #52:

```
THE MATRIX FOR THIS RANDOM WALK -
 1    2   3   4   5   6   7   8   9   10
11   12  13  14  15  16  17  18  19   20
21   22  23  24  25  26  27  28  29   30
31   32  33  34  35  36  37  38  39   40
41   42  43  44  45  46  47  48  49   50
51   52  53  54  55  56  57  58  59   60
61   62  63  64  65  66  67  68  69   70
71   72  73  74  75  76  77  78  79   80
81   82  83  84  85  86  87  88  89   90
91   92  93  94  95  96  97  98  99  100


START COORDINATES ARE: ROW  5 COLUMN  5
  45            44            53            62            52
  52            43            52            41            32
  31            22            21            12            13
  23            12            11            22            21
  21            32            23            13            24
  33            22            22            32            22
  31            21            32            31            21
  11            22            23            13            13
```

Nonuniform Probability Distributions

Many compositional algorithms entail the testing of large amounts of data obtained from BASIC's built-in random number generator, which is actually a mathematical function written to provide a uniform probability distribution of real numbers within the range 0 to 1. In practice, the likelihood of occurrence of numbers approaches uniformity only when a large number of calls is made to the RND function, but nonetheless, we normally accept short-term results as being valid for many purposes. This is because the uniform random number generator often functions only as the initial source of values which will be further filtered or tested against conditions held in a rule-base. This is known as the sample-test-discard/keep method.

Nonuniform probability distributions, on the other hand, are fundamental to another important method of composition in which the details of selected musical parameters are directly calculated without reference to table-based syntactical rules. Often, the goal of this approach is to map the characteristic curve of the distribution function onto one or more parameters; there is no further contextual or historical contingency other than the appropriate scaling of data to meet parameter-range requirements.

In understanding probability distribution functions, it is important to note that the characteristic curve exhibited by a particular distribution is cumulative in nature. That is, the curve is a summary of the likelihood of occurrence of all values falling within the generated range. The actual values are, of course, generated in random order. The two primary categories of probability distribution functions are Mathematical Distributions and Defined Distributions.

Mathematical Probability Distribution Functions

Continuous Random Variables. Each distribution function deals with either a continuous or discrete random variable. Random variables assume their values as the result of a selection process based on probabilities. A random variable is said to be continuous in nature if it can assume an unlimited number of states within the prescribed range. This is the situation with regard to real numbers such as:

.01940331 .90132563 .00019462

Discrete Random Variables. A discrete random variable, on the other hand, can only assume a limited number of states, as in the case of parameters consisting of a range of scalar integer values such as the Pitch parameter:

0 1 2 3 4 5 6 7 8 9 10 11 12 127

Even though the initial output of a particular probability distribution function may be in the form of real numbers, the values can be converted to integer form by multiplying them by the appropriate scaling factor, then truncating them to integer form using the INT instruction, as in the following program fragment,

```
10 RANDNUM = RND
20 PRINT RANDNUM
30 PITCHNUM = INT(RANDNUM * 127) + 1
40 PRINT "The Pitch is number ";PITCHNUM
```

which, when executed will produce the following screen display:

.19320226

The Pitch is number 25

Probabilities

The sum of all probabilities of all possible outcomes in a random process is always equal to 1, and is customarily expressed as a line- or bar-graph. The continuous random variable graph is typified by a solid line curve. The discrete random variable graph resembles a histogram, but differs in that a histogram records actual frequencies of occurrence, whereas the probability distribution graph represents the likelihood of occurrence of points along a continuous or discrete scale of values during execution of the algorithm. Comparison of an occurrence frequency histogram with the probability distribution graph for a specific algorithm provides a method of verifying correct program operation. It also clarifies the correlation between number of samples generated and fidelity to the ideal probability distribution. Usually, much data must be generated before the characteristic curve develops.

Program #53, the Beta Function, returns continuous, random-order real numbers > 0 and < = 1. The shape of its curve changes with the values of its controlling parameters—PROB0 and PROB1. PROB0 determines the probability of values nearest zero; PROB1 controls probabilities nearest one. Smaller parameter values produce higher probabilities at the respective boundary; if PROB0 and PROB1 are equal, the curve is symmetrical around .5, otherwise the curve tilts in favor of the smaller parameter. The mean of the distribution is:

PROB0 / (PROB0 + PROB1)

The curve produced by this function can be made to resemble the bell-shaped (normal, or Gaussian) curve by setting both PROB0 and PROB1 equal to 1. Figure 10-2 is a sample curve, where PROB0 and PROB1 are both set to .5:

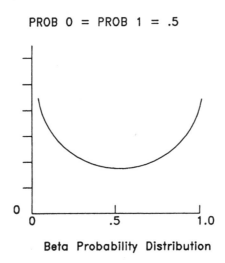

PROB 0 = PROB 1 = .5

Beta Probability Distribution

Figure 10-2.

Execute Program #53 with different values for PROB0 and PROB1 variables to observe output, then modify the program to return integer values scaled for the Pitch parameter. Listen to the results by adding the equal-tempered tuning compiler routine (Program #10) and the BASIC SOUND statement to the program.

PROGRAM #53

```
100 REM****************************************************
110 REM                       PROGRAM # 53
120 REM      Demonstration of Beta Probability Distribution
130 REM****************************************************
140    DIM X(50)
150    RANDOMIZE(-43)
160    TOTAL = 50
170    PROB0 = .4
180    PROB1 = .2
190    GOSUB 1000              '<< call Eulerian Beta distribution
200      FOR J = 1 TO TOTAL
210        PRINT X(J);" ";                 '<< sequence to screen
215        IF J MOD 4 = 0 THEN PRINT
220      NEXT J
230 END
```

```
1000 REM********************************************************
1030 REM         Eulerian Beta Distribution Function
1080 REM********************************************************
1090 REM                Variable Descriptions
1100 REM
1110 REM     Entering -
1120 REM       TOTAL: length of sequence
1130 REM       PROB0: controls occurrence of values nearer to 0
1140 REM       PROB1: controls occurrence of values nearer to 1
1150 REM     Exiting -
1160 REM       X(): array holding BETA distribution
1170 REM     Local -
1180 REM       R8: random number 1
1190 REM       R9: random number 2
1200 REM       T1: computed probability 1
1210 REM       T2: computed probability 2
1220 REM       SUM: total of probabilities 1 & 2
1230 REM       K9: loop index, pointer to array X()
1240 REM********************************************************
1250    PROB0 = 1 / PROB0
1260    PROB1 = 1 / PROB1
1270      FOR K9 = 1 TO TOTAL
1280          R8 = RND
1290          R9 = RND
1300          T1 = R8 ^ PROB0
1310          T2 = R9 ^ PROB1
1320          SUM = T1 + T2
1330          IF SUM > 1 THEN 1280 ELSE X(K9) = T1 / SUM
1340      NEXT K9
1350 RETURN
```

Execution of Program #53

.7374235	1.508907E-02	.1982958	.5404798
.8092735	.9839786	.787956	.4500791
.6320743	2.327007E-03	.9993017	.9867567
.1578648	4.570445E-03	1.895223E-03	.9999836
.8675156	.9173698	.1980324	.8315632
.9817003	.9999928	.9758412	1.191727E-04
.8533422	.9871663	.9999993	2.200857E-02
.2931527	.7608284	1	2.641087E-02
.9750708	.8355502	.9999956	.9960837
.7803568	.2853642	.9946657	.9999932
.9996375	.9984575	1	.7613421
.2004554	1.390761E-02	.9994531	.3365564
.6699975	.9900687		

Program #54 contains the Cauchy Probability Distribution routine, which returns continuously variable real numbers in a symmetrical, negative-to-positive distribution centered around the mean (0). It is similar to the Gaussian Distribution in that it is unbounded above and below the mean, but it approaches zero more slowly at the extremes. In practical terms, this causes values quite remote from the mean to have a higher occurrence probability than in a Gaussian Distribution. The control variable SPREAD determines the horizontal dispersion of values along the curve. Study Figure 10-3.

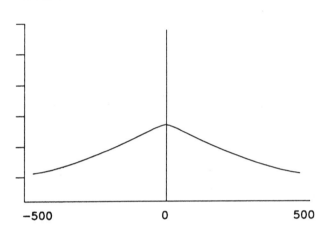

Cauchy Probability Distribution

Figure 10-3

PROGRAM #54

```
100 REM***********************************************************
110 REM                          PROGRAM # 54
120 REM        Demonstration of Cauchy Probability Distribution
130 REM***********************************************************
140     DIM X(50)
150     RANDOMIZE(31422)
160     TOTAL = 50
165     SPREAD = 2
170     GOSUB 1000              '<< call Cauchy distribution function
180        FOR J = 1 TO TOTAL
190           PRINT X(J);" ";              '<< sequence to screen
195           IF J MOD 4 = 0 THEN PRINT
200        NEXT J
210 END
1000 REM***********************************************************
1030 REM          Cauchy Probability Distribution Function
1070 REM***********************************************************
```

```
1080 REM                    Variable Descriptions
1090 REM    Entering -
1100 REM       TOTAL: length of sequence
1110 REM       SPREAD: scaling parameter
1120 REM    Exiting -
1130 REM       X(): array holding cauchy distribution
1140 REM    Local -
1150 REM       R9: uniform random number
1160 REM       K9: loop index, pointer to array X()
1170 REM*********************************************************
1171    PI = 3.1415927#
1180       FOR K9 = 1 TO TOTAL
1200          R9# = RND
1210          IF R9# = .5 THEN 1200
1220          R9# = R9# * PI
1230          X(K9) = SPREAD * TAN(R9#)
1240       NEXT K9
1250 RETURN
```

Execution of Program #54:

```
 1.435218    -3.135468     2.058527    -3.762384
-27.95866     6.063459     2.358028     3.062942
-5.187778     .9340848     1.803345     1.071952
 1.506539     2.615161     2.263138    -1.337906
 1.42068     -2.862467     1.341476     -.4193819
 12.46916     3.395561     3.760365    -35.02975
-1.565518     2.57346     -1.586209     37.2678
 2.275438     -.2182467   -4.067533     371.3344
-2.783898    -61.7626     -1.701122     .4014113
 5.449896    -16.25256    -4.052299    -1.155056
 1.304845     .5203197     31.81785     1.457217
-2.350121    -1.610642    -4.015357     .787217
 -.2709108    4.526322
```

Program #55 demonstrates the Exponential Probability Distribution. The routine returns continuously variable, random-order real numbers larger than zero. Samples closer to zero are most likely to occur, with the probabilities of higher numbers falling off exponentially.

Figure 10-4 is a representative curve. The control variable SPREAD determines the dispersion of values along the curve; larger SPREAD values increase the probability of returning a low number. Although there is no upper limit to the size of an individual sample, it is very unlikely that a large number will be generated. The distribution mean is .69315 / SPREAD.
SPREAD = 2.0

SPREAD = 2.0

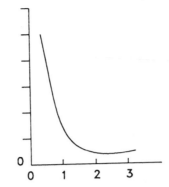

Exponential Probability Distribution

Figure 10-4

PROGRAM #55

```
100 REM*************************************************************
110 REM                          PROGRAM # 55
120 REM  Demonstration of Exponential Probability Distribution
130 REM*************************************************************
140     DIM X(50)
150     RANDOMIZE(1296)
160     TOTAL = 50
170     SPREAD = 2
180     GOSUB 1000        '<< call exponential distribution function
190       FOR J = 1 TO TOTAL
200         PRINT X(J);" ";                  '<< sequence to screen
205         IF J MOD 4 = 0 THEN PRINT
210       NEXT J .
220 END
1000 REM*************************************************************
1030 REM            Exponential Distribution Function
1090 REM*************************************************************
1100 REM                    Variable Descriptions
1110 REM     Entering -
1120 REM       SPREAD: horizontal scaling parameter
1130 REM       TOTAL: length of sequence
1140 REM     Exiting -
1150 REM       X(): array holding exponential distribution
1160 REM     Local -
1170 REM       R9 : uniform random number
1180 REM       K9: loop index, pointer to array X()
1190 REM*************************************************************
1200     FOR K9 = 1 TO TOTAL
1210       R9 = RND
1220       X(K9) = -LOG(R9) / SPREAD
1230     NEXT K9
1240 RETURN
```

Execution of Program #55:

```
.5129975          7.770826E-02       .1373043          1.540272
.2288422          .7463022           .5562524          .2861798
.212774           .1880929           .2369056          5.509907E-02
.6553798          .6811386           4.760646E-02      .6021382
.3316872          .4646425           1.072064          1.467473
.4919575          .1688508           .1593269          .126646
.1143379          3.898637E-02       .046078           2.171639
1.960498E-02      1.513713           3.757861E-02      1.422532
.111562           7.459313E-02       .1414569          1.669231
.1425321          .2525393           8.19926E-03       .7432924
.1199548          3.672071E-02       1.691136E-02      .2180869
.2021383          1.097439           .8127598          6.592536E-02
.3806464          .3525511
```

Program #56 demonstrates the Bilateral Exponential Probability Distribution Function, which returns continuous, random-order numbers centered around zero. The negative-to-positive values are distributed exponentially on either side of the mean (0), and the range is unbounded both above and below the mean. Sometimes referred to as the first law of LaPlace, this distribution is controlled by the variable SPREAD, which increases the range of generated values in inverse proportion to its magnitude (which must be greater than zero). Figure 10-5 is a sample curve, with variable SPREAD set to 1.5:

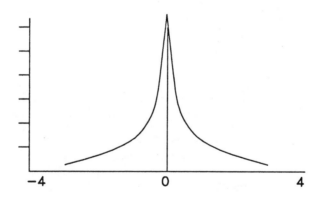

-4   0   4

Bilateral Exponential Probability Distribution

Figure 10-5

Modify Program #56 to allow the user to shift the range to positions lying above the zero-level. Listen to results of various settings for variable SPREAD applied to the Pitch parameter by converting output to integer form (use only positive values). Insert the tuning compiler routine and BASIC SOUND instruction.

PROGRAM #56

```
100 REM****************************************************************
110 REM                        PROGRAM #56
120 REM      Demonstration of Bilexp Probability Distribution
130 REM****************************************************************
140    DIM X(100)
150    RANDOMIZE(-232)
160    TOTAL = 100
170    SPREAD = 1.5
180    GOSUB 1000            '<< bilateral exponential distribution
190      FOR J = 1 TO TOTAL
200        PRINT X(J);"  ";                '<< sequence to screen
205        IF J MOD 4 = 0 THEN PRINT
210      NEXT J
220 END
1000 REM****************************************************************
1030 REM          Bilateral Exponential Distribution Function
1090 REM****************************************************************
1100 REM                 Variable Descriptions
1110 REM      Entering -
1120 REM        TOTAL: sequence length
1130 REM        SPREAD: horizontal scaling value
1140 REM      Exiting -
1150 REM        X(): array holding BILEXP real numbers sequence
1160 REM      Local -
1170 REM        R9: random number > 0 & < 2
1180 REM        K9: loop index, pointer to array X()
1190 REM****************************************************************
1200    FOR K9 = 1 TO TOTAL
1210      R9 = 2 * RND
1220      IF R9 > 1 THEN R9 = 2 - R9
1230      X(K9) = LOG(R9)/SPREAD
1240    NEXT K9
1250 RETURN
```

Execution of Program #56:

```
-7.527557E-02   -1.048221    -.501609    -.2519994
-1.250644    -2.077493    -.6291791    -.1350027
-.3317514    -.6676554    -.4461632    -.1836391
-.5460463    -1.90607    -.3781001    -4.221345E-03
-1.867456    -3.551681E-02    -3.140455    -2.288614
-.1653103    -.2016787    -1.06775    -.3859044
-.1347419    -.3660186    -.2937816    -.2585062
-1.02371    -.5031054    -9.857698E-03    -2.48315
```

```
-.8699966     -2.763871E-02      -2.032015      -.8029451
-9.554353E-02   -.664152       -.209433       -.3556865
-.0413544     -6.037871E-03    -.2083645     -1.270443
-1.196018E-02   -.5717624       -2.156488      -1.815228
-.9352418     -.7964256      -1.026462       -.3324287
-1.685562     -1.424225      -1.177418       -.1132024
-.4870833     -1.280384       -.520645      -1.106162
-.1751037     -.173508       -2.140626      -4.139423E-02
-4.881247E-03   -2.0667        -.5787996      -.5220735
-2.864639     -6.984135E-02    -.1644743      -.8086827
-.1401253     -.1342839       -.1037712     -1.231441
-.8923945     -9.915353E-02    -.0458915      -.1809691
-2.627466     -.3321272       -.8375581     -1.060364
-.2185364     -1.804743E-02    -4.740762E-02   -.4196546
-.5685414     -.2167344       -.1957427      -.2934903
-1.691944     -.4002831       -.1195477     -1.082456
-.2708417     -.3499161       -.2475746      -.1130062
```

Program #57 demonstrates the Gaussian Probability Distribution.
Also referred to as the "normal distribution" and the Gauss-LaPlace
Distribution, this algorithm generates a bell-shaped curve comprised
of random-order, real numbers larger than zero and centered around
the mean. The distribution, illustrated in Figure 10-6, is arrived at by
the summation of uniform random numbers. The standard deviation,
variable DEV, and the mean, variable MEAN, are the control parameters.

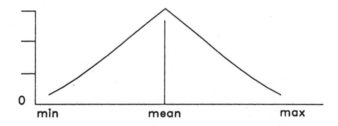

Gaussian Probability Distribution

Figure 10-6.

PROGRAM #57

```
100 REM****************************************************************
110 REM                          PROGRAM #57
120 REM      Demonstration of Gaussian Probability Distribution
130 REM****************************************************************
```

```
140      DIM X(50)
150      RANDOMIZE(-30261)
160      TOTAL = 50
170      DEV = 2
180      MEAN = 10
190      GOSUB 1000        '<< call gaussian distribution function
200        FOR J = 1 TO TOTAL
210          PRINT X(J);"   ";              '<< sequence to screen
215            IF J MOD 4 = 0 THEN PRINT
220        NEXT J
230 END
1000 REM***********************************************************
1030 REM         Gaussian Probability Distribution Function
1110 REM***********************************************************
1120 REM                      Variable Descriptions
1130 REM     Entering -
1140 REM       TOTAL: length of sequence
1150 REM       DEV: statistical standard deviation
1160 REM       MEAN: statistical mean
1170 REM     Exiting -
1180 REM       X(): array holding gaussian distribution
1190 REM     Local -
1200 REM       NUM: number of random values used in computation
1210 REM       HALFNUM: NUM / 2
1220 REM       SCALE: scaling factor    (varies with NUM as
1230 REM              SCALE = 1 / SQR(NUM/12)
1240 REM       K9: loop index, pointer to array X()
1250 REM***********************************************************
1260     NUM = 12
1270     HALFNUM = NUM/2
1280     SCALE=1
1290       FOR K9= 1 TO TOTAL
1300          SUM=0
1310             FOR L9 = 1 TO NUM
1320                SUM = SUM + RND
1330             NEXT L9
1340          X(K9) = DEV * SCALE * (SUM - HALFNUM) + MEAN
1350       NEXT K9
1360 RETURN
```

Execution of Program #57:

```
13.30657     11.70571     12.39236      9.985172
7.704356     11.74669      9.660515     10.72073
8.303805     10.26276     13.3022       7.353261
13.94866      8.597688     9.161171     10.22651
11.48268     10.09521      9.081176     11.68424
9.749614     12.09908      8.905967      8.070188
7.593204      9.953041    10.47929       9.728108
5.857204      9.000855    11.6449        9.001751
```

11.38536	10.58627	10.24655	8.234867
11.02143	10.05303	12.12798	9.771207
7.609164	8.744881	5.132949	11.95452
9.992305	8.005586	7.105201	9.128552
7.014606	9.178887		

Program #58 demonstrates the Poisson Probability Distribution. The algorithm, which starts in Line 1000, generates random-order, positive integers. The control variable, SPREAD, determines the distribution of values, which are unbounded at the upper end.

The distribution, shown in Figure 10-7, has a mean controlled by the value of the variable SPREAD, which must be larger than zero.

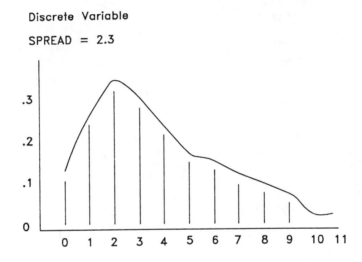

Poisson Probability Distribution

Figure 10-7.

PROGRAM #58

```
100 REM*****************************************************
110 REM                        PROGRAM #58
120 REM      Demonstration of Poisson Probability Distribution
130 REM*****************************************************
140    DIM X(100)
150    RANDOMIZE(9213)
160    TOTAL = 100
165    SPREAD = 5
170    GOSUB 1000            '<< call Poisson distribution function
180       FOR J = 1 TO TOTAL
190          PRINT X(J),              '<< sequence to screen
200       NEXT J
210 END
```

```
1000 REM********************************************************
1030 REM        Poisson Probability Distribution Function
1070 REM********************************************************
1080 REM                  Variable Descriptions
1090 REM     Entering -
1100 REM       TOTAL: length of sequence
1110 REM       SPREAD: scaling parameter
1120 REM     Exiting -
1130 REM       X(): array holding poisson distribution
1140 REM     Local -
1150 REM       NUM: Poisson value
1160 REM       R9: uniform random number
1170 REM       T9: while loop limit
1180 REM       K9: loop index, pointer to array X()
1190 REM********************************************************
1200     FOR K9 = 1 TO TOTAL
1210        NUM = 0
1220        R9 = RND
1230        T9 = EXP(-SPREAD)
1240           WHILE R9 > T9
1250              NUM = NUM + 1
1260              R9 = R9 * RND
1270           WEND
1280        X(K9) = NUM
1290     NEXT K9
1300 RETURN
```

Execution of Program #58:

7	4	7	10	4
3	6	2	6	9
3	5	3	4	2
4	3	8	5	5
3	9	10	7	5
3	4	2	3	8
3	4	4	4	7
4	6	4	5	3
2	0	8	7	3
2	2	6	8	7
6	3	4	6	7
6	3	9	5	7
7	5	6	3	0
7	5	6	8	7
6	3	6	5	9
2	7	5	3	9
1	7	3	4	11
8	5	2	4	6
3	3	3	6	4
3	10	5	3	4

Program #59 demonstrates the Linear Probability Distribution (Figure 10-8). It returns continuously variable, random-order, real numbers larger than zero and smaller than 1. Results closer to zero are most likely to occur. The range of the variable, R8, will be the same as the BASIC RND function, with a mean of .2929; however, by substituting as follows:

1210 R8 = INT(RND * RANGE)
1220 R9 = INT(RND * RANGE)

and defining the variable RANGE, the output can be converted to integer form and scaled to meet scalar parameter requirements.

A reverse linear distribution can be obtained by altering the algorithm to select the larger rather than the smaller random value in Line 1230. In this case, results farther removed from zero will more likely occur.

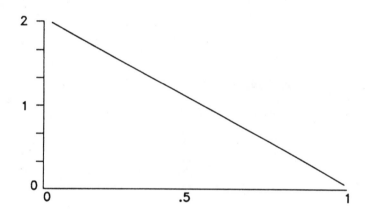

Linear Probability Distribution

Figure 10-8.

PROGRAM #59

```
100 REM************************************************************
110 REM                       PROGRAM #59
120 REM      Demonstration of Linear Probability Distribution
130 REM************************************************************
140    DIM X(50)
150    RANDOMIZE(-29454)
160    TOTAL = 50
170    GOSUB 1000                        '<< call linear distribution
180      FOR J = 1 TO TOTAL
190        PRINT X(J);"   ";             '<< sequence to screen
```

```
195             IF J MOD 4 = 0 THEN PRINT
200         NEXT J
210 END
1000 REM*********************************************************
1030 REM         Linear Probability Distribution Function
1090 REM*********************************************************
1100 REM                      Variable Descriptions
1110 REM     Entering -
1120 REM       TOTAL: length of sequence
1130 REM     Exiting -
1140 REM       X(): array holding LINEAR real number sequence
1150 REM     Local -
1160 REM       R8: random number 1
1170 REM       R9: random number 2
1180 REM       K9: loop index, pointer to array X()
1190 REM*********************************************************
1200    FOR K9 = 1 TO TOTAL
1210       R8 = RND
1220       R9 = RND
1230       IF R9 < R8 THEN R8=R9
1240       X(K9) = R8
1250    NEXT K9
1260 RETURN
```

Execution of Program #59:

```
.4456887      .2722291      .3064838      .3420551
.351074       .4640859      .7553751      .1060918
.1278117      .193983       .1276593      7.395947E-02
.2792682      .1303772      .3700039      .2647041
.2115452      1.985061E-02  .2108588      .6762706
8.201766E-02  .1416531      .3802015      .1715714
.3024199      3.498828E-02  .1224885      .2874659
.5373027      .5444416      .2117493      .197436
3.475803E-02  .3495422      .2150704      .7970608
.4743383      .3625273      9.280014E-02  .4293836
.6929202      2.369869E-02  .3738582      .5406035
.1870632      5.152357E-02  .29202        .1851393
.8570027      .6911503
```

Program #60 demonstrates the Recursive Random Probability Distribution. The algorithm uses a random decaying function to determine the distribution of random-order integers. Occurrence frequency falls off with magnitude, similar to the Exponential Probability Distribution, but with more variability. To obtain this dispersion, the random number generator is made to call itself recursively. See Figure 10-9.

Discrete Variable

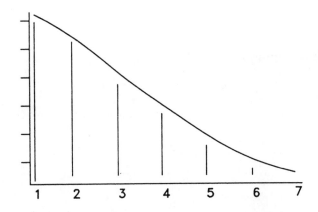

Recursive Random Probability Distribution

Figure 10-9.

PROGRAM #60

```
100 REM*********************************************************
110 REM                       PROGRAM #60
120 REM   Demonstration of Recursive Random Probability Distr.
130 REM*********************************************************
140    DIM X(50)
150    RANDOMIZE(-6729)
160    TOTAL = 50
161    LOW = 1
162    HIGH = 12
163    RANGE = HIGH - LOW + 1
170    GOSUB 1000          '<< call recursive random distribution
180      FOR J = 1 TO TOTAL
190        PRINT X(J),              '<< sequence to screen
200      NEXT J
210 END
1000 REM*********************************************************
1010 REM    Recursive Random Probability Distribution Function
1020 REM*********************************************************
1030 REM                 Variable Descriptions
1040 REM   Entering -
1050 REM     TOTAL: length pf sequence
1060 REM     RANGE: span of possible random numbers
1070 REM     LOW: lowest possible random number
1080 REM   Exiting -
1090 REM     X(): array holding number sequence
1100 REM   Local -
1110 REM     K9: loop index, pointer to array X()
```

```
1111 REM*********************************************************
1120    FOR K9 = 1 TO TOTAL
1130       X(K9) = INT(RND * RND * (RANGE)) + LOW
1140    NEXT K9
1150 RETURN
```

Execution of Program #60:

1	3	12	1	2
5	7	2	6	7
1	1	3	2	1
1	1	2	1	5
1	2	5	1	1
5	3	2	1	1
4	9	2	4	1
1	1	1	9	4
1	8	9	7	3
1	1	2	6	9

Program #61 demonstrates the Weibull Probability Distribution (Figure 10-10). It returns random-order, continuously variable real numbers larger than zero. Its curve can assume a variety of shapes according to the value of its input variable, DENSHAPE. The variable SPREAD controls only the horizontal scale. There is no upper limit to values generated.

Weibull Probability Distribution

Figure 10-10.

PROGRAM #61

```
100 REM*********************************************************
110 REM                         PROGRAM #61
120 REM      Demonstration of Weibull Probability Distribution
130 REM*********************************************************
140    DIM X(50)
150    RANDOMIZE(-212)
160    TOTAL = 50
161    SPREAD = 20
162    DENSHAPE = 1
170    GOSUB 1000            '<< call Weibull distribution function
```

```
180          FOR J = 1 TO TOTAL
190             PRINT X(J);"   ";              '<< sequence to screen
195             IF J MOD 4 = 0 THEN PRINT
200          NEXT J
210 END
1000 REM*********************************************************
1020 REM          Weibull Probability Distribution Function
1080 REM*********************************************************
1090 REM                       Variable Descriptions
1100 REM      Entering -
1110 REM         TOTAL: length of sequence
1120 REM         SPREAD: horizontal scaling parameter
1130 REM         DENSHAPE : curve shaping parameter
1140 REM      Exiting -
1150 REM         X(): array holding Weibull distribution
1160 REM      Local -
1170 REM         R9: uniform random number
1180 REM         K9: loop index, pointer to array X()
1189 REM*********************************************************
1190    FOR K9 = 1 TO TOTAL
1200       R9 = RND
1210       R9=1/(1-R9)
1220       X(K9) = SPREAD * LOG(R9)^(1/DENSHAPE)
1230    NEXT K9
1240 RETURN
```

Execution of Program #61:

40.04524	.4851622	4.304656	53.79547
10.61169	17.12798	4.832766	1.972481
13.93264	35.32088	2.844489	16.11783
26.49674	15.96843	67.06329	7.709352
44.64901	59.70074	9.911872	10.88667
24.85636	9.825422	20.45505	5.070353
44.1469	7.986445	20.25357	.5292715
8.91578	15.59778	9.748322	40.96782
32.06255	16.09293	19.19697	20.026
10.15478	8.690274	22.43852	8.365089
41.94628	8.466834	21.36433	28.97163
27.66084	16.13501	32.93699	5.288891
36.26468	1.497101		

Program #62 demonstrates the Triangular Probability Distribution (Figure 10-11). It returns real numbers, continuously variable over the range zero to one. Middle-valued results are most likely to occur. This algorithm functions by taking the average of two uniformly distributed random numbers.

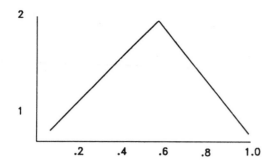

Triangular Probability Distribution

Figure 10-11.

PROGRAM #62

```
100 REM*********************************************************
110 REM                         PROGRAM #62
120 REM    Demonstration of Triangular Probability Distribution
130 REM*********************************************************
140    DIM X(50)
150    RANDOMIZE(62)
160    TOTAL = 50
170    GOSUB 1000          '<< call triangular distribution function
180      FOR J = 1 TO TOTAL
190        PRINT X(J);"   ";              '<< sequence to screen
195        IF J MOD 4 = 0 THEN PRINT
200      NEXT J
210 END
1000 REM********************************************************
1030 REM      Triangular Probability Distribution Function
1060 REM********************************************************
1070 REM                    Variable Descriptions
1080 REM      Entering -
1090 REM        TOTAL: length of sequence
1100 REM      Exiting -
1110 REM        X(): array holding triangular distribution
1120 REM      Local -
1130 REM        R8: random number 1
1140 REM
1150 REM        R9: random number 2
1160 REM********************************************************
1170    FOR K9 = 1 TO TOTAL
1180       R8 = RND
1190       R9 = RND
1200       X(K9) = .5 * (R8+R9)
1210    NEXT K9
1220 RETURN
```

Execution of Program #62:

.5038861	.5351346	.6813608	.7823095
.2550567	.5876625	.7820417	.3398041
.1348132	.2662127	.2356735	.5426083
.5411047	.6523283	.2761432	.4957022
.9187554	.2494271	.4342123	.4759416
.7594646	.4828021	.5375177	.4320569
.6018065	.1996214	.2105709	.4846534
.5312303	.6689279	.3747588	.4262118
.6800603	.5816395	.7483431	.7210875
.7274956	.5505493	.8464605	.5055108
.3996104	.6103251	.4811226	.5875874
.469354	.21751	.7612163	.9472976
.2565506	.2505219		

11

Defined Probability Distributions

Many compositional situations require the use of defined probability distributions. Programs which allow the user to determine the distribution of probabilities for each value in a parameter element list and programs which update probability tables on the basis of run-time computational results are two examples of situations in which provision must be made for the configuration and updating of probability tables.

Two elementary types of probability distribution tables are: (1) the cumulative probability table and (2) the transitional probability table.

Cumulative Probability Tables

This method begins with the assignment of probability weights to each element of a scale of parameter values. For instance, thinking in terms of the number of times each particular pitch of the C-Major diatonic scale should be expected to occur in a generated melodic sequence, it is convenient to generalize using percentages of the total number of values to be returned. Note that the projected relative proportions of occurrence are idealized; they are only approximate in reality. Over short runs the distribution of values may be quite rough compared to the ideal curve, which is approached more accurately only when a large number of values is generated.

Figure 11-1 illustrates the cumulative probability table concept.

Cumulative Probability Table Concept

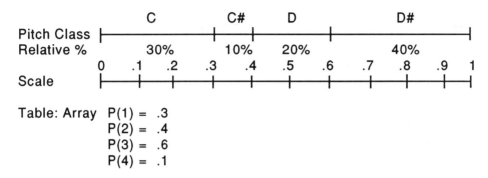

Table: Array P(1) = .3
P(2) = .4
P(3) = .6
P(4) = .1

Figure 11-1.

Event selection proceeds by testing a random number (larger than zero, but smaller than 1.0) against each value in the table. When an array value is found which is larger than the random number, the event corresponding to the table value is selected. This test takes a form similar to the BASIC instruction:

```
IF RND <= TABLE(N)
      THEN EVENT = LIST(TABLE(N))
```

The cumulative probability table concept works because the RND function generates a continuous, uniform distribution of values > 0 and < 1. Those values taking up a larger chunk of the continuum in Figure 11-1 will be selected more often, roughly in proportion to the relative percentage scale.

Relative probability weights, rather than exact percentages, are normally used to build a table of values. This method simply allows the program user to enter a number for each element to be included in the table, then the program normalizes them. For example, instead of entering the probabilities in Figure 11-1 as decimal values—.3, .1, .2, .4—(and making sure everything adds up to 1.0), the user can enter any combination of real numbers or integers—6, 2, 4, 8—and the program will do the required apportioning.

Program #63 builds, then applies, a table of probability weights to the generation of a sequence of values. The routine which begins in Line 1000 builds a cumulative probability table in array WTABLE( ). The weights are read into it from the DATA statements of Line 1220. Because the weights are relative, the program user need not be concerned with their sum (the probability calculation routine normalizes all weights to the required scale). The routine which begins in Line 2000 makes the decisions about which values will be returned by checking the array WTABLE for current probabilities.

PROGRAM #63

```
100 REM*********************************************************
110 REM                        PROGRAM #63
115 REM     Demonstrate Cumulative Probability Table
120 REM*********************************************************
130    DIM WTABLE(5), X(40)
140    RANDOMIZE(111)
150    PROBS = 5
160    TOTAL = 40
170    GOSUB 1000                  '<< call probability table subr.
180    GOSUB 2000                    '<< call table look-up & test
190       FOR J = 1 TO TOTAL
200          PRINT X(J),                  '<< send choices to screen
210       NEXT J
220 END
1000 REM*********************************************************
1010 REM     Routine to Build Table of Probability Weights
1020 REM*********************************************************
1030 REM    This subroutine reads relative weights into a
1040 REM    cumulative probability table (array).
1050 REM*********************************************************
1060 REM                    Variable Descriptions
1070 REM    Entering -
1080 REM       PROBS: number of relative probability weights
1090 REM    Exiting -
1100 REM       WTABLE(): data table containing relative weights
1110 REM    Local -
1120 REM       WSUM: holds current sum of probability weights
1130 REM       K9: loop index, pointer to array WTABLE()
1140 REM*********************************************************
1150    WSUM = 0
1160       FOR K9 = 1 TO PROBS
1170          READ WTABLE(K9)
1180          WTABLE(K9)=WTABLE(K9)+WSUM
1190          WSUM=WTABLE(K9)
1200       NEXT K9
1210 REM ++++++++++++++++++++++++++++++++++++++++++++++++++++++++
1220 DATA 1,2,3,4,5
1230 REM ++++++++++++++++++++++++++++++++++++++++++++++++++++++++
1240 RETURN
2000 REM*********************************************************
2010 REM        Routine to Apply Probability Weights
2020 REM*********************************************************
2030 REM    This subroutine generates random-order integers
2040 REM    whose occurrence frequencies are distributed
2050 REM    in proportion to weights contained in a cumulative
2060 REM    probability table.
2100 REM*********************************************************
```

```
2110 REM                    Variable Descriptions
2120 REM    Entering -
2130 REM      TOTAL: number of values to be returned
2140 REM      WTABLE(): array containing relative weights
2150 REM      PROBS: number of relative probability weights
2160 REM      WSUM: holds current sum of probability weights
2170 REM    Exiting -
2180 REM      X(): array containing selected values
2190 REM    Local -
2200 REM      WSUM: stores current sum of probability weights
2210 REM      R: random number, scaled to sum of weights
2220 REM      L9: loop index, pointer to WTABLE()
2230 REM      K9: loop index, pointer to array X()
2240 REM*********************************************************
2250        FOR K9 = 1 TO TOTAL
2260          R = RND * WSUM
2270          FOR L9 = 1 TO PROBS
2280             IF R <= WTABLE(L9) THEN 2300
2290          NEXT L9
2300          X(K9) = L9
2310        NEXT K9
2320 RETURN
```

Execution of Program #63:

4	3	4	3	5
3	5	3	2	5
4	4	4	5	4
4	5	3	5	5
5	3	5	2	4
4	4	2	3	4
4	3	4	1	3
5	2	4	5	4

Transitional Probabilities

Program #64 demonstrates the use of a transitional probability table to determine melodic pitch class order. In this algorithm, a two-dimensional array holds the occurrence frequency probabilities which make the current pitch choice conditional on the previous choice. The appropriate probabilities are entered in the matrix P( ), either as program data, or via user INPUT statements.

For output data to be accurate, it is important that the sum of each matrix column be 1.0 (Figure 11-2). Moreover, the data table should be well thought out to prevent situations with no exit. For instance, if the probability that C follows F is changed to 0.0, the probability that F follows F is changed to 1.0, and the probability that G follows F is changed to 0.0, nothing but the pitch F will be generated once F is selected.

In Figure 11-2, read columns for last pitch, rows for next pitch. For instance, if the last generated pitch was B (column 4), then the probability of the next pitch being B (row 4) is 0.1. This principle can be extended to three, four, or more dimensions, but it rapidly becomes difficult to visualize the effects of a complex transition table. Execute Program #64 several times, editing the DATA statements to produce different probabilities; then, write an interactive program that allows the user to enter data for the transition table and apply it to any musical parameter.

Transition Table Concept
LAST PITCH

		C	F	G	B
	C	0.0	0.5	0.1	0.0
NEXT	F	0.1	0.2	0.5	0.1
PITCH	G	0.6	0.3	0.1	0.5
	B	0.3	0.0	0.3	0.4

Figure 11-2.

(Program #64 includes file-writing code for use with the MusicSculptor System.)

PROGRAM #64

```
100 REM*********************************************************
110 REM                        PROGRAM #64
115 REM        Demonstration of Transitional Probability Table
120 REM*********************************************************
125 REM                       Main Routine
128 REM*********************************************************
130 REM   To change the probabilities in this program, edit
140 REM   the DATA statements which are read into the table.
150 REM*********************************************************
160     DIM P(4,4),P$(4)
161     ' next line initializes variables for MusicSculptor file
162     NOTEON=0:DURATION=60:VELOCITY=100:ARTDUR=55:CHANNEL=0
163     OPEN "O",#1,"PROG#64.SC"
164     PRINT #1,"File-ID : 2"
165     PRINT #1,"Format : 1"
170 REM >> load pitch character set
```

```
180      P$(1)="C"
190      P$(2)="F"
200      P$(3)="G"
210      P$(4)="B"
211      LOWP=60
220      TOTAL = 25
230      LASTPITCH = 3
240      PRINT
250      PRINT "CURRENT PROBABILITY TABLE --"
260         FOR J1 = 1 TO 4
270            FOR J2 = 1 TO 4
280               READ P(J1,J2)          '<< load probability table
290               PRINT P(J1,J2),              '<< send to screen
300            NEXT J2
310            PRINT
320         NEXT J1
330 REM +++++++++++++++++++++++++++++++++++++++++++++++++++++++++++
340      DATA .0,.5,.1,.0
350      DATA .1,.2,.5,.1
360      DATA .6,.3,.1,.5
370      DATA .3,.0,.3,.4
380 REM +++++++++++++++++++++++++++++++++++++++++++++++++++++++++++
390      RANDOMIZE(TIMER)
395      PRINT : PRINT "PITCH SEQUENCE --"
400      PRINT P$(LASTPITCH);" ";
401      PITCH=LASTPITCH + LOWP
402      ' now file pitches
403      PRINT #1,NOTEON;PITCH;VELOCITY;ARTDUR;CHANNEL
404      NOTEON=NOTEON+DURATION
410         FOR J = 1 TO TOTAL-1
420            GOSUB 1000          '<< call transition probability
430            PRINT P$(NEXTPITCH);" "; '<< send choice to screen
431            PITCH=NEXTPITCH   + LOWP
432            ' now file pitches
433            PRINT #1,NOTEON;PITCH;VELOCITY;ARTDUR;CHANNEL
434            NOTEON=NOTEON+DURATION
440            LASTPITCH = NEXTPITCH
450         NEXT J
451      ' write EOF flag
452    PRINT #1,0;-1;0;0;0
453    CLOSE #1
460 END
1000 REM****************************************************
1030 REM    First-order Transition Probabilities Routine
1240 REM****************************************************
1450 REM                Variable Descriptions
1460 REM    Entering -
1470 REM       LASTPITCH: holds last note choice
1480 REM    Exiting -
```

```
1490 REM      NEXTPITCH: holds the current note choice
1500 REM   Local -
1510 REM      U: uniform random number
1520 REM      T9: threshold test value
1530 REM      K9: loop index, pointer to data table
1540 REM*******************************************************
1550    U = RND
1560    T9 = 0
1570       FOR K9 = 1 TO 4
1580          T9 = P(K9,LASTPITCH) + T9
1590          IF U <= T9 THEN 1610
1600       NEXT K9
1610    NEXTPITCH = K9
1620 RETURN
```

Execution of Program #64:

```
CURRENT PROBABILITY TABLE --
 0              .5             .1             0
 .1             .2             .5             .1
 .6             .3             .1             .5
 .3             0              .3             .4


PITCH SEQUENCE --
G B B F F G F G B G G C G F G F C G C G F G G F F
```

Musical Fractals   *Algorhythm written by Voss.*

Fractal designs have recently gained broad popularity in the
computer graphics field. They are also applicable to musical materials, as demonstrated by Program #65. Fractals are an example of what
is called 1/f (one-over-f) fractional noise. In practical terms, this
means that integer patterns generated by the fractal routine will
exhibit self-similarity. Many composers consider fractals to be more
useful than other types of randomly generated sequences, because
they closely seem to resemble the melodic patterns found in traditional
music. The fractal routine output consistently reflects a high degree
of microformal/macroformal relatedness, in that the patterns on the
large scale are similar to nested, internal patterns. Moreover, a group
of values selected from the end of the sequence will seem to be close
variants of a group of values chosen from the beginning of the
sequence. To test this, compare the number and types of melodic
interval sizes present between the internal values of each sequence
segment. Each 1/f value returned by the routine is conditional on the
previous one generated, and all constituent values correlate logarithmi-
cally with the past, which is why the process is said to have long-term
memory.

(Program #65 includes file-writing code for use with the MusicSculptor System.)

PROGRAM #65

```
100  REM*******************************************************
110  REM                       PROGRAM #65
120  REM        Demonstrate Generation of Fractal Patterns
125  REM*******************************************************
130  REM                      Main Routine
135  REM*******************************************************
140     DIM X(50)
141       ' next line initializes variables for MusicSculptor file
142     NOTEON=0:DURATION=60:VELOCITY=100:ARTDUR=55:CHANNEL=0
143     OPEN "O",#1,"PROG#65.SC"
144     PRINT #1,"File-ID : 2"
145     PRINT #1,"Format : 1"
150     RANDOMIZE(TIMER)
151     LOWP = 60
160     TOTAL = 50
170     LAST = 24
180     GOSUB 1000         '<< call one-over-f distribution function
190        FOR J = 1 TO TOTAL
200            PRINT X(J) + LOWP;            '<< sequence to screen
201            PITCH=X(J) + LOWP
202            ' now file pitches
203            PRINT #1,NOTEON;PITCH;VELOCITY;ARTDUR;CHANNEL
204            NOTEON=NOTEON+DURATION
210        NEXT J
211     ' write EOF flag
212     PRINT #1,0;-1;0;0;0
213     CLOSE #1
220  END
1000 REM*******************************************************
1080 REM                     Fractals Routine
1090 REM*******************************************************
1100 REM                   Variable Descriptions
1110 REM     Entering -
1120 REM        TOTAL: length of sequence
1130 REM        LAST: last value generated
1140 REM     Exiting -
1150 REM        X(): array holding one-over-f distribution
1160 REM     Local -
1170 REM        FRACT: current one-over-f value
1180 REM        HALFVALS: 1/2 the number of possible values
1190 REM        PROB: 1 / number of possible values
1200 REM        R9: uniform random number
1210 REM        S9: stores in-progress computation
1220 REM        K9: loop index, pointer to array X()
```

```
1230 REM****************************************************************
1240 REM
1250 REM
1260    FOR K9 = 1 TO TOTAL
1270       FRACT = 0
1280       HALFVALS = 16  ' = 1/2 number of poss values
1290       PROB = .03125 ' = 1/num poss values
1300          WHILE HALFVALS > = 1
1310             S9 = INT(LAST/HALFVALS)
1320             IF S9 = 1 THEN LAST = LAST-HALFVALS
1330             R9 = RND
1340             IF R9 < PROB THEN S9 = 1-S9
1350             FRACT= FRACT + S9 * HALFVALS
1360             HALFVALS = HALFVALS/2
1370             PROB = PROB * 2
1380          WEND
1390       X(K9) = FRACT
1400       LAST = FRACT
1410    NEXT K9
1420 RETURN
```

Execution of Program #65:

25	24	25	24	25
25	26	26	26	26
26	30	23	20	28
30	29	25	25	25
24	25	29	29	28
28	29	28	29	28
28	29	30	30	30
30	20	23	20	21
23	23	21	21	21
23	18	19	19	1

Procedure for Creating MIDI-format Output Score Files

The simplest way to play the output of a BASIC program on MIDI synthesizers is to choose commercial sequencing software which will accept a properly formatted text file and convert it to a Standard MIDI File sequence. The author uses the MusicSculptor Interactive Composition System, developed at the North Texas Research Institute, University of North Texas, Denton, Texas 76203, USA. The MusicSculptor System includes complete recording, playback, and editing software as well as standard MIDI-file import/export and text file-reading capabilities.

Adaptation of BASIC programs to MIDI-format. The steps to be followed in creating an output file, converting it to MIDI-format, and playing it on the synthesizer are:

(1) Add text file-writing instructions to the BASIC program, then execute the program to produce an output text file;

(2) Load commercial sequencing software capable of reading text score-files; and

(3) Import the text file and play it as a sequence on a MIDI synthesizer.

Step (1) involves the addition of statements at strategic points in the BASIC program to print the note-event data records to a disk file. This file can be thought of as the music score, because it will contain complete information for the performance of the sequence, first note to last.

A disk file is created and opened by the statement:

```
120 OPEN "O",#1,"PROG.DAT"
```

It is important to tell the program user where to look for the output file, so usually a prompt precedes it:

```
110 PRINT  "Output filename for MusicSculptor-format";
    "text scorefile will be <PROG.DAT>"
```

Next, values must be assigned to a number of variables required by each note-event record. If you are only interested in listening to the pitch result of an algorithm, then fixed values can be assigned for the Volume (Velocity), Rhythm, and Articulation parameters, and for the channel assignment of the note as follows:

```
1030  CHANNEL = 0 'assign channel (0-15)
1050  DURATION = 120 'MIDI quarter-note (in clock ticks)
1060  ARTDUR = 102 'sound the note for 85% of allowed
      time (gate)
1070  VELOCITY = 127 'strike the note with maximum force
```

Then, at the point in the program where you would normally print the Pitch parameter to the CRT screen, add statements to get the current pitch value, advance the note-on (event start-time), and print one record to the disk text file:

```
2000  PITCH = P ' prepare to file original pitch
2010  PRINT #1, NOTEON; PITCH; VELOCITY; ARTDUR;
      CHANNEL
2020  NOTEON = NOTEON + DURATION
```

Notice that the variable DURATION is not part of filed information in this case; it is added to the original start-time (in clock ticks) to calculate the start time of the next note-event. The variable ARTDUR holds the shortened (articulated-duration) DURATION value; this is to provide adequate synthesizer gate time in situations where each voice of an 8-voice polyphonic synthesizer is assigned to a separate part. If the synthesizer is set to allow the playing of chords, then the note start times may be allowed to overlap in time.

Selected MIDI-compatible Programs

Program #66 demonstrates the aforementioned MIDI-format text file writing principles. Study it to be sure you understand the function of all the variables, then execute it a number of times using different pitch ranges.

(Program #66 includes file-writing code for use with the MusicSculptor System.)

PROGRAM #66

```
10  REM*********************************************************
20  REM                       PROGRAM #66
30  REM
40  REM       Demonstrate MIDI-format file-writing procedures
45  REM
50  REM       The Program generates a note-event list of random
60  REM       numbers to be interpreted as MIDI Pitch numbers.
70  REM       The numbers are displayed to the user in integer
80  REM       form and as Pitch Characters with octave registration.
90  REM
100 REM
110 REM*********************************************************
120 REM                      Main Routine
130 REM*********************************************************
140     GOSUB 1000             'call program user help subroutine
150     GOSUB 2000     'call program variables initialization subr.
160     GOSUB 4000                   'call MIDI initialization
170     GOSUB 3000           'call pitch table initialization subr.
180     GOSUB 5000     'call subr. to generate random number array
190     GOSUB 6000             'call subr. to print rnd. num. array
200     GOSUB 7000'call subr. to print rnd. num. array as pitches
210     GOSUB 8000                   'call MIDI data filing subr.
220 END
1000 REM*********************************************************
1010 REM                   User Help Routine
1020 REM*********************************************************
1030  PRINT "1. This program generates 100 random-order integers"
```

```
1040    PRINT " over the range 60-90, prints them to the screen"
1050    PRINT " as numbers, then prints them as pitch characters. "
1070    PRINT
1080    PRINT "2. It then files the numbers, along with uniform"
1090    PRINT " values for the other MIDI parameters, as"
1100    PRINT " MIDI pitch numbers."
1110    PRINT
1160    RETURN
2000 REM******************************************************
2010 REM        Routine to Initialize Program Variables
2020 REM******************************************************
2030    RANDOMIZE          'user enters a seed for the rnd. generator
2040    DIM NOTELIST(200)  'array to hold random nmbrs (note list)
2060    LOWPITCH = 60      'set lowest possible pitch to number 60
2070    HIGHPITCH = 90     'set highest possible pitch to number 90
2080    PITCHRANGE = HIGHPITCH - LOWPITCH + 1   'set rnd.gen.range
2090    TOTAL = 100        ' request a notelist of 100 numbers
2100 RETURN
3000 REM******************************************************
3010 REM        Routine to Load Pitch-Character Table
3020 REM******************************************************
3030    DIM PITCH$(128)         'an array to hold pitch characters
3040    PRINT "Here is a number/pitch equivalence display:"
3050     FOR COUNT = 0 TO 127
3060       READ PITCH$(COUNT)    'fill array with pitch characters
3070       PRINT COUNT;"=";PITCH$(COUNT),         'send to screen
3080     NEXT COUNT
3090     PRINT
3100     DATA C0,C#0,D0,D#0,E0,F0,F#0,G0,Ab0,A0,Bb0,B0
3110     DATA C1,C#1,D1,D#1,E1,F1,F#1,G1,Ab1,A1,Bb1,B1
3120     DATA C2,C#2,D2,D#2,E2,F2,F#2,G2,Ab2,A2,Bb2,B2
3130     DATA C3,C#3,D3,D#3,E3,F3,F#3,G3,Ab3,A3,Bb3,B3
3140     DATA C4,C#4,D4,D#4,E4,F4,F#4,G4,Ab4,A4,Bb4,B4
3150     DATA C5,C#5,D5,D#5,E5,F5,F#5,G5,Ab5,A5,Bb5,B5
3160     DATA C6,C#6,D6,D#6,E6,F6,F#6,G6,Ab6,A6,Bb6,B6
3170     DATA C7,C#7,D7,D#7,E7,F7,F#7,G7,Ab7,A7,Bb7,B7
3180     DATA C8,C#8,D8,D#8,E8,F8,F#8,G8,Ab8,A8,Bb8,B8
3190     DATA C9,C#9,D9,D#9,E9,F9,F#9,G9,Ab9,A9,Bb9,B9
3200     DATA C10,C#10,D10,D#10,E10,F10,F#10,G10
3210 RETURN
4000 REM******************************************************
4010 REM        Routine to Initialize Variables
4020 REM        and Open File for MIDI-Format Data
4030 REM******************************************************
4051    OPEN "O",#1,"PROG#66.SC"
4052    PRINT #1,"File-ID : 2"
4053    PRINT #1,"Format : 1"
4060    CHANNEL = 0       'set MIDI channel number (0-15 possible)
4080    NOTEON = 0        'set initial note start time in clock tics
4090    PITCH = 0                           'MIDI pitch variable name
```

```
4095    WHOLENOTE = 480 'nmbr of clock ticks to make whole-note
4100    DURATION = WHOLENOTE / 8    'set note-length to 8th-note
4110    ARTDUR = INT(DURATION * .85)'articulate the note slightly
4120    VELOCITY = 127                   'use maximum MIDI volume
4130 RETURN
5000 REM*******************************************************
5010 REM     Routine To Generate Array of Random Integers
5020 REM*******************************************************
5030    FOR COUNT = 0 TO TOTAL - 1
5040       RANDNOTE = INT(RND*PITCHRANGE) + LOWPITCH
5050       NOTELIST(COUNT) = RANDNOTE
5060    NEXT COUNT
5070 RETURN
6000 REM*******************************************************
6010 REM     Routine to Print Random Number Array
6020 REM*******************************************************
6030    PRINT
6040    PRINT "Here is the array of random-order integers:"
6050    FOR COUNT = 0 TO TOTAL - 1
6060       PRINT NOTELIST(COUNT),
6070    NEXT COUNT
6080 RETURN
7000 REM*******************************************************
7010 REM  Routine to Print Random Numbers as Pitch CHaracters
7020 REM*******************************************************
7030    PRINT
7040    PRINT "Here is the integer array converted to pitches:"
7050    FOR COUNT = 0 TO TOTAL - 1
7060       PRINT PITCH$(NOTELIST(COUNT)),
7070    NEXT COUNT
7080 RETURN
8000 REM*******************************************************
8010 REM              Routine to File MIDI Data
8020 REM*******************************************************
8030    PRINT "The pitch (integer) data is being filed on disk,"
8040    PRINT "along with constant values for rhythm and volume."
8050    PRINT
8060    PRINT "       Type ---------     "
8070    PRINT "                 SYSTEM <ENTER>"
8080    PRINT "       to leave BASIC,"
8090    PRINT
8100    PRINT "       then Type ---------- "
8110    PRINT
8120    PRINT "                 TYPE PROG#66.SC <ENTER>"
8130    PRINT "       to view the file."
8140    FOR COUNT = 0 TO TOTAL - 1
8150       PITCH = NOTELIST(COUNT)  'get a pitch for MIDI message
8160      PRINT #1,NOTEON;PITCH;VELOCITY;ARTDUR;CHANNEL
8170       NOTEON = NOTEON + DURATION  'advance noteon start time
8180    NEXT COUNT
```

```
8181    ' write EOF flag
8182    PRINT #1,0;-1;0;0;0
8190    CLOSE #1
8200 RETURN
```

Program #67 is a shell program which contains dummy routines for
the generation of Pitch, Rhythm, Velocity, and Timbre (Program
Change) MIDI parameters. The routines as they stand simply call the
random number generator to get data within user-determined range
limits. Execute the program several times to be sure you understand
its operation, then devise more sophisticated algorithms for data
shaping and insert them in place of the provided routines.
(Program #67 includes file-writing code for use with the MusicSculptor
System.)

PROGRAM #67

```
10  REM************************************************************
11  REM                        PROGRAM #67
12  REM          Shell Program for User-Written MIDI Routines
13  REM
14  REM       This program outline contains dummy routines which
15  REM       call the uniform random number generator to get
16  REM       data for the MIDI parameters Pitch Rhythm, Velocity,
17  REM       and Program Change (Timbre).
18  REM
19  REM       (MusicSculptor System file-writing code has been
20  REM         provided.)
30  REM************************************************************
40  REM                        Main Routine
50  REM************************************************************
60  DIM P(500),R(500),D(500),V(500)
89  ' next lines set up the outfile to be read by MusicSculptor
90  OPEN "O",#1,"PROG#67.SC"
91  PRINT #1,"File-ID : 2"
92  PRINT #1,"Format : 1"
95  RANDOMIZE
96  GOSUB 1000                                'get user parameters
100 CHANNEL = CHANNEL - 1
110 NNMESS = -20      'set non-note message to program change
130 NOTEON = BEGIN + 200 : PORT = 0
140 CLOCK = 480                              'quarter-note duration
150 ARTICRANGE = ARTICLONG-ARTICSHORT + 1'note articulation range
160 VELOCRANGE = MAXVELOC-MINVELOC+1          'key velocity range
170 PITCHRANGE = HIPITCH-LOPITCH + 1
180 DURANGE = SHORTDUR-LONGDUR+1             'note-duration range
190 METSCALE = METLEVEL * CLOCK          'metrical scaling factor
200 PRINT "HOW MANY NOTES?"
```

```
210 INPUT NOTES
220 GOSUB 3000                         'call pitch generation routine
230 GOSUB 4000                        'call rhythm generation routine
240 GOSUB 5000                       'call velocity generation routine
250 PRINT #1,NOTEON-4;NNMESS;VOICENUM;0;0;  'set patch #
260  FOR X = 1 TO NOTES
270     PITCH = P(X)
280     ARTDUR = R(X)
290     VELOCITY = V(X)
300     DURATION = D(X)
310     IF X = 1 THEN VOICENUM = VOICENUM
              ELSE IF VELOCITY > 0 AND RND <   PROGCHANGE
              THEN GOSUB 2020
320     PRINT #1,NOTEON;PITCH;VELOCITY;ARTDUR;CHANNEL
330     NOTEON = NOTEON + DURATION   'advance note-on (start) time
340  NEXT X
341  ' write EOF flag
342  PRINT #1,0;-1;0;0;0
343  CLOSE #1
350 END
1000 REM*************************************************************
1010 REM          Routine to Get User-Input Data
1020 REM*************************************************************
1040 INPUT "Enter channel # (1-16) ",CHANNEL : PRINT
1050 INPUT "Enter start time (an integer 0-1000) ",BEGIN : PRINT
1060 INPUT "Enter short and long articulation range limits
              (integers between 10 and 85)",
              ARTICSHORT,ARTICLONG : PRINT
1070 INPUT "Enter min,max velocity range (integers 0 - 127)",
              MINVELOC,MAXVELOC : PRINT
1080 INPUT "Enter low,high pitch range (0-127)",
              LOPITCH,HIPITCH : PRINT
1090 PRINT "Note duration is an integer -n- which serves as the "
1100 PRINT "denominator of a fraction whose numerator";
              " is always - 1 -."
1110 INPUT "Enter long,short note-duration range (1-64) ",
                   LONGDUR,SHORTDUR : PRINT
1120 INPUT "Enter percentage of rest ",REST : PRINT
1130 REST = REST/100
1140 PRINT
1150 INPUT "Enter percentage of program table (voice)changes ",
                   PROGCHANGE : PRINT
1160 IF PROGCHANGE < 1 THEN 1200
1170 PROGCHANGE = PROGCHANGE/100 : PRINT
1180 INPUT "Enter low,high integer range for program table: ",
                   TABLO,TABHI : PRINT
1190 TABLRANGE = TABHI-TABLO+1
1200 INPUT "Enter voicenumber to begin notelist: ",
                   VOICENUM : PRINT
1210 INPUT "Enter metrical level (1-10) ",METLEVEL
```

```
1220 RETURN
2000 REM**********************************************************
2010 REM    Program Change Routine (insert your own algorithm)
2020 REM**********************************************************
2030    PRINT "PROGRAM TABLE CHANGE";
2040    VOICENUM = INT(RND*TABLRANGE) + TABLO
                 : PRINT "NUMBER ";VOICENUM
2050    PRINT #1,NOTEON-4;NNMESS;VOICENUM;0;CHANNEL
2060 RETURN
3000 REM**********************************************************
3010 REM    Pitch Generation Routine (insert your own algorithm)
3020 REM**********************************************************
3030    FOR Y = 1 TO NOTES
3040       P(Y) = INT(RND*PITCHRANGE)+LOPITCH
3050    NEXT Y
3060 RETURN
4000 REM**********************************************************
4010 REM    Rhythm Generation Routine (insert your own algorithm)
4020 REM**********************************************************
4030   FOR Y = 1 TO NOTES
4040      DURATION = INT(METSCALE/(INT(RND * DURANGE)+LONGDUR)+.5)
4050      ARTICULATION = INT(RND * ARTICRANGE) + ARTICSHORT
4060      R(Y)   = INT(DURATION * (ARTICULATION/100))
4070      D(Y) = DURATION
4080   NEXT Y
4090 RETURN
5000 REM**********************************************************
5010 REM    Velocity/Rest Generation Routine
5020 REM**********************************************************
5030    FOR Y = 1 TO NOTES
5040       IF RND < REST THEN V(Y)=0
                 ELSE V(Y)=INT(RND*VELOCRANGE)+MINVELOC
5050    NEXT Y
5060 RETURN
```

Program #68 outputs register-specific pitches as the result of a melody-oriented strategy. Probabilities (in percentages) are entered for each octave-contained interval except the unison, as well as range limits and a bias factor which will skew (deflect) melodic direction upward or downward. The user enters an initial pitch from which interval computation begins.

The direction bias causes the resulting melodic line to be shaped in an overall upward, neutral, or downward direction, depending on the user-input bias value. This feature can be used to create a feeling of directionality in the melodic line, as opposed to the rather aimless sound of drifting random values.

Execute Program #68 several times, then make the following revisions:

(1) Modify this program to use relative, instead of absolute, probability weights;

(2) Reorganize the program from in-line code form to subroutine form;

(3) Visually articulate the program using white space, indentation of FOR...NEXT loops to provide a more intelligible result;

(4) Add REMarks to clarify code function;

(5) Add a Variable Description section to the program to aid the user who wishes to read the program; and

(6) Convert all mnemonic (single- or double-letter) variables to descriptive variables.

(Program #68 includes file-writing code for use with the MusicSculptor System.)

PROGRAM #68

```
10 REM*************************************************************
11 REM                     PROGRAM #68
12 REM*************************************************************
20 REM THIS PROGRAM GENERATES RANDOM ORDER INTERVAL SEQUENCES
30 REM OVER AN 8-OCTAVE RANGE, AND ALLOWS THE USER TO SPECIFY
40 REM THE PROBABILITY DISTRIBUTION OF THE INTERVALS.
50 REM*************************************************************
60 DIM P(12),P$(96)
61       ' next line initializes variables for MusicSculptor file
62 NOTEON=0:DURATION=60:VELOCITY=100:ARTDUR=55:CHANNEL=0
63 OPEN "O",#1,"PROG#68.SC"
64 PRINT #1,"File-ID : 2"
65 PRINT #1,"Format : 1"
70 FOR X = 1 TO 8
80 FOR Z = 1 TO 12
90 DATA C,C#,D,D#,E,F,F#,G,G#,A,A#,B
100 READ P$(Z +(X - 1)*12)
110 NEXT Z
120 RESTORE
130 NEXT X
140 PRINT "ENTER PERCENTAGES FOR EACH OF THE 12 INTERVALS"
145 PRINT "WITHIN THE OCTAVE:"
150 FOR I = 1 TO 12
160 PRINT I
170 INPUT P(I)
180 P(I)= P(I)/100 + S
190 S = P(I)
200 PRINT "TOTAL % INCLUDING INTERVAL";I " IS ";S*100
210 NEXT I
220 PRINT
230 PRINT "YOU MAY DETERMINE PITCH RANGE LIMITS FOR THE SEQUENCE."
```

```
240 PRINT "WHEN PROMPTED ENTER 2 NUMBERS WITHIN RANGE 1-96)."
250 PRINT "DO YOU NEED A PITCH/NUMBER DISPLAY?"
260 INPUT A$
270 IF A$="N" THEN 310
280 FOR X = 1 TO 96
290 PRINT X"="P$(X);INT(1 +(X - 1)/12),
300 NEXT X
310 PRINT
320 PRINT "ENTER LOW/HIGH RANGE LIMITS: (COMMA BETWEEN)"
330 INPUT L,H
340 PRINT "YOU MAY SELECT A DOWNWARD, NORMAL, OR UPWARD
350 PRINT "DIRECTIONAL BIAS BY ENTERING .3, .55, OR .7"
360 PRINT
370 PRINT "ENTER DIRECTION BIAS (.3, .55, OR .7)"
380 INPUT D
390 PRINT
400 PRINT "HOW MANY NOTES TO BE RETURNED?"
410 INPUT N
420 PRINT
430 PRINT "ENTER START NUMBER (WITHIN RANGE LIMITS "L"-"H"):"
440 INPUT U
450 PRINT
460 RANDOMIZE
470 FOR J = 1 TO N
480 R = RND
490 FOR I = 1 TO 12
500 IF R > P(I) THEN 520
510 GOTO 530
520 NEXT I
530 F = RND
535 IF F < D THEN 560
540 U = U - I
550 GOTO 570
560 U = U + I
570 IF U > H THEN U = U - 12
580 IF U < L THEN U = U + 12
590 PRINT P$(U);INT(1 +(U - 1)/12),
591       PITCH=U
592       ' now file pitches
593       PRINT #1,NOTEON;PITCH;VELOCITY;ARTDUR;CHANNEL
594       NOTEON=NOTEON+DURATION
600 NEXT J
607 ' write EOF flag
608 PRINT #1,0;-1;0;0;0
609 CLOSE #1
610 END
```

Program #69 is a package of routines which allows the user to enter probabilities (in percentages) for all parameter values and provides a choice between melodic interval-sequence and pitch-class generation modes. Its output is in notelist format (each line has complete information for a single note-event).

Execute Program #69 several times, then make the following revisions:

(1) Modify this program to use relative, instead of absolute, probability weights;
(2) Visually articulate the program using white space, indentation of FOR...NEXT loops to provide a more intelligible result;
(3) Add REMarks to clarify code function;
(4) Add a Variable Description section to the program to aid the user who wishes to read the program;
(5) Convert all mnemonic (single- or double-letter) variables to descriptive variables.

(Program #69 includes file-writing code for use with the MusicSculptor System.)

PROGRAM #69

```
10 REM*******************************************************
11 REM                     PROGRAM #69
12 REM
13 REM*******************************************************
20 REM THIS PROGRAM USES SUBROUTINES TO 'PACKAGE USER OPTIONS
30 REM AND PROCESSING MODULES.
40 REM IT PRINTS PITCH/OCTAVE REGISTER, RHYTHM, ARTICULATION,
50 REM AND VOLUME LEVEL DATA.  THE USER CAN OPT FOR A RANDOM
60 REM ORDER PITCH CLASS GENERATION MODE, OR A RANDOM ORDER
70 REM INTERVAL SEQUENCE GENERATION MODE.
80 REM OTHER PARAMETERS ALLOW THE INPUT OF SPECIFIC VALUES FOR
90 REM PROCESSING BY RND FUNCTION.  USER PROVIDES PROBABILITY
100 REM WEIGHT FACTOR FOR ALL PARAMETERS.
110 REM*******************************************************
130 REM                   Main Routine
135 REM*******************************************************
136 OPEN "O",#1,"PROG#69.SC"
137 PRINT #1,"File-ID : 2"
138 PRINT #1,"Format : 1"
141 CLOCK = 480 '(whole note reference duration)
142      ' next line initializes variables for MusicSculptor file
143 NOTEON=0:DURATION=0:VELOCITY=0:ARTDUR=0:CHANNEL=0
144 PRINT "Output file for MusicSculptor data will be PROG#69.SC"
150 GOSUB 250
160 IF A = 1 THEN GOSUB 430 ELSE GOSUB 670
170 GOSUB 920
180 GOSUB 1080
190 GOSUB 1240
200 GOSUB 1400
```

```
201 ' write EOF flag
202 PRINT #1,0;-1;0;0;0
203 CLOSE #1
210 END
220 REM************************************************************
230 REM                 Initialization Routine
240 REM************************************************************
250 DIM A(10),B(10),D(20),E2(20),H(10),K(10),O(8),P(12),P$(96)
260 FOR X = 1 TO 8
270 FOR Z = 1 TO 12
280 DATA C,C#,D,D#,E,F,F#,G,G#,A,A#,B
290 READ P$(Z +(X - 1)*12)
300 NEXT Z
310 RESTORE
320 NEXT X
330 PRINT "ENTER NUMBER OF NOTES TO BE RETURNED:"
340 INPUT N
350 PRINT "DO YOU WISH TO PROCESS PITCH DATA AS 1) WEIGHTED"
360 PRINT "PITCH CLASSES WITH 8-TAVE REGISTERS SPECIFIED, OR"
370 PRINT "2) INTERVAL (SIZE 1-12) SUCCESSIONS WITH WEIGHTED"
375 PRINT "PROBABILITIES? (ENTER 1 OR 2:)"
380 INPUT A
390 RETURN
400 REM************************************************************
410 REM  Routine to Set Pitch Class/Octave Register Probabilities
420 REM************************************************************
430 PRINT "ENTER PERCENTAGES FOR EACH OF THE 12 PITCH CLASSES:"
440 FOR I = 1 TO 12
450 PRINT P$(I)
460 INPUT P(I)
470 P(I)= P(I)/100 + S
480 S = P(I)
490 PRINT "TOTAL % INCLUDING PITCH ";I;" ("P$(I)") IS ";S*100
500 IF S = 1 THEN 520
510 NEXT I
520 S = 0
530 PRINT "ENTER PERCENTAGES FOR EACH OF THE 8 OCTAVE REGISTERS:"
540 FOR L = 1 TO 8
550 PRINT "OCTAVE ";L
560 INPUT O(L)
570 O(L)= O(L)/ 100 + T
580 T = O(L)
590 PRINT "TOTAL % INCLUDING OCTAVE "L;" IS ";T*100
600 IF T = 1 THEN 620
610 NEXT L
620 T = 0
630 RETURN
640 REM************************************************************
650 REM  Routine to Set Interval Succession Probabilities
660 REM************************************************************
```

```
670 PRINT "ENTER PERCENTAGES FOR EACH INTERVAL WITHIN THE OCTAVE"
680 FOR I = 1 TO 12
690 PRINT I
700 INPUT P(I)
710 P(I)= P(I)/100 + S
720 S = P(I)
730 PRINT "TOTAL % INCLUDING INTERVAL ";I;" IS ";S*100
740 IF S = 1 THEN 760
750 NEXT I
760 PRINT "ENTER LOW/HIGH RANGE LIMITS (COMMA BETWEEN):"
770 INPUT L,H
780 PRINT "YOU MAY SELECT A DOWNWARD, NORMAL, OR UPWARD"
790 PRINT "DIRECTIONAL BIAS BY ENTERING .3,.55, OR .7 WHEN PROMPTED"
800 PRINT
810 PRINT "ENTER DIRECTIONAL BIAS (.3, .55, OR .7):"
820 INPUT D
830 PRINT
840 PRINT "ENTER START NUMBER (WITHIN RANGE LIMITS "L"-"H"):"
850 INPUT U1
860 S = 0
870 PRINT
880 RETURN
890 REM*********************************************************
900 REM    Routine to Set Duration Values and Probabilities
910 REM*********************************************************
920 PRINT "ENTER NUM OF DIFFERENT DURATIONS YOU WILL USE (20 MAX)
930 INPUT D1
940 PRINT "ENTER ";D1" DURATION VALUES AND THEIR WEIGHTS."
950 PRINT "ENTER 1 VALUE AND ITS WEIGHT (COMMA BETWEEN) PER LINE"
960 FOR I = 1 TO D1
970 INPUT E2(I),D(I)
980 D(I)= D(I)/100 + S
990 S = D(I)
1000 PRINT "TOTAL % INCLUDING VALUE";I;"IS";S*100
1010 IF S = 1 THEN 1030
1020 NEXT I
1030 S = 0
1040 RETURN
1050 REM*********************************************************
1060 REM    Routine to Set Articulation Vals and Probabilities
1070 REM*********************************************************
1080 PRINT "HOW MANY ARTICULATION VALUES WILL YOU USE?"
1090 INPUT G
1100 PRINT "ENTER "G" ARTICULATION VALUES AND THEIR WEIGHTS"
1110 PRINT "ENTER 1 VALUE AND ITS WEIGHT(COMMA BETWEEN) PER LINE"
1120 FOR I = 1 TO G
1130 INPUT A(I),B(I)
1140 B(I)= B(I)/100 + C
1150 C = B(I)
1160 PRINT "TOTAL % INCLUDING VALUE ";I;" IS ";C*100
```

```
1170 IF C = 1 THEN 1190
1180 NEXT I
1190 C = 0
1200 RETURN
1210 REM**********************************************************
1220 REM     Routine to Set Volume Values and Probabilities
1230 REM**********************************************************
1240 PRINT "HOW MANY VOLUME VALUES WILL YOU USE (10 MAX):"
1250 INPUT V1
1260 PRINT "ENTER ";V1;" VALUES AND THEIR WEIGHTS:"
1270 PRINT "ENTER 1 VALUE AND ITS WEIGHT(COMMA BETWEEN) PER LINE"
1280 FOR I = 1 TO V1
1290 INPUT H(I),K(I)
1300 K(I)= K(I)/100 + E: E = K(I)
1320 PRINT "TOTAL % INCLUDING VALUE ";I;" IS ";E*100
1330 IF E = 1 THEN 1350
1340 NEXT I
1350 E = 0
1360 RETURN
1370 REM**********************************************************
1380 REM     Routine to Generate Parameter Values
1390 REM**********************************************************
1400 RANDOMIZE
1410 PRINT "PITCH","DURATION","ARTICULATION","VOLUME"
1420 REM**********************************************************
1430 REM MODULE TO GENERATE DATA FOR PITCH CLASS SEQUENCE ******
1440 FOR J = 1 TO N
1450 IF A = 2 THEN 1610
1460 R = RND
1470 FOR I = 1 TO 12
1480 IF R > P(I) THEN 1500
1490 GOTO 1510
1500 NEXT I
1510 T$= P$(I): R = RND
1520 FOR X = 1 TO 8
1530 IF R > O(X) THEN 1560
1540 GOTO 1570
1550 NEXT X
1560 O2 = X : PITCH= I+ (12*O2)
1570 IF A = 1 THEN 1760
1590 REM**********************************************************
1600 REM MODULE TO GENERATE DATA FOR INTERVAL SEQUENCE *********
1610 R = RND
1620 FOR I = 1 TO 12
1630 IF R > P(I) THEN 1650
1640 GOTO 1660
1650 NEXT I
1660 F = RND
1665 IF F < D THEN 1690
1670 U1 = U1 - I
```

```
1680 GOTO 1700
1690 U1 = U1 + I
1700 IF U1 > H THEN U1 = U1 - 12
1710 IF U1 < L THEN U1 = U1 + 12
1720 T$= P$(U1)
1730 O2 = INT(1 +(U1 - 1)/12)
1740 REM******************************************************
1750 REM MODULE TO GENERATE DURATION DATA   ********************
1760 R = RND
1770 FOR I = 1 TO D1
1780 IF R > D(I) THEN 1810
1790 X1 = E2(I)
1800 GOTO 1840
1810 NEXT I
1820 REM******************************************************
1830 REM MODULE TO GENERATE ARTICULATION DATA ******************
1840 R = RND
1850 FOR I = 1 TO G
1860 IF R > B(I) THEN 1890
1870 Z1 = A(I)
1880 GOTO 1920
1890 NEXT I
1900 ******************************************************
1910 REM MODULE TO GENERATE VOLUME DATA ********************
1920 R = RND
1930 FOR I = 1 TO V1
1940 IF R > K(I) THEN 1970
1950 Q1 = H(I)
1960 GOTO 1980
1970 NEXT I
1980 PRINT T$;O2,X1,Z1,Q1
1981 VELOCITY = Q1 : DURATION = INT(CLOCK /X1)
1982 ARTDUR = INT(DURATION * (Z1/100))
1983 PRINT#1,NOTEON;PITCH;VELOCITY;ARTDUR;CHANNEL
1989 NOTEON = NOTEON + DURATION
1990 NEXT J
2000 RETURN
```

Automated Composition

Program #70 is a very simple program which makes compositional
decisions, then proceeds to generate data for a melodic sequence
without interaction of any kind from the user (except for approval of
the decisions).

Execute Program #70 several times, then make the following revisions:

(1) Convert the program from its present state to structured subroutine form; eliminate the GOTO statements;
(2) Visually articulate the program using white space, indentation of FOR...NEXT loops to provide a more intelligible result;
(3) Add REMarks to clarify code function;
(4) Add a Variable Description section to the program to aid the user who wishes to read the program;
(5) Convert all mnemonic (single- or double-letter) variables to descriptive variables; and,
(6) Expand the program to include routines for the automatic generation of data for the other MIDI parameters (Rhythm, Velocity, Articulation, etc.).

(Program #70 includes file-writing code for use with the MusicSculptor System.)

PROGRAM #70

```
10 REM*******************************************************
11 REM                    PROGRAM #70
12 REM*******************************************************
20 REM THIS PROGRAM MAKES RANDOM MACROCOMPOSITIONAL DECISIONS
30 REM RELATIVE TO PITCH SELECTION, RANGE AND REGISTER,
40 REM SUBSECTION AND SECTION LENGTH.
45 REM*******************************************************
47 PRINT "RUN THIS PROGRAM WITH CapsLock ON!!!"
48 RANDOMIZE
50 DIM A(97),B(97),C(97),K(97),P$(97)
51 PRINT "Output filename for MusicSculptor will be <PROG#70.DAT>"
52        ' next line initializes variables for MusicSculptor file
53 NOTEON=0:DURATION=60:VELOCITY=100:ARTDUR=55:CHANNEL=0
54 OPEN "O",#1,"PROG#nn.SC"
55 PRINT #1,"File-ID : 2"
56 PRINT #1,"Format : 1"
57 VELOCITY = 127 ' highest MIDI loudness
60 FOR X = 1 TO 8
70 FOR Z = 1 TO 12
80 DATA C,C#,D,Eb,E,F,F#,G,Ab,A,Bb,B
90 READ P$(Z +(X -1)*12)
100 NEXT Z
110 RESTORE
120 NEXT X
130 FOR X = 36 TO 97
140 B(X) = 0
150 NEXT X
160 PRINT "NEED SCREEN OUTPUT AS NUMBERS OR PITCHES? (N/P)"
```

```
170 INPUT L$
190 FOR Y = 36 TO 97
200 R = INT(RND*62) + 36
210 IF B(R) = 1 THEN 200
220 B(R) = 1
230 K(Y) = R
240 NEXT Y
250 FOR Z = 36 TO 97 STEP 2
260 IF K(Z) > K(Z + 1) THEN GOSUB 840
270 A(Z) = K(Z)
280 A(Z + 1) = K(Z + 1)
290 NEXT Z
300 PRINT "HERE ARE THE RANGES SELECTED BY THE COMPUTER:"
310 IF L$ = "P" THEN 340
320 PRINT " L - H       L - H       L - H       L - H       L - H"
330 GOTO 350
340 PRINT "LOW    TO    HIGH"
350 FOR X = 36 TO 97 STEP 2
360 IF L$ ="P" THEN 390
370 PRINT A(X);A(X + 1),
380 GOTO 400
390 PRINT P$(A(X));INT(1 + (A(X) -1)/12),P$(A(X + 1));
     INT(1 +(A(X + 1) - 1) / 12)
400 NEXT X
410 PRINT
420 PRINT "OK? (Y/N)"
430 INPUT O$
440 IF O$ = "N" THEN 130
450 PRINT
460 PRINT "NEED NON-REPEATING SERIES? (Y/N)"
470 INPUT S$
480 T = 0
490 FOR Z = 36 TO 97 STEP 2
500 L = A(Z): H = A(Z + 1)
520 IF L$="P" THEN 560
530 PRINT "L=";L, "H=";H,
540 PRINT
550 GOTO 580
560 PRINT "L=";P$(L);INT(1 +(L - 1)/ 12),
570 PRINT "H=";P$(H);INT(1 +(H - 1) /12),
580 IF S$="Y" THEN 610
590 N = INT(RND*62)+ 1
600 IF S$="N" THEN 620
610 N =(H + 1)- L
620 PRINT "N=";N
630 PRINT
640 FOR J = 1 TO N
650 M = INT((RND*(H + 1)- L)+ L)
660 IF S$="N" THEN 690
670 IF C(M)= 1 THEN 650
```

```
680 C(M)= 1
690 IF L$="P" THEN 720
700 PRINT M,
701 PITCH = M+36 'bring up to middle MIDI range
702 PRINT #1,NOTEON;PITCH;VELOCITY;ARTDUR;CHANNEL
710 GOTO 730
720 PRINT P$(M);INT(1 +(M - 1)/ 12),
721 PITCH = M+36  ' bring up to middle MIDI range
722 PRINT #1,NOTEON;PITCH;VELOCITY;ARTDUR;CHANNEL
730 T = T + 1
735 NOTEON = NOTEON + DURATION 'advance start time for next note
740 NEXT J
750 PRINT
760 PRINT
770 FOR W = 36 TO 97
780 C(W)= 0
790 NEXT W
800 NEXT Z
810 PRINT
820 PRINT "TOTAL DATA = ";T
827 ' write EOF flag
828 PRINT #1,0;-1;0;0;0
829 CLOSE #1
830 END
831 REM*********************************************************
835 REM****************    SWAP SUBROUTINE    ******************
836 REM*********************************************************
840 A(Z)= K(Z + 1)
850 A(Z + 1)= K(Z)
870 RETURN 290
```

Ideas for Further Programming

There are many other MIDI messages that you can experiment with besides Pitch, Rhythm, Velocity, and Program Change. Review the material from earlier in the text which covers the control of Pitch Bend, Main Volume Controller, Sustain Pedal, and other control parameters.

It is best to develop and test routines for a new program in an isolated environment; that is, write a simple Driver Program to test each routine individually before trying to insert it into a large program, then build the Master Program up one routine at a time until you reach your goal. In this way, programming errors will be kept to a minimum and the amount of debugging time spent should be within reason.

Idea 1:

Write a program based on Program #70 which is self-determining with regard to probability weights assigned to Pitch, Rhythm, Velocity, and Articulation values. Parameter ranges may be input by the user or unalterably set within the program. Allow for the inclusion of a "rest" probability to allow for occasional silence.

Idea 2:

Write a program which uses the last two random intervals generated to determine the probability weight for the next interval to be generated.

Add a probability weight factor to shape the melodic contour as a function of melodic sequence-length, so that the curve chosen corresponds to varied-length phrases.

Idea 3:

Design a program which returns motif-oriented phrases over a wide range of synthetic scale structures (use sieves or scale transforms). Allow the user to choose transposition, inversion, rhythmic augmentation and diminution, etc. to create diversity of material.

APPENDIX

MusicSculptor Text File Format Information

1) MusicSculptor SCORE Files (*.SC). Score (*.sc) files are those containing complete data for all note-event parameters:

Noteon timing; Pitch; Velocity; Articulation; Channel

   Line1 : File-ID : 2 (The exact characters should appear on the
                                  first line of your SC files specifying the format
   Line2 : Format : f of the SC file)

wherein -

f = 1 : a SC file using cumulative Time_On stamp in ticks
f = 2 : a SC file using the interval in ticks between note attack points

   Line3   The note events
.
.   *Time_On*   *Pitch*   *Velocity*   *Duration*   *Channel*
.
. ** Time_On : Either Cumulating or Time_On interval stamps
. ** Pitch   : 0—127 regular notes
.   : -20 Program Change - |
.   : -21 PT Bend |
.   : -22 Main Volume Change |
.   : -23 After Touch |
.   : -24 Foot Controller | Followed by their
.   : -25 Sustain | non-note values in
.   : -28 Modulation Wheel | the Velocity field
.   : -29 Breath Wheel |
.   : -30 Sostenuto |
.   : -31 Soft Pedal - |
. ** Velocity : 0—127
. ** Duration : 0—65535
. ** Channel : 0—15
.
LastLine: You should put an end mark at the end of the file in the form—

X -1 X X X

—by setting the 2nd field of the line to be -1. X can be any number (0 is suggested)

2) MULTI-FIELD File format (*.MUL). Multi-field files are those which may contain data for fewer than five parameters:

Line1 : File-ID : 3 (The exact characters should appear on the first line of your MUL files)

Line2 : Map : T P V D wherein -

T = 0 No Time_On field in this file
T = 1 Cumulative Time_On stamp
T = 2 Attack Interval Time_On stamp
P = 0 No pitch field in this file
P = 1 Has Pitch field in this file
V = 0 No Velocity field in this file
V = 1 Has Velocity field in this file
D = 0 No duration field in this file
D = 1 Has duration field in this file

Line4 : The event lines : Your desired data fields should have been
 . indicated on the field Map and follow the
 . proper order of Time_On, Pitch, Velocity
 . and then Duration if anyone exists.
 . *Time_On*   *Pitch*   *Velocity*   *Duration*
 .
 . ** Time_O : Either cumulative or attack interval
 . Time_On stamps
 . ** Pitch : 0—127 regular notes
 . : -20 Program Change
 . : -21 PT Bend
 . : -22 Main Volume Change
 . : -23 After Touch
 . : -24 Foot Controller
 . : -25 Sustain
 . : -28 Modulation Wheel
 . : -29 Breath Wheel
 . : -30 Sostenuto
 . : -31 Soft Pedal DY

(Each of the preceding values should be followed by Velocity for their non-note values)

 . ** Velocity : 0—127
 . ** Duration : 0—65535
 . ** Channel : 0—15
 .

Lastline: You should put an end mark at the end of the file in the form—

X -1 ? ? ?

—by setting the 2nd field of the line to be -1. X can be any number (0 is suggested).

MusicSculptor SCORE Files (*.SC) Examples

Multiple Channel Score File Example:

```
File-ID : 2
Format : 1
120 33 44 55 0
120 33 44 55 1
120 33 44 55 2
240 55 66 77 0
180 55 66 77 1
180 55 66 77 2
300 66 77 88 2
200 66 77 88 1
123 66 77 88 0
0 -1 0 0 0
```

Multiple Channel Score File With Non-note message Example:

```
File-ID : 2
Format : 1
120 -20 44 55 0
120 -21 44 55 1
120 -22 44 55 2
240 23 66 77 0
180 -24 66 77 1
180 -25 66 77 2
300 -28 77 88 2
200 -29 77 88 1
123 -30 77 88 0
0 -1 0 0 0
```

MusicSculptor Multi-Field Files (*.MUL) Examples

Multi-Field File : Non-accumulating-Time_On, Pitch and Duration Example

```
File-ID : 3
Map : 1 1 0 1
120 33 55
120 33 55
120 33 55
240 55 77
180 55 77
180 55 77
300 66 88
200 66 88
123 66 88
0 -1 0
```

Multi-Field File : Time_On Interval Stamp, Pitch and Duration Example

File-ID : 3
Map : 2 1 0 1
120 33 55
120 33 55
120 33 55
240 55 77
180 55 77
180 55 77
300 66 88
200 66 88
123 66 88
0 -1 0

Multi-Field File : With Pitch and Duration fields (To Load this file, you
should have set the Time_On Parameter already)

File-ID : 3
Map : 0 1 0 1
33 55
33 55
33 55
55 77
55 77
55 77
66 88
66 88
66 88
60 6000
0 -1

REFERENCES

Barnsley, M. F. 1989. *Fractals Everywhere*. New York: Springer-Verlag.

Cope, David. 1991. *Computers and Musical Style*. Madison, WI: A-R Editions, Inc.

Dodge, C. and T. Jerse. 1985. *Computer Music Synthesis, Composition, and Performance*. New York: Schirmer Books.

Forte, Allen. 1973. *The Structure of Atonal Music*. New Haven: Yale University Press.

Hiller, L. and L. Isaacson. 1959. *Experimental Music*. New York: McGraw-Hill, Inc.

Peitgen, H.-O., and P. H. Richter. 1986. *The Beauty of Fractals*. Berlin: Springer-Verlag.

Rahn, John. 1980. *Basic Atonal Theory*. New York: Longman, Inc.

Roads, C. 1979. "Grammars as Representations for Music." *Computer Music Journal* 3(1): 48–55.

Winsor, Phil. 1989. *The Computer Composer's Toolbox*. Blue Ridge Summit, PA: Windcrest Books/McGraw-Hill, Inc.

Winsor, P. and G. DeLisa. 1991. *Computer Music in C*. Blue Ridge Summit, PA: Windcrest Books/McGraw-Hill, Inc.

Wuorinen, Charles. 1979. *Simple Composition*. New York: Longman, Inc.

Xenakis, I. 1971. *Formalized Music*. Bloominton, IN: Indiana University Press.

INDEX

Defined Probability Distributions, 273
Deterministic Algorithms, 99
Digital information recorders, 25
DIM Statement, 85
Discrete Random Variables, 252–53
Disruptive shuffle routine, 241

Ecological (sonic environment) Acoustics, 5, 9
Editing a program, 45
Encoding of Musical Data, 18–23
Entering a Program, 44
Equal-Temperament Tuning System, 112
Error-detection, 67
Error message, 40
Esthetic Perception, 5, 9–10
Eulerian Beta Distribution Function, 255
Event vector, 18, 69
Executing a program, 47
Experimental Music, 270
Expert Systems, 5, 7, 14, 15
Exponential Distribution Function, 257
Exponential Probability Distribution, 257

Fibonacci numbers, 169
Fixed (hard) disk drive, 40
Foot Controller, 35
FOR...NEXT Loop, 81
Formalized Music, 240
Forte, Allen, 173
FORTRAN, 6, 26
Fractal designs, 279
Function library, 42
Functional tonality, 14
Future Research, 11

Gauss-LaPlace Distribution, 261
Gaussian Probability Distribution, 261
GOSUB Instruction, 74
Grammar, 14
GWBASIC, 39, 40

Hiller, Lejeran A., 6, 240
Histogram, 253
Hybrid computer music system, 24

IBM-PC, 39
Iconic Mapping, 111–12
Ideas for Further Programming, 299
IF...THEN Instruction, 75
Information Theory, 5, 9–10
"Information Theory and Esthetic Perception," 9, 10
Information Transmission, 28
INKEY$ Instruction, 62–63
INPUT Instruction, 68–69

Integerize function, 42
Integrative Procedures, 153
Interactive Programs, 67
Interval Alteration, 201
Interval-set, 116
Interval-size, 103
Iterative Processing, 78–79

Josephus' Problem, 185

Linear Probability Distribution, 265
Linear unsorted table search, 212
List-element rotation, 159
Logical Operators, 76–77
Logical Sieve Theory, 145–46

Machine Learning, 76
Macintosh computer, 24, 39
Main Volume, 36
Main Volume Controller, 36
Mapping, 101
Mapping Concept, 111
Mapping Levels, 112
Mapping pitches onto characters, 219
Mapping Programs, 118
Mapping techniques, 117
Mathematical Algorithms, 162–72
Mathematical curves, 162
Mathematical functions, 42
Mathematical Probability Distribution Functions, 252
Matrix random walk, 250
Melodic patterning, 116
Melodic shape, 116
Melodic Transformation, 197
Melody, 116
Microsoft BASIC, 39
MIDI, 11, 12
MIDI channels, 30, 31
MIDI codes, 28, 29
MIDI Communications, 13
MIDI-compatible Programs, 283
MIDI controllers, 35
MIDI data to standard music notation, 38
MIDI file specification, 283
MIDI-format Output, 281
MIDI fundamentals, 23
MIDI implementation of music scores, 23
MIDI keyboard synthesizers, 24–25
MIDI "Language", 28, 29
MIDI Manufacturer's Association, 10
MIDI messages, 299
MIDI Note Parameter Scales, 28, 33
MIDI notelist file format, 30, 283
MIDI parameters, 286
MIDI protocol, 12, 26

Automated Music Composition

If you are intrigued with the possibilities of the programs included in *Automated Music Composition*, consider having the ready-to-run disk containing the software application. You will save the time and effort of typing the programs, as well as eliminate the possibility of errors that can prevent the programs from functioning.

Available on either 5.25" or 3.5" disk at $24.95, plus $3.05 shipping and handling. You need an IBM PC or compatible and DOS version 2.0 or higher.

Yes, I'm interested. Send me:

_____ copies 5.25" BASIC program disk, $24.95	$_____
_____ copies 3.5" BASIC program disk, $24.95	$_____
(Add $3.05 per copy S & H)	$_____
Texas residents add 7.25% sales tax	$_____
Total	$_____

Send check or postal money order (U.S. Currency) payable to:

Phil Winsor
College of Music
University of North Texas
Denton, Texas 76203